ELT, Gender and International Development

© **Mixed Sources**
Product group from well-managed
forests, controlled sources and
recycled wood or fibre
www.fsc.org Cert no. SA-COC-002112
© 1996 Forest Stewardship Council

FSC

CRITICAL LANGUAGE AND LITERACY STUDIES

Series Editors: **Professor Bonny Norton**, (*University of British Columbia, Canada*), **Professor Alastair Pennycook**, (*University of Technology, Sydney, Australia*), **Professor Brian Morgan**, (*York University, Canada*).

Critical Language and Literacy Studies is an international series that encourages monographs directly addressing issues of power (its flows, inequities, distributions, trajectories) in a variety of language- and literacy-related realms. The aim with this series is twofold: (1) to cultivate scholarship that openly engages with social, political, and historical dimensions in language and literacy studies, and (2) to widen disciplinary horizons by encouraging new work on topics that have received little focus (see below for partial list of subject areas) and that use innovative theoretical frameworks.

Full details of all our other publications can be found on http://www.multilingual-matters.com, or by writing to Multilingual Matters, St Nicholas House, 31–34 High Street, Bristol BS1 2AW, UK.

Other books in this series

Collaborative Research in Multilingual Classrooms
Corey Denos, Kelleen Toohey, Kathy Neilson and Bonnie Waterstone
English as a Local Language: Post-colonial Identities and Multilingual Practices
Christina Higgins
The Idea of English in Japan: Ideology and the Evolution of a Global Language
Philip Seargeant
Language and HIV/AIDS
Christina Higgins and Bonny Norton (eds)
China and English: Globalization and the Dilemmas of Identity
Joseph Lo Bianco, Jane Orton and Gao Yihong (eds)
Bodies and Language: Health, Ailments, Disabilities
Vaidehi Ramanathan
Hybrid Identities and Adolescent Girls: Being 'Half' in Japan
Laurel D. Kamada
Decolonizing Literacy: Mexican Lives in the Era of Global Capitalism
Gregorio Hernandez-Zamora
Contending with Globalization in World Englishes
Mukul Saxena and Tope Omoniyi (eds)

CRITICAL LANGUAGE AND LITERACY STUDIES
Series Editors: Bonny Norton, Alastair Pennycook
and Brian Morgan

ELT, Gender and International Development
Myths of Progress in a Neocolonial World

Roslyn Appleby

MULTILINGUAL MATTERS
Bristol • Buffalo • Toronto

For Tom, Nick and Lucy
without whom this book would have been written much sooner.

Library of Congress Cataloging in Publication Data
Appleby, Roslyn.
ELT, Gender and International Development: Myths of Progress in a Neocolonial
World / Roslyn Appleby.
Critical Language and Literacy Studies: 10
Includes bibliographical references and index.
1. English language—Study and teaching—Foreign countries. 2. English
language—Study and teaching—Foreign speakers. 3. Women teachers. I. Title.
PE1128.A2A57 2010
428'.0071-dc22 2010025412

British Library Cataloguing in Publication Data
A catalogue entry for this book is available from the British Library.

ISBN-13: 978-1-84769-304-4 (hbk)
ISBN-13: 978-1-84769-303-7 (pbk)

Multilingual Matters
UK: St Nicholas House, 31–34 High Street, Bristol BS1 2AW, UK.
USA: UTP, 2250 Military Road, Tonawanda, NY 14150, USA.
Canada: UTP, 5201 Dufferin Street, North York, Ontario M3H 5T8, Canada.

The policy of Multilingual Matters/Channel View Publications is to use papers that
are natural, renewable and recyclable products, made from wood grown in
sustainable forests. In the manufacturing process of our books, and to further support
our policy, preference is given to printers that have FSC and PEFC Chain of Custody
certification. The FSC and/or PEFC logos will appear on those books where full
certification has been granted to the printer concerned.

Typeset by Integra Software Services Pvt. Ltd, Pondicherry, India
Printed and bound in Great Britain by Short Run Press Ltd

Contents

v

List of Figures

Acknowledgements

I am grateful to the many colleagues, students, and friends who have provided immense support for my research endeavours and the writing of this book.

My thanks go to the wonderful teachers and students who generously participated in my research; and to Alastair Pennycook, for intellectual exchanges, collegial advice, and critical comments on my ideas.

My research has benefited from the material support provided by the ELSSA Centre at the University of Technology, Sydney, and I am grateful for the encouragement generously offered by my current and former colleagues at the Centre, including Ross Forman, Constance Ellwood and Cynthia Nelson. Thanks also to the Faculty of Arts and Social Sciences at the University of Technology, Sydney, for the provision of a dissemination grant to assist with the final stages of production.

I gratefully acknowledge the Faculty of Arts and Social Sciences, Universiti Brunei Darussalam, for permission to reprint short excerpts from my 2005/2006 article 'Mobilising and disabling the desire for empowerment: English and the transition to independence in East Timor', which was published in *Southeast Asia: A Multidisciplinary Journal*, 6 (1), 3–12; and the School of Liberal Arts, King Mongkut's University of Technology Thonburi, Thailand, for permission to reprint short excerpts from my 2007 article 'Not my place: Gender politics and language teaching in East Timor', which was published in *Trends and Directions: Proceedings of the 12th International English in South-East Asia Conference* (pp. 1–9).

Preface

In this important book, Ros Appleby brings together three domains of work that have to date received relatively little attention in English language teaching and applied linguistics, and have certainly not been addressed in relation to each other. The first area is language and development, the second concerns gender in language teaching, and the third addresses theories of space in language education. In the area of language and development, there is a small body of published work (Rassool, 1999, 2007), including a special issue of *TESOL Quarterly* in 2002, and a number of edited books (e.g. Kenny & Savage, 1997; Lo Bianco, 2002), based around the Language and Development conferences organized by the Asian Institute of Technology in Bangkok and held in various parts of South East (and later Central) Asia over the last 15 years. Yet both the field itself and the understanding of its significance to the larger domain of global English language teaching is only just beginning to make an impact, particularly with respect to literacy and development (Djite, 2008; Muthwii & Kioko, 2004; Ramanathan, 2005; Street, 2001). The central questions raised by a focus on language and development urge us to ask several questions: What *is* development? How can we escape models of development that simply collude with the wider agenda of the major donor nations? How can we develop local models of cooperative change that really assist local people? For whom is Aid really beneficial?

Such questions force language education to engage with the wide and multidisciplinary field of development studies, which in turn draws in political science, anthropology, economics, environmental studies and more. For ELT, however, further questions need to be asked, and these go to the heart of many of the issues we need to take up seriously in our understanding of the global role of English in the world. How, when, in what ways and for whom does the learning of English bring advantage? We still do not have good answers to this basic set of questions. Of course, we know that learning English can bring advantage on an individual basis, and that to deny access to English may limit opportunities for change. But we also need to consider on the one hand the waste of resources in mass English teaching: What gets left out when so much time and money is put into education in English? And on the other hand we need to ask what the effects of English education might actually be. In order to understand this, we have to look at English in terms of class, and thus at poverty alleviation not in terms of individual escape from poverty but in terms of larger social and economic relations (Appleby et al., 2002). We need to be clear about whether we are looking at individual rights to English or whether we are looking at how access to English can alleviate poverty across a broader domain. The question, then, is how English may be related to economic change. As Tollefson (2000) warns, 'At a time when English is widely seen as a key to the economic success of nations and the economic well-being of individuals, the spread of English also contributes to significant social, political, and economic inequalities' (p. 8).

Bruthiaux (2002) argues convincingly that for many of the world's poor, English language education is 'an outlandish irrelevance' and 'talk of a role for English language education in facilitating the process of poverty reduction and a major allocation of public resources to that end is likely to prove misguided and wasteful' (pp. 292–293). Grin (2001), one of the few to study the relationship between English and economic gain in any depth, argues that there is also an issue of diminishing returns here, since the more people learn English, the less the skill of knowing English will count. And bringing a novel economic analysis to the question of global English, Lysandrou and Lysandrou (2003) argue that 'the embrace of the English language is to the detriment of the majorities of communities the world over insofar as it contributes to their systematic dispossession' (p. 230). As Tupas (2006) points out in the context of the export of labour from the Philippines, for example, the 'hierarchy of skills (including English language skills) that governs the deployment of labour actually perpetuates, rather than reconfigures, both the Philippine social structure (which, in turn, also reproduces such hierarchy), as well as the globalized unequal structure of relations between the Philippines as a labour-producing country and labour-using countries and corporations' (p. 101). Thus we need to distinguish very clearly between individually oriented access arguments about escape from poverty, and class-oriented arguments about large-scale poverty reduction. The challenge here is to get beyond liberal arguments for access, and look instead at the broad effects of educational provision in all their complexity.

When a newly emergent country such as East Timor chooses Portuguese and Tetum as its official languages, and yet young students demand access to English, how should we understand what is at stake here in terms of the economic and political agendas of those asking and those willing to provide? Alongside such economic questions, we also need to explore the relation between English and particular cultural and ideological formations (Newfield & Stein, 2006; Papen, 2004; Phan, 2008; Prinsloo, 2005; Tembe & Norton, 2008). We know that English is commonly perceived as a (or the) language of modernity, technology, mobility and so forth. What happens, then, in the context of development when English is tied up with the complex social and ideological transformations implied by supposed moves from tradition to modernity, from poverty to affluence, from ignorance to knowledge, from underdevelopment to development? English and its teachers are caught up in this, purveyors of far more than the packaged languages they are employed to transmit. This book explores the daily dilemmas of English language teaching in development aid, and situates the classroom practices of the teachers within the context of these sometimes neocolonial relations. What happens, asks Appleby, when white Western men and women come in to rebuild former colonies in Asia? What happens in the daily encounters between white and brown, rich and poor, women and men, First World and Third World? How does a bag of English language lessons translate, or disintegrate, in a radically different world? How is English teaching linked to ideas of progress?

The second area that Ros Appleby brings to the table here is gender, since a particular focus of this book is on women teachers in development contexts. The role of gender in development has been widely discussed, from the benefits of making loans to women, to ensuring women receive education and are freed from domestic chores (Robinson-Pant, 2000; Visvanathan *et al.*, 1997). But the role of women in English language teaching, and particularly in the context of development, has received little attention. Teacher (rather than student) identity has recently emerged as an important focus of study (Morgan, 2004; Varghese *et al.*, 2005), though only a few scholars (e.g. Clarke, 2008) have taken up such concerns in majority world contexts. Research in applied linguistics has in recent times made gender a focus of serious interest (rather than being either invisible or a 'variable'), looking at the portrayal of women in textbooks, participation in classrooms, or the struggle that immigrant women may face in learning languages while managing work and families (Norton, 2000; Norton & Pavlenko, 2004; Sunderland, 2000). Yet, as Appleby points out, although female teachers dominate the language teaching professions, there is little literature that explores their perceptions and experiences as gendered professionals. Thus the roles and identities of women English teachers in majority world contexts have still to be explored in any depth. By looking at white women teachers in the context of development work, Appleby opens up this field of gender, bodies, disparity and ELT.

When gender and language in development are brought together, we are presented with hard questions about the role of white Western women taking on the role of English teachers in development contexts. This has, first of all, a long colonial history, since language teaching has long been seen as 'women's work', as the leftover from the more serious colonial projects of the male domain. The role of women in such work also takes us into those complex relations between, on the one hand, race, privilege and development – these women enjoy undeniable privileges in this context of development – and, on the other hand, gender relations with both local people and the development workers. As Appleby shows, this is difficult and treacherous territory for these women to negotiate, enjoying the benefits of salaries, comforts and lifestyle that accrue to those on the right side of the development divide, while also being threatened, harassed and subject to all those patronizing and misogynist behaviours that can be the daily life of working women.

Here, in the context of ELT and development, we also see the intersections between gender and race, as these white women struggle to come to terms with the task they have taken on. As Kubota and Lin (2009) note, race – from colonial contexts to current debates about native speakers – has been strangely absent from serious discussion of ELT. In the interwoven narrative recollections of women English teachers, this book presents the daily experiences of white female teachers in bars, beaches and classrooms: How will they handle the hostility and harassment provoked by their whiteness and suspect sexuality? How will their trusty lessons and methods survive the radically different realities of East Timor and Indonesia? Can they find a better way of connecting, relating and just 'being there'? Their stories provide the flesh for an insightful examination of language, race and gender as problems that too often remain silent partners in the story of development as white man's endeavour.

The treacherous territory that these women negotiate brings us to the third area that Appleby deals with: space. While research on classrooms and multimodality (e.g. Bhattacharya *et al.*, 2007) has raised awareness of the spatial elements of the classroom in relation to what they call the 'textual cycle', the rise of spatial theory in the social sciences has still received little attention in ELT and applied linguistics (Pennycook, 2010). At the core of the spatial turn is the observation that rather than being a neutral setting, a backdrop, a blank canvas against which social relations are acted out, space is a central interactive part of the social. For Soja (1996), space is the 'third existential dimension' (p. 3) that needs to be considered alongside, as well as deeply interwoven with, the social and the historical. This spatiality/historicality/sociality nexus, argues Soja, affects not only the ways in which we consider space but also the ways in which we understand history and society. Recent thought on space, therefore, has sought to move beyond the remnants of a Kantian version of space as fixed and immutable towards space that also encompasses a notion of time and change, space as process. From this point of view, we can look at 'practice as an activity creating time-space not time-space as some matrix within which activity occurs' (Crang, 2001: 187).

Hadi-Tabassum's (2006) use of spatial theory to better understand bilingual classrooms shows how basic divisions we may make – scheduling different languages at different times of the day, or creating spatial boundaries around languages in classrooms – may have major implications for the development and use of languages. Where a dual immersion class divides English and Spanish into two equal halves in the curriculum, for example, this dichotomy 'produces a linguistic differentiation through its border-making design in which each language is separated and segregated into its own discrete space and time and is not allowed to mix with the other' (p. 5). Taking such insights further, Appleby shows in this book how a focus on time and space can shed light on relations of gender, development and ELT. There is a particular temporal and spatial logic to ELT in relationship to developmentalism, in which development is seen as change in a specified modernist direction, with expertise imported from elsewhere to effect this change. Time, with its particular links to progress, curriculum and masculinity, is favoured over space and a far more localized understanding of gender, difference and teaching practices. Unless we understand the ways in which the social, political and the spatial are mutually constituted, we will fail to establish a more complex understanding of how ELT and gender operate as politicized spatial practices.

Appleby's research – combining English language teaching, development, gender and space, and based on the narratives of women teachers as well as her own ethnographic notes – takes us into the very real context of teaching English in the context of Dili, ravaged by a bitter and destructive war for independence from Indonesia. We start to feel what it is like to teach in the battered classrooms on the campus, with wood smoke and the sounds of roosters drifting through the broken windows; we are given a close portrait of the disparity between the adversity of the locals and the comfort of the expats on the development 'gravy train'; we learn of the extraordinary hardships some of these students have faced, and their courage and pain in taking up education again. Appleby presents us with a critical analysis of language teaching that interrogates the ways in which inequality can be perpetuated through the very processes of international development, and the place of English language within those processes; she shows how and why certain practices of English language teaching persist, and how they may 'crash and burn' in practice; she links the local experiences of language teaching, gender relations and development with the ambiguous location of women in the language and development industries, and offers fresh insight into social, political and historical understandings of English language and gender in a globalised world.

Alastair Pennycook
Bonny Norton
Brian Morgan

References

Appleby, R., Copley, K., Sithirajvongsa, S. and Pennycook, A. (2002) Language in development constrained: Three contexts. *TESOL Quarterly* 36 (3), 323–346.

Bhattacharya, R., Gupta, S., Jewitt, C., Newfield, D., Reed, Y. and Stein, P. (2007) The policy-practice nexus in English classrooms in Delhi, Johannesburg, and London: Teachers and the textual cycle. *TESOL Quarterly* 41 (3), 465–488.

Bruthiaux, P. (2002) Hold your courses: Language education, language choice, and economic development, *TESOL Quarterly* 36 (3), 275–296.

Clarke, M. (2008) *Language Teacher Identities: Co-constructing Discourse and Community*. Clevedon: Multilingual Matters.

Crang, M. (2001) Rhythms of the City: Temporalised space and motion. In J. May and N. Thrift (eds) *Timespace: Geographies of Temporality* (pp. 187–207). London: Routledge.

Djite, P. (2008) *The Sociolinguistics of Development in Africa*. Clevedon: Multilingual Matters.

Grin, F. (2001) English as economic value: Facts and fallacies. *World Englishes* 20 (1), 65–78.

Hadi-Tabassum, S. (2006) *Language, Space and Power: A Critical Look at Bilingual Education*. Clevedon: Multilingual Matters.

Kenny, B. and Savage, W. (eds) (1997) *Language and Development: Teachers in a Changing World*. London: Longman.

Kubota, R. and Lin, A. (eds) (2009) *Race, Culture, and Identity in Second Language Education: Exploring Critically Engaged Practice*. New York: Routledge.

Lo Bianco, J. (ed.) (2002) *Voices from Phnom Penh: Development and Language: Global Influences and Local Effects* (pp. 3–22). Melbourne: Language Australia.

Lysandrou, P. and Lysandrou, Y. (2003) Global English and proregression: Understanding English language spread in the contemporary era. *Economy and Society* 32 (2), 207–233.

Morgan, B. (2004) Teacher identity as pedagogy: Towards a field-internal conceptualization in bilingual and second language education. *Bilingual Education and Bilingualism* 7 (2&3), 172–188.

Muthwii, M. and Kioko, N. (2004) *New Language Bearings in Africa*. Clevedon: Multilingual Matters.

Newfield, D. and Stein, P. (Guest eds) (2006) English education in Africa [Special Issue]. *English Studies in Africa*, 49 (1).

Norton, B. (2000) *Identity and Language Learning: Gender, Ethnicity and Educational Change*. London: Longman.

Norton, B. and Pavlenko, A. (2004) Addressing gender in the ESL/EFL classroom. *TESOL Quarterly* 38 (3), 504–514.

Papen, U. (2004) Literacy and development: What works for whom? Or, how relevant is the social practices view of literacy for literacy education in developing countries? *International Journal of Educational Development* 25, 5–17.

Pennycook, A. (2010) *Language as a Local Practice*. London: Routledge.

Phan, L.H. (2008) *Teaching English as an International Language: Identity, Resistance and Negotiation*. Clevedon: Multilingual Matters.

Prinsloo, M. (2005) New literacies as placed resources. *Perspectives in Education* 23 (4), 87–98.

Ramanathan, V. (2005) *The English-Vernacular Divide: Postcolonial Language Policies and Practice*. Clevedon: Multilingual Matters

Rassool, N. (1999) *Literacy for Sustainable Development in the Age of Information*. Clevedon: Multilingual Matters.

Rassool, N. (2007) *Global Issues in Language, Education and Development: Perspectives from Postcolonial Countries*. Clevedon: Multilingual Matters.

Robinson-Pant, A. (2000) Women and literacy: A Nepal perspective. *International Journal of Educational Development* 20, 349–364.

Soja, E.W. (1996) *Thirdspace: Journeys to Los Angeles and Real-and-Imagined Places*. Oxford: Blackwell.

Street, B. (ed.) (2001) *Literacy and Development: Ethnographic Perspectives*. New York: Routledge.

Sunderland, J. (2000) Issues of language and gender in second and foreign language education. *Language Teaching* 33, 203–223.

Tembe, J. and Norton, B. (2008) Promoting local languages in Ugandan primary schools: The community as stakeholder. *Canadian Modern Language Review* 65 (1), 33–60.

Tollefson, J. (2000) Policy and ideology in the spread of English. In J.K. Hall and W. Eggington (eds) *The Sociopolitics of English Language Teaching* (pp. 7–21). Clevedon: Multilingual Matters.

Tupas, R. (2006) Anatomies of linguistic commodification: The case of English in the Philippines vis-à-vis other languages in the linguistic marketplace. In P. Tan and R. Rubdy (eds) *Language as Commodity: Global Structures, Local Marketplaces* (pp. 90–105). London: Continuum.

Varghese, M., Morgan, B., Johnston, B. and Johnson, K.A. (2005) Theorizing language teacher identity: Three perspectives and beyond. *Journal of Language, Identity, and Education* 4 (1), 21–44.

Visvanathan, N., Duggan, L. Nisonoff, L. and Wiegersma, N. (eds) (1997) *The Women, Gender and Development Reader* (pp. 7–13). London: Zed Books.

Introduction: This is Where it Crashed and Burned

...*every story is a travel story – a spatial practice*
de Certeau, 1984: 115

Elly: We were TESOL teachers and most of us had travelled and taught in other countries, but the TESOL system is kind of a tight circuit system where English is taught in a particular way, and I think most people just thought we were just going to another country. We decided what we were doing before we went in, it was planned out, we went through it, and the students fitted in, really, and that was our TESOL training, you can go anywhere, pretty much, and do the same thing. And that's where it crashed and burned in Timor, you know. Well, like, you've been to Siberia and you've taught English, and you've been in Australia and you've taught English and it works, and you've been to Indonesia and taught English and it works. And then you to Timor and it doesn't bloody work! So like, what the hell's going on here?!

Elly and I had arrived in East Timor with a group of fellow teachers in the tumultuous period after a popular consultation set the world's newest nation on the path to independence. As part of Australia's aid effort, we had been engaged by a non-government organisation (NGO) to work as English language teachers, and the task of our project was to teach English language and computer skills to a thousand Timorese tertiary students prior to the reopening of the national university. The 'outputs' of the project were clearly stated: our objective was to improve students' English language skills by one step on an international language proficiency scale. The English language we taught was to be 'in context', and to be relevant to the students' educational and vocational needs. We were to use a communicative approach, focusing on speaking, which was expected to be the students' weakest skill. We brought our expertise in curriculum design around competencies, functions and genres. We knew that there would be few resources in terms of textbooks available; most of these had been destroyed in a wave of conflict and violence, so we had come prepared with a range of familiar English language teaching course books, grammar books, pronunciation books, favourite lessons, and so on. We knew the books and lessons would need to be adapted to the context of East Timor and to the needs of our students. But what were those 'needs'? The needs analysis that had been sent to the students ahead of our arrival had not been returned, so we drew on our experience and knowledge of language teaching methods: in the days after our arrival we made our plans for teaching, developing a curriculum, discussing diagnostic tests to organise class groups, deciding whether we would plan lessons according to themes or competencies, and noting what functions and genres these would cover. We had the expertise. This is how we would fill our two-month course. As qualified and experienced English language teachers, there was so much we 'knew' ahead of our arrival. Yet as one teacher aptly observed, over that short period 'we found out how much we didn't know', or to use Elly's phrase, this is where what-we-already-knew 'crashed and burned'.

Specific circumstances shaped Elly's and my experiences of English language teaching in East Timor at that time: a fluid linguistic landscape, an uncertain role for English, a severely disrupted education system, a fragile infrastructure, an influx of international aid agencies in a territory that had been virtually closed to external engagement for decades. A new nation was in the process of being built, and various interests – local, national and international – were vying for influence. The campus in which we taught was located on a street that carried peace-keeping troops to and from the border with Indonesia, and lessons were frequently interrupted by the rattle of tanks and buzz of helicopters overhead. International military forces had quelled the violence that arose in the wake of Indonesian withdrawal, but the ongoing threat of political volatility and militia attacks meant that, in many ways, this was a man's world.

Elly: *As a woman it was probably one of the freakiest experiences of my life. What is it, like nine men to one woman in Dili at the time. Oh my god, yeah, look that was full on. The whole bar scene, the pick up in the bars, like those World War II movies. And men, those truckloads of soldiers looking like predators, looking at us like predators. [. . .] It did restrict my movement, but I was pretty careful anyway, at night time, well we all were I guess. Just because of the general climate of people saying be careful, and you'd feel a bit nervous. I felt that we were almost a bit of an anomaly. The whole set-up was still kind of quite patriarchal because* *it was still so war-oriented. It felt like, kind of 'watch out, it's males that operate here'.*

The experiences of Elly and her fellow teachers in East Timor, both inside and outside the classroom, raise a number of questions that are central to this book. These are questions about the 'tight circuit system' of English language teaching, its reliance on methods and texts, and the confusions that arise when the system is transferred from one place to another; about the consequences of predetermined goals and measurable outputs in language teaching; about the place of English language in international development; about the global interests that are represented in development and in military interventions; and about the ways in which gender is experienced by language teachers in development contexts. An exploration of these questions informs this book, and underpins its quest to extend understandings of the relationship between English language teaching and gender relations in the context of international development.

The Purpose, Aims and Focus on this Book

This book presents the narrative accounts of English language teachers working in development aid projects and provides an original discussion of the key challenges they face both inside and outside the classroom: engaging in the processes of international development, practising the conventions of English language teaching (ELT), participating in teacher education, and negotiating gendered interactions within development communities and classrooms. With these challenges in mind, the central questions addressed by the book are posed from the perspective of professional practitioners:

- How does English language teaching fit into the world of development?
- How and to what extent are English language teaching practices contextualised in development?
- What are the conflicts between the principles and practices of English language teaching and development, and how are they resolved?
- How is English language teaching in development experienced through discourses of gender and ethnicity?

To address these questions, the teachers' experiences and perspectives, together with my own observations and reflections, are considered through a unique theoretical and interpretive framework that focuses on time, space and place as key concepts and themes. Through this lens, the world inside the classroom is seen as situated within the larger world of development, and teachers' accounts of classroom practices are mapped onto more abstract macro relations and sociopolitical forces. Using this framework, the book critiques the discourses of modernisation and temporal progress that underpin mainstream policies and practices, and perpetuate economic, cultural and political inequalities at the core of development thinking. With this approach, the book seeks to contribute to a growing project of critically locating English language teaching in diverse social, cultural and political contexts.

The central argument of the book is that widespread modernist paradigms of gender, development and disciplinary knowledge dominate ELT practice and share in a metanarrative that privileges 'time', in its guise as teleological history and progress, over 'space', and its alignment with the particularities of place and context. This privileging of time, which I refer to as an overarching temporal (time-based) narrative, shapes everyday practices inside and outside the classroom, in social spaces conceived as contact zones 'where cultures meet, clash, and grapple with each other, often in highly asymmetrical relations of domination and subordination' (Pratt, 1992: 4). A temporal narrative places the 'developed' nations ahead of 'developing' nations; supports the reproduction of linguistic, colonial and patriarchal discourses and hierarchies; enables the disconnection of disciplinary knowledge and pedagogical practice from students' lived experience; and inhibits teachers' engagement with local places and spaces, and with the broader cultural and political contexts of their work. An alternative paradigm, one that engages with diverse spatial practices in the contact zone of development, enables a more critical and complex engagement between English language teaching, gender issues, and the cultural and political dimensions of local spaces and places of learning.

Previous studies in the emerging field of language in development have offered valuable insights into the workings and achievements of language teaching in development (see, for example, studies collected in volumes edited by Kenny & Savage, 1997; Shaw et al., 2000; Lo Bianco, 2002; Coleman et al., 2005). In recent years, many of the projects on which these studies are based have taken up the rhetoric of critical approaches to development, in particular emphasising the crucial importance of collaboration, participation and the inclusion of local knowledges. This is particularly so in literacy projects influenced by Freirean approaches to critical pedagogy (see Archer & Cottingham, 1997; Archer & Newman,

2003). At the same time, accounts of the great majority of programmes, both mainstream and critical, are inevitably framed as stories of success, if only to ensure continuing funding from donors for future projects. Closer scrutiny suggests, however, that despite the rhetoric of participation and connection to local contexts, language and literacy projects designed according to Freirean ideals may continue to be underpinned by a drive to bring 'First World' methods of language teaching, and 'modern' practices of knowledge construction, to developing countries through the expertise offered by foreign development workers (Bowers, 1983; Fiedrich & Jellema, 2003). As such, these accounts tend to demonstrate, on the whole, a continuing instrumental connection between English language teaching and international development as processes of modernisation.

This book marks a departure from these earlier studies. First, it aims to engage a critical analysis of language teaching that interrogates the ways in which inequality can be perpetuated through the very processes of international development and the place of English language within those processes. Second, it is concerned with the dilemmas and struggles of professional practitioners as they attempt to introduce 'modern' ways of ELT as a means of addressing the inequalities that characterise development domains; it explores how and why certain practices of English language teaching persist, and how they may 'crash and burn' in practice. By engaging an interdisciplinary approach to concepts of space and time, I aim to bring these theoretical and practical concerns together, and to construct new ways of understanding, and transforming, the links between everyday practices of ELT in development and wider relations of power and global inequality.

This book is also distinctive in its focus on the dynamics of gender in the contexts of ELT and international development, and takes up the perspective of female language teachers in its empirical analysis. Although female teachers dominate the language teaching professions, there is little literature that explores their perceptions and experiences as gendered professionals. Recent studies concerning gender and English language education have mostly centred on empirical studies of learners (rather than teachers); have been located in immigrant, 'First World'[1] contexts rather than in the (majority) 'developing' world; and can tend to imply assimilation to 'First World' feminist norms. Studies of gender inequality within the domain of international development have tended to focus on gender as a 'problem' located in Third World communities although, more recently, studies that adopt a postcolonial perspective have pointed to the impact of a prevailing masculinist regime in the development industry. However, on the whole, development studies have tended to neglect the gender relations experienced by donor communities, and have not explored gender as an issue for language teaching and learning.

Bringing these fields together, this book incorporates a critical approach to English as an international language, and furthers disciplinary thought in relation to gender, English language teaching and development. It is grounded in empirical research that is historically and geographically contingent, being based on the narratives of Western, female teachers, and their experiences of development aid programmes in East Timor and Indonesia (see Figure I.1). At the same time, the analyses presented in the book point to a way of rethinking gender and English language teaching that is more widely applicable. It links the local experiences of language teaching, gender relations and development with the ambiguous location of women in the language and development industries, and offers fresh insight into social, political and historical understandings of English language and gender in a globalised world.

In the following sections of this chapter, I introduce the teachers and the projects in which they worked, and describe the nature of the empirical research in which they participated. Finally, I provide an overview of the structure of the book, and the arguments that unfold in each chapter.

Foreign Teachers in East Timor and Indonesia

A background to this study

Writing from a white Australian perspective, a key concept I work with is that an understanding of language teaching in the context of development requires, in the first instance, 'not a clearer understanding of "them", but an ongoing and thoughtful unpacking of the values and fears that constitute "us"' (Philpott, 2001: 371). Accordingly, I focus on teachers as foreign aid workers, rather than on students as the recipients of development aid: I examine Australian teachers' perceptions and understandings of themselves as participants in a wider development community, as Australians and professionals, and as transient residents in host communities. Although the specific geographical context of this study locates teachers' work in East Timor and Indonesia (see Figure I.1), the teachers' experiences are relevant to many locations across the globe where different transnational and translocal cultures come into contact.

The narrative accounts that form the basis of this book are derived from my interviews and written correspondence with nine teachers, which explored their gendered and pedagogical experiences of teaching English in development aid projects in East Timor and Indonesia. My discussion

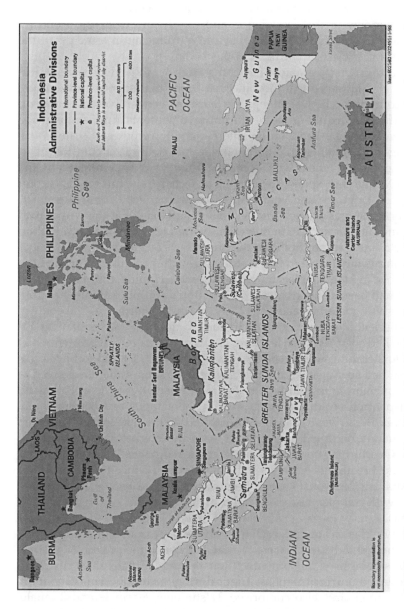

Figure I.1 Map of Indonesia and East Timor (available online at http://permanent.access.gpo.gov/lps35389/2000/index.html)

of their accounts is informed by my own experiences of teaching in East Timor during the nation's transition to independence, and I return here to an overview of that experience, and the themes emerging from my initial analysis of that experience, before introducing in more detail the teachers and projects at the heart of this book.

It was my own experience of teaching English in a development project located in a tertiary institution in East Timor that sparked my interest in the connections between language teaching, gender and development. While the plan for the project – to improve students' English language proficiency by one band on an internationally recognised scale – was seemingly straightforward, the material and political circumstances of the project environment were complex. The project was initiated by the United Nations in response to lobbying by tertiary students for instruction in English language and computer skills, in the face of moves to institute Portuguese as the new national language following the withdrawal of the Indonesian regime. In line with the trend towards decentralisation of development responsibilities, the project was taken up by an NGO that had won a competitive bid for Australian government funds, but had little experience in language teaching programmes. Finding a location for the project had been difficult: most of the nation's educational infrastructure and teaching materials had been destroyed; students across the country had experienced disruption to their studies; and most Indonesian nationals who had comprised the teaching profession prior to independence had fled. Our teaching was eventually conducted in a disused tertiary campus that had been a site of political struggle between students involved in the East Timorese resistance and the Indonesian government. Following the suspension of educational activities, the campus had been partially destroyed in the wave of violence surrounding the referendum, and then subsequently occupied as a military base by international intervention forces. Overturning conventional hierarchies of power between staff and students, the campus was now in the hands of a politically active tertiary students' organisation. Plans for English language teaching had come face to face with complex historical, political and linguistic contingencies and agendas.

The two classes I taught, each for 4 hours a day from Monday to Friday over a period of 8 weeks, were typical of those in the project. My morning class comprised 30 students, 9 female and 21 male, most of whom had attended university in East Timor during the Indonesian occupation. My afternoon class also comprised 31 students, 8 female and 23 male. The majority of male students in this class had previously attended universities elsewhere in Indonesia, either in Java or Bali. As a whole, the university students were highly politicised: they had played an important part in the independence movement, and were eager to engage with the establishment of the new nation. Some discord was apparent between those students who had undertaken studies outside Timor and those who had remained enmeshed in the independence struggles within the territory. All students had suffered serious disruption in their education, particularly in the years immediately before and after independence. All spoke at least two languages, Tetum and Bahasa Indonesia, usually in addition to at least one other indigenous language, and most had an elementary proficiency in English.

My own reflections on the project (see Appleby, 2004; Appleby *et al.*, 2002) were based on daily observations recorded in a journal, responses to my students' writing and a range of administrative documents. Selected accounts from my personal observations and experiences have been included as boxed texts throughout later chapters in the book. As I struggled to situate and explain my own disorienting, challenging and exhilarating experiences, I sought to construct an understanding of the way the practices and interactions I observed inside and outside the classroom related to broader theories of ELT, gender and development. My observations and reflections formed a significant basis for the enquiries that underpin this book, and gave me a thirst for conversations with colleagues who had taught in similar circumstances, either as language teachers or as teacher educators.

A central theme arising from my experiences concerned the apparent mismatch between the development project's singular focus on achieving quantifiable measures of student progress and what was *going on* inside and outside the classroom. Inside the classroom, I recognised that my performance as a teacher was tied up with conventions and practices of ELT that not only emphasised my place as an alien in that environment, but also appeared inadequate in connecting with the lived experiences of my students. It seemed the conventions of ELT and the proprieties of development bureaucracy combined to actively exclude from the space of the classroom other (more political) discourses that might be realised in the language. However, rather than those institutional conventions determining the limits of language use, the concerns emerging in students' own journal writing formed what I came to see as a parallel syllabus, one in which the students could 'recognise themselves in the acquisition of English' (Thesen, 1997: 509). In blank exercise books, provided to encourage written fluency and to enable a relatively free expression of ideas in English without the constraints imposed by a teacher-set task, the students wrote on topics of their own choice. Although the students' unstructured writing was not a prior goal of my teaching and did not have an official or natural(ised) place in the classroom, it remained as a potent sign of political discourses that washed across the border of the classroom wall. While the focus of the book remains on teachers' perspectives, a small number of selected extracts from students' journal writing have also been included in later chapters. In addition, I had recognised that students appeared more actively involved when we were *outside* the classroom, exploring places that were not structured by the disciplining formalities of classroom space (cf. Holliday, 2005). These contrasts suggested that the orthodox classroom space offered, through the effects of professional and bureaucratic discourses, a particularly circumscribed performance of language use and learning for both teacher and students.

From my reflections emerged two broad themes: of *place* (in terms of the meanings attached to, and produced in, the specific and complex relation between the classroom, the teacher and students, and the world outside); and *change* (in terms of the characterisation of teachers as change-agents – an oft-used term in development literature – and critical questions regarding who controlled and who would benefit from the changes envisaged in the programme). These twin themes indicated sites of tension and struggle, and provided a starting point for a further phase of enquiry involving interviews and correspondence with a range of teachers who had worked in the same or similar programmes in East Timor and Indonesia.

An emergent framework of space and time

My subsequent interviews and written correspondence with female English language teachers about their experiences of teaching in development projects form the basis of this book. Through my analysis of teachers' accounts, a broader conceptual framework of space and time has developed, which builds on my earlier reflective themes of *place* and *change*. Spatial perceptions and patterns emerged in the teachers' constructions of encounters between the various social groups in the development context, in their embodied experiences as gendered subjects, and in their reflections on the flow between the world outside and inside the classrooms. Temporal perceptions and patterns emerged in the way teachers conceived of their roles within the development context, and in the way they constructed the ordered temporality of their classrooms. The usefulness of a time–space framework in interpreting, conceptualising and organising the research data arises from its integration with social life, its mobilisation in micro and macro aspects of social and political organisation, and its importance for epistemology and ontology. The framework is intended to bring into dialogue the discursive and the material effects of embodiment and emplacement in the 'discomfort zone' of intercultural contact (Somerville & Perkins, 2003: 253), and to conceptualise notions of being-in-place in a way that is central to the enactment of ELT across the globe.

An interpretive analysis of teachers' accounts

My interviews and written exchanges with teachers explored how they saw and performed their role as English language teachers, how they perceived and responded to challenges of teaching in their specific contexts, and their relationships with development and host communities. Drawing from these interviews and correspondence, the teachers' words are included throughout the book in *'quoted italics'*. Considering the open, passionate and sometimes intimate nature of participants' stories, they could be characterised more as conversations between participants who had shared similar experiences than formal events with predetermined response categories. I considered teachers' accounts of critical incidents to be particularly interesting in terms of situating lived experiences into a wider social and political setting, and suggesting possible points of tension between the various assumptions and discursive regimes that interacted in the contexts of study. By bringing these narratives together with my own experiences, I've aimed not for triangulation or consensus, but have sought to construct a 'crystallised' image and a 'deepened, complex, thoroughly partial understanding of the topic' (Richardson, 1997: 92). This multifaceting was extended through the reading of letters emailed to family and friends by one of the interviewed teachers, and by two others who were not interviewed, during their periods of development work, and by email correspondence between myself and several of the participants relating to issues arising from our conversations.

The teachers and projects

Throughout the book, I am interested in unpacking the discourses, regulatory regimes and practices, particularly those related to time and space, that produce teachers' subjectivities, that shape teachers' understandings and practices of English language teaching in the world of development, and that situate teachers among the various participants in development communities. My focus is therefore on discursive constructions, on temporal and spatial regimes, on teachers' positioning in relation to others, rather than on individual teachers as fully 'fleshed out', stable personalities and autonomous identities. As a general guide, teachers' locations and projects are summarised below, with further details provided in Appendix A.[2]

Location	Teacher[3]	Project
East Timor	Elly Dana Fay Carol Roslyn	ELT for university students
East Timor	Helen	ELT for university students
East Timor	Ann	ELT and teacher training
East Timor	Jane Kate	ELT and teacher training
Indonesia Bali Ambon Sulawesi	 Carol Bree Ann	 ELT in vocational and teacher training colleges

All the projects were indirectly funded by Australian government agencies, with the exception of the project at the East Timor teachers college, which was funded by an Australian Catholic organisation. In line with the shift towards privatisation and decentralisation in the delivery of aid programmes, the organisations responsible for administering the projects were non-government agencies.

All the interviewed teachers were Caucasian Australians; all were experienced English language teachers and first-language speakers of English. Four also spoke one of the languages used by their students or by some sections of the local community: Ann, Bree and Carol spoke Bahasa Indonesia, and Helen spoke Portuguese. The teachers had between 5 and 25 years experience in ELT, and ranged in age between late 20s and late 50s at the time of the interviews. Teachers' ELT training varied from certificates in teaching adult English as a Foreign Language (EFL), to ESL teaching degrees and postgraduate qualifications. Immediately prior to the appointments that were the subject of these interviews, all but one were teaching English language in government or commercial establishments in Australia, mostly in full-time casual positions. They had worked in a variety of institutions, including universities, government technical colleges and private English language colleges, language centres for migrant adults and children, and Australian primary and high schools.

Some of the teachers' accounts related to their initial experiences of teaching English language in development projects. This was true for Ann, Bree and Carol's appointments as volunteers in Indonesia and for Dana, Elly, Fay, Jane and myself in East Timor. On the other hand, Ann, Carol, Helen and Kate all had considerable international experience by the time of their appointments in East Timor. Rather than seeing a lack of development experience as a drawback, I considered that this could potentially provide a fresh outlook on a new context, before teaching practices became sedimented through familiarity.

Bree, Carol and Ann were interviewed regarding their English language teaching in three separate locations across Indonesia. Of those teaching in East Timor, Carol, Dana, Elly and Fay were interviewed about their experiences in the same tertiary programme in which I was engaged. Helen taught in a follow-up programme at the same institution. Ann taught in a variety of locations in East Timor, at first temporarily in a tertiary institution, but then the majority of her work was with small groups of Timorese school teachers, providing classes in English language and teaching methodology. Ann also taught groups of school children on an ad hoc voluntary basis. Jane and Kate taught small classes (fewer than twelve students) in a teacher training institution established with Australian funding and located in a regional centre in East Timor. As part of this project, Jane also travelled to rural schools where she taught English and language teaching methodology for another group of Timorese teachers.

An Overview of the Book: Bringing together Language, Development and Gender

The book is structured in two parts. Following the introduction, Part 1, 'Understanding English Language Teaching in Development', focuses on the two theoretical frames that underpin this study, and then situates the study in its geopolitical context. Chapter 1 sets out different ways of understanding development and English language teaching; Chapter 2 introduces the analytical framework of time and space; Chapter 3 presents the broader historical, political and linguistic contexts of teachers' work in Indonesia and East Timor, and considers the cultural and geopolitical relationship between those countries and Australia. Part 2 of the book, 'Teachers' Narrative Accounts', interweaves theory and context with accounts of professional practice. Chapter 4 explores teachers' reflections of living amongst development communities; Chapter 5 focuses on teachers' accounts of classroom language teaching practice; and Chapter 6 discusses the ways in which teachers negotiate gender as a dynamic of language teaching.

INTRODUCTION		
PART 1	Understanding English Language Teaching in Development	Chapter 1 Development, English language and ELT
		Chapter 2 Space and time as overarching concepts
		Chapter 3 Historical, geopolitical and linguistic contexts of East Timor, Indonesia, Australia
PART 2	Teachers' Narrative Accounts	Chapter 4 Outside the classroom: teachers in the development context
		Chapter 5 Inside the classroom: professional practices of ELT
		Chapter 6 Inside the classroom: negotiating gender
CONCLUSION		Chapter 7

The narrative accounts of teachers, and of my own experiences in East Timor, are discussed throughout the book in the light of several intersecting angles of enquiry. The following provides a more detailed overview of the book's structure and unfolding argument.

An overview of chapters

Chapter 1 outlines competing mainstream, critical and alternative models of English language teaching and gender in the context of international development. It charts the inception of the development age from the end of the Second World War, and identifies the legacy of colonialism that underpins mainstream development discourses of progress, modernisation and Westernisation. These discourses inflect development programmes designed to introduce advanced methods of English language teaching and promote gender equality. Taking a different perspective, critical analyses have demonstrated the ways in which discourses of international development have constructed a binary divide between 'developed' nations defined in terms of their advanced technical, economic and political status, and 'developing' nations defined in terms of their comparable deficiencies, thereby perpetuating colonial hierarchies and justifying interventions based on the supposed expertise offered by foreign development workers. Similar critical analyses point to the ways in which the spread of English language in the developing world fosters a colonial legacy of social and economic inequalities. In the face of these critiques, alternative models of English language teaching in development have proposed participatory approaches that emphasise the agency of local communities, and value of diverse knowledge practices. Despite the adoption of rhetoric emerging from alternative understandings of development, it seems that mainstream institutional and pedagogical practices of language teaching and gender development programmes continue to support Western models of progress and modernisation, and tend to neglect approaches that relate classroom practice to critical analyses of broader economic, cultural, historical and political concerns.

Chapter 2 introduces a macro framework of time and space as a means of understanding the discourses that drive development and English language teaching, and explaining the disjuncture between teaching practices, and the specificities of places in which those practices are introduced. Drawing on theories of space and time contributes to a more complex understanding of the historical, developmental and pedagogical discourses that shape teacher subjectivities and practices. This innovative theoretical framework lays the groundwork for the twin arguments that underpin the book. First, that English language teaching in international development contexts is governed by a modernist narrative that favours time, and occludes a comparable educational engagement with the specificities of space, place and context; second, that this temporal narrative supports the reproduction of colonial and patriarchal discourses that shape development work as a masculine endeavour, thus creating significant personal and professional challenges for a largely female teaching workforce.

Ideas about time and space may at first appear quite abstract, yet they underpin our perceptions, experiences and constructions of professional and personal life, and have the capacity to relate these everyday experiences to larger geopolitical forces. The language of time and space resonates with understandings of our social and political place in the world, and spatial regimes organise and regulate educational practice. So, for example, notions of time are central to our ideas about curriculum planning, the sequencing of lesson activities, the importance of efficiency, and the proper development of language acquisition; concepts of time shape our beliefs about progressive improvements in teaching methods, and our ideas about the contribution English language can make to economic, scientific and technological development. Similarly, notions of space and spatial boundaries as socially constituted underpin the division between schooling and community life, and naturalise the separation of students into discrete classes based on proficiency levels. Social and spatial expectations secure the authority of the teacher in controlling the space of the classroom; spatial arrangements, both physical and symbolic, affect the way teachers interact with students, colleagues and supervisors.

Discourses which take the politics of space and location as central, aim to destabilise taken-for-granted concepts of time as the primary explanatory framework for social and educational development. Focusing on practices that engage with the social and political dimensions of space and place also aims to enable a more complex conceptualisation of the interaction between English language teaching, gender relations and the cultural and political dimensions of context. Drawing primarily on insights from postcolonial, feminist and cultural geography, a focus on spatiality – an understanding of space as socially and politically constituted – is intended to challenge prevailing Western notions of progress that legitimise the imposition of externally generated disciplinary practices in diverse locations across the globe. By asserting the importance and specificity of space, my intention is to move beyond assumptions about context as something language teachers already know and already incorporate into language teaching: context as a given set of variables or local scenes, or context as taken-for-granted notions of social relevance and social progress. By prioritising concepts of time and space, there is the potential to relate quotidian life, and pedagogical practices, to broader social, economic and political relationships (Gulson & Syme, 2007; Moss, 2006), and to think in new ways about the dynamic interaction between global/local engagements, gender regimes and English language teaching. In effect, I argue that understandings of time and space may be used to politicise, revitalise and extend the notion of context in English language teaching, particularly within the domain of international development.

Chapter 3 turns from the more theoretical understandings of temporality and spatiality to focus on the specific historical, geographic and linguistic relationship between East Timor, Indonesia and Australia. This relationship contextualises my discussion of Australian teachers' experiences of international development interventions in Indonesia and East Timor, undertaken during periods of external engagement and change in language policy and teaching practice. The teachers' appointments are also framed within a broader global relationship between 'the West' and 'the rest', exemplified in Australia's strategic interests in, and ambivalence towards, Indonesia and East Timor. Throughout these relationships, we see the centrality of spatial concepts: realised in regional interests, borders and territorial claims and, on an everyday level, in teachers' perceptions of their positioning in the discomfort zones of development work.

Chapters 4, 5 and 6 focus on teachers' narratives, and readers who are more interested in these empirical accounts may prefer to skip to those chapters. In Chapter 4, teachers' narratives constitute development contexts as complex contact zones, characterised by particular patterns and hierarchies of gender, ethnicity and economic status within communities of foreign workers, and between foreigner and host communities. From the teachers' perspective these socio-spatial constructions produce dislocation between donor and host communities, and tend to reproduce a hegemonic, colonial masculinity that effectively controls women's bodily performance and mobility while reinforcing racial stereotypes. Yet teachers' narratives also demonstrate how distance and detachments may be ameliorated through a re-engagement with a local sense of place.

Chapter 5 considers how teachers' perceptions of the development world outside the classroom relate to their pedagogical practices, and focuses on the flow of bodies, practices and ideas across the walls of the classroom. It explores the ways in which naturalised concepts of time and space shape pedagogical practices in ELT, reproduce development hierarchies and isolate classrooms from a political engagement with context. It demonstrates that although calls to relate teaching and language to local contexts are widely acknowledged amongst teachers, teaching performances are nevertheless shaped by instrumental educational discourses and technologies that promote Western teaching methods as universally applicable. These approaches tend to focus classroom activities on 'the main task of describing [and teaching] text and talk' (van Dijk, 2006: 160) at the expense of interaction with salient alternative discourses emerging from local places and spaces beyond the classroom walls. This chapter considers the interaction and disorientating effects of these competing discourses in the space of the classroom, and the extent to which teachers either conform to a temporal paradigm that privileges a limited vision of progress or engage with the spatiality of context.

Chapter 6 extends this focus on the educational domain and illustrates the way gendered spatial discourses, together with the civilising legacies of colonialism in ELT, affect the teachers' negotiation of gender in the course of language teaching. Although the promotion of gender equity is now a mainstream imperative in international development policies, its realisation in the classroom is shown to be constrained by a range of spatial paradoxes concerning the outsider status of foreign teachers, conflicting expectations of pedagogical nurturance and authority in both public and private domains, and ambiguous gendered hierarchies between teachers and students. The teachers' struggles within these spatial conditions nevertheless suggest some productive and flexible ways to approach gender relations through practices that take into account the interests, values and investments of students and teachers.

The final chapter draws together the arguments developed throughout the book and considers the implications that might be drawn more generally for the English language teaching profession. It concludes that orthodox ELT principles and practices, underpinned by modernist temporal narratives, provide an inadequate basis for a critical orientation towards language, gender and the global context of development. Building on the teachers' narratives, it discusses the possibilities for spatial enquiry as a tool for interrogating the social and political dimensions of pedagogy, and opens possibilities for revitalising connections between language study, context and imagined futures.

Notes

1. For convenience, I have used the terms 'First World' and 'Third World', 'developed' and 'developing countries', but acknowledge that these are contentious labels and subject to intense debate.
2. A limited amount of information is given about each project and teacher in order to restrict the likelihood of identification.
3. All teacher and student participants are referred to by pseudonym.

Part 1
Understanding English Language Teaching in Development

Chapter 1
Models of Development and English Language Teaching

The teachers' narratives at the heart of this book are about their work as English language teachers in international development programs. To see how the teachers' experiences are shaped within broader political and professional discourses, in this chapter I outline, in broad terms, different paradigms or ways of understanding development, ways of understanding gender in development, and ways of understanding the spread of English language as aspects of development work. In the later part of the chapter, I discuss in more detail the professional practices of English language teaching, explore the distinction between functional and critical approaches, and raise pertinent questions regarding the adoption of appropriate pedagogies for language teaching in development.

Models of International Development

The inception of the development age was concurrent with the post-World War II processes of reconstruction and decolonisation, and set a new international agenda on the basis of a world divided into 'developed' (First World) and 'undeveloped' (Third World) nations. The new global organisation, attuned to the economic interests of the USA (Rist, 2002), and in part aimed at the containment of communism (in the Second World), opened up markets from the dismantling of colonial empires and, in many ways, perpetuated the interests and hierarchies of colonialism. Colonial expenditure that had been aimed at expanding the trade opportunities of colonial powers gave way to financial investments referred to as aid, and tended to be concentrated in countries where donors had strategic political or past colonial connections. Previously colonised countries tended to be viewed as lacking the means to modernise and develop, thus justifying the need for the First World's ongoing intervention in 'less advanced' nations in the form of economic assistance and the transfer of modern scientific and technical knowledge (Escobar, 2004; Kingdon, 1999).

In broad terms, development means the planned process of change intended to improve the material and social conditions of life for people and states outside the wealthy, industrialised world (Kingsbury, 2004a). However, development remains a highly contentious term, and there is much disagreement at all levels as to its meaning, the nature of the problems to be solved, and the selection of appropriate remedies. The primary focus on economic growth in the early postwar period has shifted over succeeding decades, and development has expanded to encompass a range of meanings and priorities. Goals related to improved governance, health, equity, democratisation, and environmental protection now sit alongside economic measures of development. In the following discussion, different ways of thinking about international development are represented, for the sake of simplicity, in three broad categories, which are then mapped against different ways of viewing gender and English as an international language, with these two elements representing important aspects of many development programmes. The models or paradigms described here are intended as a broad overview, and do not represent complete, or discrete, ways of approaching either development or the spread of English language. My aim here is not to present a conclusive definition of development, nor an exhaustive accounts of shifts in development theory, but rather to consider the broader discourses that influence the ways in which language teachers understand their work in development enterprises.

Three broad categories that have been influential in understanding the processes and ideologies of international development are described here as modernisation, dependency and alternative development. Each of these broad frameworks is associated with particular approaches to education, language and literacy.

Modernisation discourses of development

The dominant paradigm of development established in the early postwar years depicts the developing countries of the Third World as following a pre-established pattern of economic, political and social change in order to ameliorate poverty and achieve progress towards the material standards of living attained in developed, First World nations. In the era of decolonisation, modernisation offered an apolitical justification for why some nations were rich and others poor, identified the transition from traditional to modern societies as the key to progress, and proposed a set of planned interventions to achieve that transition (Fiedrich & Jellema, 2003: 40).

Economic growth, stimulated by capital investments, has for the most part been central to the modernisation theory that continues to pervade mainstream development thinking, and is designed to move societies 'on a linear path from [traditional] subsistence agricultural systems to industrialized economies and market production' (Visvanathan, 1997: 6). In the early postwar decades, the work of Rostow (1960) in describing the stages of growth that would lead traditional societies towards economic maturity and mass consumption led to a belief that every country would follow the path to prosperity mapped by developed nations. Development in this sense is seen as synonymous with modernisation, a process that includes not only progress towards industrialisation, the inculcation of economic and organisational efficiency, and the establishment of formal political institutions, but also the adoption of 'modern' attitudes and behaviours in relation to education, health and employment.

Integral to this model of development is the view, held by most donor countries and international agencies, that the only workable paradigm for development is the normative, externally established, Western model of advanced, globally integrated market economies. This view has been strengthened since the collapse of the 'Second World' and the end of the Cold War, which has left only one broad mainstream blueprint for development being promoted worldwide (Kingsbury, 2004a). Recent decades have seen purely economic measures of development expanded to include concern with the elimination or reduction of inequality and unemployment, and improvements in health, education and environmental sustainability (Todaro & Smith, 2009). Nevertheless, in mainstream institutional discourses, these factors have remained firmly within, and contributing to, the framework of economic growth (Rist, 2008). Sidestepping potentially unpalatable political and ideological issues that might arise from an externally imposed model of economic development, poverty is usually approached as a series of technical problems for which technical solutions may be offered by more developed economies.

In the mainstream paradigm, the value of education as a means of human resource development lies in its contribution to 'economic growth, sound governance, and effective institutions' (AusAID, 2007: 5). This instrumental relation between education and economic growth was highlighted in the *Education for All* speech delivered by the then Australian Minister for Foreign Affairs at the end of the international decade of 'Education for All'[1]:

In both developed and developing nations education is the key to growth. It is an absolute necessity if we are to reduce poverty and achieve development. It is, in fact, development's most basic building block. Education develops knowledge and skills and contributes to the strengthening of civil society, to national capacity and to good governance. These elements are critical in the effective implementation of sound economic and social policies necessary for the alleviation of poverty. Education makes further contributions to the alleviation of poverty through its impact on economic growth. Better educated workers are more productive and the accumulation of knowledge increases the rate of technological change – thus accelerating economic growth. Education and training are instrumental in ensuring the supply of a skilled labour force in ever changing markets. (Downer, 2000)

Prominent in Australia's aid policy during that time was also the notion of knowledge transfer from the West to institutions of higher education in developing countries. These were seen as 'conduits for the transfer, adaptation and dissemination of knowledge generated elsewhere in the world', and thereby 'contribute to increases in labour productivity and higher long-term growth' (Downer, 1996: 11). From this perspective, education interventions thus aim to transfer skills, knowledge and attitudes for a more productive workforce, raising the level of income per head and thereby stimulating economic activity.

Contributing to human resource development, a threshold level of basic, functional literacy was claimed to be necessary for workers to maximise their productivity levels and facilitate economic growth towards Rostow's 'take-off' stage of development and modernisation (1960). External funding for functional literacy, seen as a neutral set of decoding skills existing autonomously outside culture and society, became part of the modernisation project in the 1970s. More recently, developing countries that are seen to have performed best, such as the newly industrialised countries of East Asia, are those where economic growth has been propelled by heavy investments in education and training (Kingsbury, 2004b). In particular, OECD data has suggested that language and literacy education is 'critically involved in making some economies more competitively successful than others' (Lo Bianco, 2002: 4), but in the age of globalisation, support for a more complex level of literacy combined with technical assistance to improve employment opportunities has been identified as an essential requirement of educational development.

Over the 60 years of the development age, aspects of modernisation theory have been subject to ongoing revision. However, since the mid-1980s the influence in mainstream development thinking of neoliberal, market-based solutions has supported the rise of neomodernisation models that maintain a focus on Western style economic growth. In this sense, neoliberalism represents a return to the 'the often unstated belief that there is one path to development that all nations can follow in a series of stages . . . a simple movement toward modernity that is portrayed as so successful in the West' (McKay, 2004: 61). Under this regime, targeted development programmes have been linked to market restructuring conditions demanded by funding bodies such as the World Bank and the International Monetary Fund that aim to remove 'traditional barriers to growth' such as government intervention (McKay, 2004: 61). By improving global capital flows and trade opportunities, these reforms purport to 'extend the benefits of economic globalization' and alleviate poverty by integrating developing countries into a worldwide, market-driven, economic system (Griffin, 2003: 790). In the mood of the times, although mainstream development programmes have incorporated notions of equity and sustainability borrowed from alternative development paradigms, the principles of the economic growth model have remained intact, alongside 'value neutral' functional literacy programmes focused on vocational or work skill competencies (Rassool, 1999).

Critical discourses of development

In a second paradigm, originally influenced by Marxist scholars such as Frank (1969), economic development and modernisation are thought to represent ongoing forms of Western political domination and exploitation, with development aid objectives designed to support the political, strategic, military and commercial objectives of donor countries. Development itself is seen as an essentially political process that involves local, national and international communities' choices about the production, allocation and use of resources. This political interpretation of development suggests that the process of decolonisation continued the economic 'war' between the colonial North (the wealthy, powerful *core* regions) and colonised South (the impoverished *periphery*) over resources and markets (McKay, 2004).

The assumptions of the capitalist economic development model are said to contain an inherent tension between donor altruism and economic self-interest that renders impossible the goal of achieving a more just and equitable global society through the extension of economic growth (Rist, 2002: 214). Instead, continued development through a capitalist system of economic growth is said to reproduce spatial patterns of uneven development in favour of donor countries' interests, a process that fails to achieve the broader goal of a more just and equitable global society (Harrison, 2004). From this perspective, underdevelopment thus remains rooted in historically generated structures of the capitalist world system and colonial dependency, with systemic inequality maintained by national and international elites who benefit from previous and present concentrations of power.

Critiques of development informed by Foucauldian discourse analysis suggest that a conflation of discourses on progress, modernisation and Westernisation has produced a 'Third World' where people are defined and measured by deficiencies and lack, thus perpetuating colonial images of the pagan 'Other' as backward and ignorant (Escobar, 1995; Spurr, 1993). In this sense, development is seen as an heir of colonialism and its dichotomous construction of Self and Other: of European superiority, and 'Otherness' as a lack of qualities associated with 'Europeanness' (Gillen & Ghosh, 2007). Economic growth models of development which aim to correct such deficiencies in recipient communities tend to present poor people as 'objects of someone else's policy and not as active participants in the improvement of their individual and community lives' (Zachariah, 1997: 483), thus 'reinforcing rather than addressing sources of discrimination and social exclusion' (Mayo, 1997: 22). Such policies support notions of First World superiority and assume that foreign 'experts', who have identified the gap in skills or knowledge, can then prescribe and implement an appropriate solution based on Western cultural models. Moreover, the association of expert knowledge with Western science in the professionalisation of development enables the removal of problems from the political and cultural realms, recasting them in terms of the apparently more neutral realm of science. The discourses of development are thus seen to establish particular hierarchical social, cultural and knowledge relations that 'set the rules' of development practice, determining 'who can speak, from what points of view, with what authority, and according to what criteria of expertise' (Escobar, 1995: 45). 'The rules' also determine the way in which problems are identified and categorised, and what solutions are to be enacted.

In terms of educational aid, dependency is linked to the adoption of Western educational forms and models, the preferential use of Western languages, especially in higher education, and reliance on Western academic books and journals, practices that combine to make periphery universities consumers of knowledge from the centre rather than producers of locally mediated knowledge (Altbach, 1998; Coleman & Sigutova, 2005). Development assistance for education through these means has been critiqued as a form of cultural imperialism that has secured allegiance between national and transnational bourgeois elites (Arnove, 1980; Carnoy, 1980). Possibilities for resisting metropolitan forms of knowledge and influence are limited, because the types of educational development offered by foreign consultants and aid agencies are said to be compromised by their incorporation into the economic and political objectives set by donors. Within an ideological framework determined by an external funding body such as the United Nations, the World Bank, a foreign government or a large corporation, many agencies responsible for the delivery of aid adopt educational programmes and 'specific pedagogical models' that 'implicitly articulate and underwrite particular views of social development' (Rassool, 1999: 92). Reliance on international agencies and consultants in educational development can thus lead to an external form of governance and quasi-privatisation of the education system, with implications for the control of literacy provision, and for the status of languages through decisions about the language of instruction.

In recent years, a neodependency school has denounced the claims that development will be enhanced by economic globalisation, which is identified as a means of further expanding the economic and political interests of international capitalism at the expense of underdeveloped countries (Escobar, 2004; Petras & Veltmeyer, 2002). Moreover, critical theorists have argued that donor countries have profited since the end of the Cold War by an increasing association between aid and military intervention in conflict zones such as Rwanda, Sudan, Sri Lanka and East Timor (Addison, 2000; Clarke, 2006; German & Randel, 2002; Jeffreys, 2002). In these situations, aid is seen as a 'will to govern', to support donor countries' geopolitical interests, and to instil order in areas of the globe construed as unstable, barbaric borderlands where underdevelopment is associated with threats to global and regional security (Duffield, 2002). In particular, since September 11, 2001, critics have argued that increased development assistance has been used as one ingredient in the war on terror, and an element in establishing a 'new imperial' order of 'asymmetrical and spatialized violence' and 'territorial control' (Escobar, 2004: 18) ultimately designed to meet US security and economic objectives.

A growing body of work is now emerging in regard to the role of educational aid in conflict or postconflict environments. After food and water, shelter and health care, education has become a crucial element of humanitarian response in emergency situations (Kagawa, 2005); nevertheless, in any reconstruction effort, tension exists between the drive for a return to 'business as usual' via speedy restoration of the education system, and the urge for significant long-term curricular reform as a means of ameliorating underlying economic, political and social causes of discord (Paulson & Rappleye, 2007; World Bank, 2005). The World Bank recognises that the process of reconstructing and reforming education systems is a means of 'reshaping the future', but questions remain about *whose* plan of reform and *whose* vision of the future should be implemented.

Alternative discourses

A diffuse range of alternative development theories has grown out of dissatisfaction and disillusionment with both modernisation and dependency paradigms. Alternative approaches have broadened the concerns of development to include 'bottom-up', grass-roots interests, and an emphasis on democratic structures of community participation, self-reliance and empowerment, social justice and equality (particularly in regard to gender), and environmental sustainability and alternative cultural values. Favouring local, indigenous knowledges, and influenced by feminism, these approaches have helped to challenge Western economic and scientific bias in development thinking and to encourage alternatives that 'imagine other forms of existence' (Rist, 2002: 244).

Proponents of alternatives known as reflexive development and critical globalism (Neverdeen Pieterse, 1995, 2001) reject the either-or dichotomisation of both 'top-down' mainstream and 'bottom-up' critical approaches, and present a complex view of development as a process of global–local interaction, rather than as a coherent, linear project (Harrison, 2004). From this point of view, some aspects of globalisation are seen as oppressive, but others have the potential to be enabling and transformative. Rather than focusing on oppression, exploitation, deficiencies and needs, such approaches aim to harness people's potential to shape their own identity and destiny. As Amartya Sen (1999: 14) has argued, economic growth is not an end in itself, and 'development has to be more concerned enhancing the lives we lead and the freedoms we enjoy'. In a complex reciprocal relationship, economic freedom can help to promote political, social and cultural opportunities, such that 'freedoms of different kinds can strengthen one another' (Sen, 1999: 11). Within this more complex picture, development is understood as an on going, contingent, trial-and-error process of integrating multiple knowledges in a larger framework against which a critical stance should be maintained (Craven, 2002).

Alternative approaches to development vary in their degree of accommodation or opposition to mainstream development, and their underlying approach to social, political and economic reform. A key point of difference arises, for example, in regard to the aims and means of increasing participation and empowerment: an emphasis on increased participation may, in some development domains, aim to *incorporate* marginalised individuals into mainstream social, political and economic structures; in other enterprises, increased participation may be envisaged as a means of overturning entrenched social structures by building alliances that *transform* the mainstream. In recent years, concerns have been expressed that participatory approaches have been co-opted into the mainstream and have promoted a model of incorporation into 'disempowering agendas', and, as a result, have failed to achieve meaningful change to inequitable social, economic and political structures at both local and global levels (Hickey & Mohan, 2005: 238).

Alternative educational responses to Westernisation in development are often aimed at the promotion of critical understanding and empowerment, the construction of new identities and, ideally, the creation of cultures of resistance and social transformation (Kingsbury, 2004b). Associated approaches to adult literacy aim to support participation in the democratic processes of a complex, globalised society, and require a more sophisticated range of literacy and communicative skills than those necessary for performing a functional role in the economy. In alternative development theories literacy is integrally linked with ideology, culture, knowledge and power, and includes the ability to read the interaction between social systems, historical relations and global networks as part of a process of self-identification and cultural transformation (Rassool, 1999). Influenced by Freirean ideals, postcolonial critique and dependency theory, critical literacy is recognised as an important part of the struggle for independence and political enfranchisement, and as a means of contributing to human rights through 'economic and political redress in relation to historical forms of control and exploitation' (Rassool, 1999: 86). These concerns with the meaning and value of literacy are taken up again later in this chapter.

Questioning the effectiveness of development aid

Despite concerted criticisms and revisions of development policy and practice over recent decades, there has been no consensus as to the causes of, or the means and strategies for alleviating, continuing world poverty. Indeed, critiques of development aid focusing on its failure to reduce world poverty suggest that through colonialism, neocolonialism, and more recently the effects of neoliberal globalisation, the West has become ever richer at the expense of the Third World. As Kingsbury (2004a: 8) observes, while 'development fads have changed... the lives of many poor people remain much the same', and indeed recent measures of development demonstrate that global inequalities are increasing. Since the fall of the Soviet Union, a more complex global political order has emerged in which Western capitalist states and multinational institutions dominate, while poorer states are beholden to routine and pervasive intervention from international financial agencies (Harrison, 2004: 1042). Moreover, the rise of globalisation has meant that nation states now have greater difficulty in addressing problems of poverty because the state no longer controls the flow of finance across national borders. Indeed, financial flows associated with speculative global currency and commodity trading now dwarf official development assistance, and have led to greater volatility and instability in national economies (Hunt, 2004; Watkins & Fowler, 2002).

Meanwhile, development assistance programmes intended to alleviate the effects of uneven development have spawned a billion dollar multinational industry with an enormous bureaucratic infrastructure. The flow of aid funds and a proliferation of development programmes are seen to mask a form of neocolonialism that reproduces the activities of colonial administrators, missionaries, international investment and trading companies and merchant gamblers (Remenyi, 1994). Benefits accrue to donor countries through the effects of 'boomerang aid', whereby funds allocated for development are returned to the donor country through the purchase of services (in the employment of consultants) and products (such as textbooks) supplied by donor countries (Aidwatch, 2005). The flow of such funds may, in turn, be used to promote power elites within recipient countries, and to support the conspicuously comfortable lifestyles of foreign consultants and experts. One significant outcome of this, and of the recent devolution and commercialistion of aid, is that individual project failures are not openly acknowledged or discussed, since recipients and NGOs have a vested interest in presenting a public façade of success so as not to jeopardise lucrative government contracts for future projects. Moreover, necessary compliance with donor imperatives also means that projects remain politically safe, rather than encouraging host communities to raise questions about donor institutions' vested interests in prevailing socio-economic-political structures (Slater & Bell, 2002).

In one of the few detailed reviews of English language teaching in development, Savage (1997: 318) refers to a litany of parasitic macro and micro abuses that are 'symptomatic of the overall macro-failure of development assistance'. Rather than addressing the involvement of educational aid in these failures and abuses, Savage claims that 'most people involved in educational development assistance are genuinely interested in collaborating towards the improvement of their particular sector' through the provision of 'the best and most up-to-date' resources and training for host countries (p. 320). These views tend to reflect the myth of ELT as an autonomous, apolitical and beneficial activity, thus avoiding any notion of complicity between ELT and the social, political and economic 'failures' of development assistance.

Competing interests in development

Central to the debate over the effectiveness of development is the question of who sets the agenda for spending the development aid dollar. The various categories of 'players' in development projects, including diplomats and politicians, development bureaucracies, NGOs, implementers and participants, have different objectives that may not always coincide. On the one hand, the aid objectives of donors may be designed to support the political, strategic, military and commercial objectives of donor countries (Escobar, 2004). Thus, Australia's overseas aid policy, focusing on economic growth and liberalisation, also fosters Australian trade and strategic foreign policy interests. On the other hand, language teachers in development, employed by a range of NGOs, may be concerned with linguistic objectives, or a range of professional and personal goals, with little awareness or interest in wider strategic and political concerns (Denham, 1997; Toh, 2003); or they may come to develop a profound sense of the politics surrounding their role. These conflicting interests and objectives may cause tension during the implementation or evaluation of a programme when the various agendas of players are given material expression.

Adding to this complexity, the number of players in development enterprises has been significantly increased since the 1970s and 1980s by the neoliberal devolution of aid delivery and consequent proliferation of decentralised and often poorly coordinated NGOs (Neverdeen Pieterse, 1996). These organisations purport to represent the interests of civil society, and their political effects rely on their ability to operate at the juncture between the centre and the periphery (Abeles, 2008). The role of NGOs is important in the debate over agenda setting, since they may act either as a force for challenging existing orders of power or as agents in support of foreign and internal government objectives (Petras & Veltmeyer, 2002). Certain NGOs, promoting participation, drawing on grass-roots support and functioning outside government control, may be 'counter-hegemonic in their practices or overtly critical of government policy' in their aim of transforming societies from within (Rassool, 1999: 91). Other NGOs function more as public service contractors, as the representatives of conservative evangelical movements, or as commercial enterprises bidding for lucrative government development contracts (Craven, 2002; Neverdeen Pieterse, 1996).

Thus, despite their grass-roots origins, over the last decade there has been considerable debate about whether the independence of such organisations has been compromised by their dependence on powerful funding bodies that ultimately set the agenda for development aid. In their continuing search for funds, NGOs have become increasingly 'professionalised' businesses (Abeles, 2008), complicit in development's neoliberal hegemony, and providing more effective instruments to 'advance external interests and agendas while further concealing the agency of outsiders' and elites (Mosse, 2004: 643; Townsend *et al.*, 2002). In sum, the widely accepted 'principles of project success: engage with local realities, take your time, experiment and learn', have been eroded by a dangerous mix of weaker governments, greedy private interests and coopted NGOs, subject to heavy bureaucratic preconditions and donor demands, and shackled by attitudes of 'short-termism, control orientation and standardisation' (Edwards, 1999: 86).

Gender and Development

Increased emphasis on participation and social equity in mainstream development policies has highlighted the necessity for engagement with the experiences of women in development. In recent decades, gender equality has been incorporated as a key goal in international development programmes and enshrined in international commitments, including the Millennium Development Goals. 'Gender mainstreaming', which requires the inclusion of a gender perspective in all development programmes, has become the primary strategy for improving the situation of women; however, these principles have not always been realised in the practice of programme design and delivery. On the whole, a lack of institutional commitment and an inability to transform entrenched social and power relations has meant that the rate of change towards equality has been glacial (Charlesworth, 2005; Thomas, 2004).

In the modernisation paradigm, an interest in participation and gender equality has often centred on women's inclusion in education and employment as an essential element in enhancing economic growth. Nevertheless, despite decades of global economic growth, feminist activists have claimed that global inequalities, environmental degradation and increasing militarisation have had negative consequences for women's struggle to gain a more equitable share of available wealth. Women's labour in low-paid work for multinational corporations and in the global care chain has shown that unbridled economic growth does not always favour gender equity, and a critical consensus has emerged that gender mainstreaming has largely failed in achieving greater gender equality and transforming gender power structures. Indeed, feminist critiques (e.g. Charlesworth, 2005; Orford, 2002; Pearson & Jackson, 1998) claim that the incorporation of gender awareness into mainstream development policies has tended to produce an institutionalised, unreflective pursuit of formal equity through a range of technocratic and administrative interventions that have depoliticised what is at base a political struggle. Rather than empowering women, such interventions 'may secure control by both governments and international agencies and "encircle" . . . those who are its targets' (Manderson & Jolly, 1997: 20). As Eisenstein (2007) has argued, on a broader scale, gender mainstreaming may also be used as a 'decoy' to legitimise conservative militarist and free-market agendas that ultimately exacerbate conditions of inequality for women. Neglecting gender problems associated with hegemonic, militarised masculinities, such interventions may secure control over women as objects of programmes designed by governments and international agencies. Within the economic frameworks set by transnational institutions, women may be 'developed' as resources to promote the efficiency of the market, yet without a commitment to political transformation, the 'mainstream remains masculine' (Thomas, 2004: 5).

Alternative approaches to gender in development have resisted universal frameworks of feminism and international human rights, and have instead been formulated within feminist debates over the way gender interests are conceived, represented and investigated. In particular, as Mohanty (1988) has pointed out, 'Third World woman' has been unhelpfully represented as poor, ignorant and tradition-bound, in contrast to Western women who are implicitly represented as educated, modern and free. Such postcolonial critiques have served to complicate approaches to gender and implicate white women – including those in international aid work – in the paternalistic, colonial discourses of development. However, Hunt (2004) has cautioned that a response that involves a retreat to culture and tradition in order to dismiss racist or colonial interference has, in some circumstances, prevented women overcoming ingrained inequalities. In refusing global solutions and essentialist notions of gender, feminist poststructuralists have emphasised the importance of engagement with multiple axes of difference, and with women's local, everyday struggles and rhizomatic practices of resistance, to develop an emancipatory politics

(Yeoh *et al.*, 2002). These emancipatory politics aim to avoid 'essential-ist notions of and transhistorical claims about gender' (p. 2) in favour of 'situated', contextualised analyses that consider the intersection of gender/power relations with other axes of difference in the politics of change. These debates and issues will be further explored in relation to the experiences of teachers in Chapters 4 and 6.

Models of English as an International Language

The three broad paradigms of development outlined above correspond in many ways to theoretical models explaining the spread of English as an international language. As with the different paradigms of development, it is important to note that these models represent neither discrete entities nor a linear progression, but can coexist and enjoy a different status in different domains.

In the predominant modernist paradigm, the global spread of English is seen as the fulfilment of a utopian desire for a shared language of international communication (Tollefson, 2000: 8). According to this model, English is favoured for its link to worldwide communication among governments, in business and industry, science and technology, and edu-cation. By association, English is presented as the language of moderni-sation and development, and is seen as a natural, neutral and beneficial adjunct to economic globalisation and progress. In keeping with these views, English language training in development projects is mostly aimed at specific instrumental purposes such as the teaching of academic and vocational skills.

A second, more critical model of the spread of English holds that the predominant paradigm fails to recognise the matrix of social, his-torical, cultural and political relationships in which that spread operates (Phillipson, 1992). English is described as a language of imperialism and class interests which poses a threat to indigenous languages and plays a role as a gatekeeper to socioeconomic advantage and influence in many societies. In this view, policies that secure the hegemony of English are seen to reproduce global inequalities that enable core countries to maintain political, economic and cultural domination over the periph-ery. Such domination ensures unequal distribution of benefits from the spread of English, bringing positive rewards for some people, mostly in centre countries, and harmful effects to others, mostly in the periph-ery. Although this critical model offers a more comprehensive analysis of global relations than the modernist approach, it has shortcomings related to the socioeconomic determinism and reductionism in which it is situated. Most importantly, its structural basis disregards the resistant and appropriating actions of periphery communities; it tends to perpetuate a homogeneous, culturally fixed view of the Other, and a view of language itself as a fixed, abstract entity separable from its environment (Makoni & Pennycook, 2007).

Both modernist and critical models of English language spread have been re-evaluated as part of the shift in the way we conceptualise world order away from universal truths and Enlightenment notions of modernity, positivism and the unified rational subject. Thus, a third, alternative, paradigm of English language spread has emerged which attempts to avoid simplistic centre–periphery or global–local models and which resists the notion that 'a universal theory of socioeconomic relations can account for all global relationships and that people are passive consumers of hegemonic cultural forms' (Pennycook, 1995: 48). Alternative models offer a way forward for communities faced with the challenges posed by the hegemony of English as an international language by engaging with the appropriation and disinvention of English, and the construction of transgressive counter-discourses realised in specific social, economic, cultural and political contexts of use. Thus, the 'intention is not to *reject* English, but to *reconstitute* it in more inclusive, ethical, and democratic terms' (Canagarajah, 1999: 2). While acknowledging the potential regulation of people's lives by dominant forms of language, culture and discourse, this paradigm recognises the vigour of human agency at work in the way people resist and produce their own forms in the global flow of 'language mixing, transidiomatic practices and refashioned identities' (Pennycook, 2007: 117).

However, as Canagarajah has warned (1993), analyses that overemphasise agency and locate the demand for English solely within recipient communities risk underestimating the hegemonic, colonising power of English and its central role in maintaining economic, cultural and political inequalities. In his review of language in development programmes, Savage (1997) counters the difficult accusations of linguistic imperialism by asserting that the demand for English is driven by recipient countries, who are therefore themselves responsible for overcoming any resultant internal economic and social injustice. This shifting of agency and responsibility locates problems within the developing nations and implies that the reproduction of inequality should not be of particular concern to international teachers in these contexts. Although Brutt-Griffler's (2002) study of world English similarly emphasises the agency rather than domination of periphery communities, it does identify imperialist tendencies in the spread of centre-driven methodologies for English language teaching and in the continuing privilege accorded to native speakers.

English as the language of necessity

From its early diffusion, imposition or importation through colonialism, and its spread in the service of economic advancement, the growth of English in periphery countries has now gained its own momentum within the forces of globalisation, and has become a substantial part of education in aid programmes for donor countries such as Australia (AusAID, 2007). In periphery communities, then, one of the tensions in addressing the demand for English in language planning arises from the double movement of decolonisation and globalisation: whereas decolonisation and the establishment of the nation state may entail resisting English in favour of establishing a new national identity, globalisation has partially dissolved national boundaries and reinserted the importance of English through the spread of 'multinationals, market forces, pop culture, cyber space, and digital technology' (Canagarajah, 2005: 196). Despite the rich linguistic diversity of many development contexts, and official policies and initiatives that value multiple national languages, many developing countries, including Indonesia and East Timor, have experienced an unplanned boom in demand for English as the language of necessity. For social and economic advancement, for accessing foreign aid money, for the chance to escape grinding poverty, or for passing gate-keeping examinations, it is purportedly 'what parents and governments want – English by popular demand' (Kennett, 2002: 239).

Professional practices of international English language teaching

The ideologies that underpin the spread of English have been associated with the shaping of an international English language teaching industry, and point to key concerns for ELT practitioners in development and commercial enterprises. In his critique of English language teacher training, Phillipson (1992) notes that Centre-trained ELT 'experts' are skilled in techniques that are presented as being universally relevant, and employed by commercial interests aiming 'to establish physical territory' at home and abroad (Holliday, 2005: 28). Almost two decades on, Phillipson's critique still holds weight, as professionals continue to be sent throughout the world to promote a raft of 'expert' TESOL techniques, train periphery teachers in the latest methodologies, develop teaching materials, and solve training needs in government and higher education.

The notion of universal relevance, fundamental to the image of Centre ELT expertise, is implicated in the disconnection of ELT from specific local contexts, and is said to contribute to the failure of language and literacy programmes to achieve their goals (Phillipson, 1992). Disconnection can be seen in a lack of awareness of the political, economic, social and cultural framework in which ELT operates, and a lack of engagement with the meaning and role of English language in each context. Moreover, although the acquisition of cultural and linguistic insight into a complex local context cannot be achieved by foreign experts in a few weeks of training, a feature of many aid programmes involving ELT has been the restriction to unrealistically short time frames and a narrowing focus on measurable outputs, accountability and efficiency (Holliday, 2005; Sharp, 1998). These restrictions militate against the flexibility and responsiveness required for teachers to develop an awareness of the language, cultural politics and existing educational environment in which they are working.

Further impediments to political and social connection are embodied in the tenets of ELT, including the bias towards monolingualism in methodology and materials, the importance attributed to the native speaker teacher, and the myth of learner-centred ideals that mask teacher-centred authority. These foundations, critics claim, are based on false assumptions about language pedagogy and serve to uphold the power of core countries in the spread of ELT in the periphery. An examination of the assumptions on which these and related language teaching practices are based suggests that they are not neutral aspects of classroom methodology but cultural practices which are sometimes at odds with the sociocultural, attitudinal, pragmatic and economic realities of recipient communities.

Method

The concept of method, at the heart of ELT pedagogy, has been interrogated in recent years for its claim to represent a series of scientific advancements in techniques for imparting and acquiring knowledge. Critical analysis demonstrates that methods, rather than representing some inexorable progress towards efficiency, tend to recycle a set of basic options in an alternating shift between formal, grammatical approaches and more 'natural' behavioural approaches (Pennycook, 1989: 604). Like other ELT practices, dominant methodologies are based on a Western ideal which sets the conditions for a process-oriented, task-based, inductive, collaborative, communicative teaching methodology that may not always be suitable in host countries and cultures with different educational values, aims and preferences.

For some time now, communicative language teaching (CLT) has been promoted as the most advanced methodological development in language teaching (Canagarajah, 2002: 137). Communicative methods are claimed to be central to ELT in development, which has been described as 'change oriented, experiential, pro-autonomy, collaborative and communicative' (Savage 1997: 283). In Savage's analysis, communicative language teaching is associated with 'sound pedagogical practice' and 'established theories of learning' (Henderson *et al.*, 1997, cited in Savage 1997: 307), and is set in opposition to 'conventional teaching approaches' and 'outdated' techniques such as repetition, memorisation and grammar explanations, which supposedly encourage learner passivity and 'dependence' (p. 307–308). Such reliance on scientific justifications serves to consolidate the myth of ELT as an autonomous, apolitical and beneficial activity, and reproduces the discursive distinction between advanced/Western and traditional pedagogies, through which learners must be progressed to avoid remaining mired in 'the old inefficiency of chalk-and-talk' (Kennet, 2005: 101). The superior status accorded to centre-generated methods thus fixes certain negative identities on students and teachers in periphery locations, helping to reinforce notions of tradition and backwardness versus enlightenment and progress. At the same time, an emphasis on technical efficiency and progress circumvents any notion of complicity between ELT and potentially negative social, political and economic effects of development assistance. Demands for efficiency have, ironically, also seen communicative teaching goals of activating language use in real situations superseded by the development of fixed syllabuses based on set language functions and practised in contrived activities and games. These in turn may contribute to the deskilling of teachers, have a reductionist and limiting effect on language use, and neglect the need for learners to develop critical methods of understanding and using English for their own purposes.

On the other hand, blanket criticisms of CLT as inappropriate in periphery contexts may run the risk of perpetuating fixed cultural generalisations of particular students and societies. In practice, as Larsen-Freeman (2000) observes, classroom teachers adapt methodologies freely according to context, and there is potential value in exposing and challenging students with a variety of classroom approaches including communicative practices. Moreover, an uncritical acceptance of more traditional teaching practices which focus on grammar, translation, written examinations and a lack of free L2 communication in the classroom, combined with limited input outside the classroom, may provide inadequate education in language skills for communication with speakers of English from other countries and access to future jobs, thereby perpetuating the marginalisation of students in periphery communities (Canagarajah, 1993; Pham, 2000). Moving away from a notion of progressive development in methods, a 'postmethod condition' has more recently been put forward that rejects the imposition of any 'pre-conceived method on local teaching contexts' (Canagarajah, 2002: 138). Instead, an inductive, context-driven strategy is endorsed that 'frees teachers to see their classrooms and students for what they are and not envision them through the spectacles of approaches and techniques' (Canagarajah, 2006: 20). Yet such ideals are not easy to achieve in practice, particularly in development contexts where foreign teachers, as outsiders with their own socially and politically constructed perceptions of the classroom, may struggle to fully appreciate the contextual dimensions of students' learning. Moreover, in order to make contextual sense of their activities, teachers need to become reflexively aware of and engaged in the larger, conflicting sociopolitical discourses that shape understandings of English language education and the contexts in which it occurs.

Textbooks

International English language teaching is also associated with a reliance on globally marketed materials and textbooks that support a profitable centre-based publishing industry. The pervasiveness of textbook-based teaching can be seen in accounts of ELT practice where, often for reasons of practicality and institutional convenience, the textbook becomes the *de facto* curriculum. Donated and pirated copies of Western textbooks abound in poor countries and, in situations where resources are scarce, the possession of an English textbook may be seen as an important priority (Do, 2000). Such textbooks tend to emphasise either an Anglo-centric or international cultural and social situations, and present a sanitized, synthetic, 'one size fits all' content. They are apt to reduce the complexities of the world to a simplified Western viewpoint which generally assumes 'a materialistic set of values' in which a moneyed lifestyle of international travel, entertainment and leisure are the norm (Gray, 2002). Such textbooks, argues Canagarajah (1993), can have the unintended effects of deprivileging knowledge derived from practice at a local level, and of introducing irrelevant or problematic social, moral and cultural values.

The selection and presentation of situations, tasks and values in textbooks also shape social roles for students and teachers. In this regard it is important not only to consider explicit social identities which are drawn for learners but also to reflect on what is excluded from textbooks and curricula. Particularly in contexts of socioeconomic deprivation, the absence of depictions and learning tasks involving the necessity to confront inequitable economic and social situations suggests a lack of engagement with learners' needs and experiences, thus potentially reinforcing a sense of individual and community helplessness. Of course, both learners and teachers of English can be actively involved in evaluating, adapting and 'talking around' textbooks (Sunderland *et al.*, 2000); however, we might be sceptical about the degree to which foreign teachers can identify and step out of their own cultural and political frames to locate or explicate alternative values in teaching materials.

In an attempt to avoid the restrictions of textbook teaching, some language in development projects have adopted task-based and experiential learning projects which are designed to create opportunities for learners to engage with contextually relevant content for vocational skills development (e.g. Kenny & Laszewski, 1997) However, where such activities comply with desires to integrate learners into a system that supports mainstream, neoliberal economic goals they, too, may construct learners in terms of deficiencies that need correction, and promote acceptance rather than interrogation or transformation of an inequitable social, economic and political status quo.

Appropriate pedagogies for change?

The notion of transformation, or change, is identified by Kenny and Savage (1997) as one of the characteristic features of language in development projects, and is closely associated with the development of an alternative vision of the future. Given that any educational endeavour bears our vision for the future encoded in curricula and pedagogy (Simon, 1987), it is crucial to ask *whose* curriculum and pedagogy teachers employ, and *whose* vision of the future is enacted in development classrooms. In development practice, however, Eversole (2003: 792) claims that a focus on *how* to achieve change has long outweighed a serious examination of 'who is defining and driving change, and how the motivations and relationships of different people and groups influence the change process'. Although Savage suggests that teachers in language and development projects 'should see themselves as change-agents' (1997: 285), case studies in this field suggest that the teachers' agency is harnessed to the production of particular types of change, and limited visions of the future. Indeed, even in literacy programmes designed around the ideals of participatory education, teachers (and learners) become aligned to broader discursive forces of progress that tend to promote change towards Western models of knowledge and practice rather than a critical appraisal of the interests served in such processes (Fiedrich & Jellema, 2003). For reasons that I discuss throughout this book, it seems that English language projects in development appear to run along instrumental lines that sustain a mainstream, Western model of development. In this regard, the label of change-agent, co-opted from alternative development, appears to be the current term for an externally appointed authority who can design and deliver strategies to resolve problems in developing communities, but with the proviso that these comply with donor objectives.

Given the drive for change, an important though largely unanswered question concerns how English language teachers in development might construct a more complex, dialogic connection with specific places and communities, *and* maintain a critical awareness of the broader ideological and macro sociopolitical forces that shape the work they do. The remainder of this section looks at some of the proposals that have aimed to reconnect language and literacy teaching with sociopolitical dimensions of the local and global (or, more accurately, translocal²) context. In this regard, I outline in more detail below the contrasting approaches towards literacy education referred to earlier in this chapter. These are discussed in two broad (and therefore inevitably reductive) groups: first, instrumental and approaches, often associated with modernisation discourses of development; and second, critical approaches, mostly associated with critical and alternative theories of development. Both approaches link language and literacy teaching to context in particular ways, and aim to promote change and empowerment. I then consider the relationship between these approaches and English language teaching in development, and point to some of the tensions and paradoxes arising for teachers in this context.

Functional approaches to literacy

One range of functional approaches presents literacy in development as a neutral set of skills that contribute to the improvement of individual life chances and, at the same time, promote social and economic growth through increased workforce productivity (Rassool, 1999). Underpinning such approaches is the view that literacy functions as an autonomous technology of the intellect, promoting superior cognitive capacity for abstraction and rational thought, and contributing to the development of more complex social and political systems (Goody, 1986; Ong, 1982). From this perspective, literacy itself is seen as an agent of progress, and is empirically connected to various developmental measures of wealth, health, nutrition, and child survival. For target-driven policy providers and donors concerned with the achievement of predetermined outcomes, functional literacy programmes that measure achievement in terms of the mastery of a particular set of skills can meet the need for quantitative measurement and monitoring of progress. However, the notion that literacy will automatically lead to certain benefits reflects, in the words of Robinson-Pant (2008: 786), an instrumental, depoliticised 'input-output model' favoured by development policies: a 'literacy first' view that assumes 'social change can be planned and predictable, initiated by literacy providers rather than participants'.

Alternative functional approaches see literacy not so much as an autonomous skill, but rather as a range of social practices informed by their location in specific institutional and cultural contexts (Street, 1984). Related pedagogical approaches are often concerned to bring language and literacy teaching in line with prevailing contextual constraints and, in development contexts, include the adoption of an 'appropriate methodology' designed to more efficiently incorporate periphery educational cultures into a system of centre-derived language teaching practice (Holliday, 1994). Also drawing on understandings of literacy as socially situated are text-based or genre-based models of language and literacy instruction that relate texts to particular academic or vocational contexts of use. Often presented as more advanced than teaching methods that focus on isolated grammatical structures at sentence level, genre-based approaches have been widely adopted by language and literacy teachers in Australian educational institutions, and aim to empower marginalised students through explicit instruction in the 'powerful' forms of writing and speaking deemed necessary for access to dominant social and economic strata (Cope & Kalantzis, 1993; Martin, 1993). Nevertheless, a more critical scrutiny suggests that this apprenticeship model of teaching, in aiming to assimilate learners to existing disciplinary forms, can also tend to be conservative of prevailing social, cultural and political norms (A. Luke, 1996). In development projects, where foreign teachers may be working with students who are marginalised within dominant global social, economic and political structures, accommodation to existing norms may not always be desirable.

Critical approaches

In contrast, critical approaches to language and literacy education focus specifically on the connection between language and its _political_ context; that is, the way languages and texts construct particular ideological positions and maintain power relationships between individuals and groups in particular cultural situations. Within these approaches, language and literacy education are seen to be 'complex matters that invoke issues of identity, nation, culture, ideologies of belonging, religion and international allegiances, and conflicted histories' (Lo Bianco, 2002: 6). Critical approaches to language and literacy education are grounded in a transformative social analysis; they contest the utilitarian and vocational meanings that frame functional concepts of language and literacy, and propose to challenge the marginalisation which is structured into language use in specific contexts. This is a very different notion of context, change and empowerment than that put forward in functional approaches to language and literacy. Indeed, some critical scholars have emphasised that a political commitment and engagement with context must *precede* considerations of literacy: if functional models propose 'literacy first', critical models can be said to provide 'literacy second'; that is, literacy *follows* from an interrogation of learners' lived experiences, undertaken within the broader aim of collaborative action for social and political transformation (Rogers, 1999, 2000). This approach of foregrounding social and political analysis is evident in some later studies of language in development projects, such as that discussed by Copley *et al.* (2005), and demonstrates an emphasis on teachers' listening and learning, rather than providing prepackaged solutions.

One stream of critical approaches to language and literacy education, inspired by theories of critical pedagogy developed in the work of Paolo Freire, recommends that teachers and learners resist accommodation to the status quo by engaging in a critical analysis of the social framework in which they live. Freire (1972) argued that a traditional 'banking' model of education, in which the teacher acts as the dispenser of knowledge, works to 'domesticate' rather than 'liberate', and thereby reproduces existing structures of societal oppression. In periphery contexts, 'banking' education facilitates the process of 'cultural invasion' by powerful colonial and neocolonial interests, which renders learners and communities dependent on external visions of social change (Mayo, 1995: 366). In contrast, Freire proposed a process of 'conscientization', engaging learners in the rational analysis and critique of their lived experiences with a view to grass-roots transformative action. In place of top-down methods of instruction, teachers (as facilitators) and students (as participants) would be involved in a 'problem-posing' education, and a reciprocal, dialogical process of learning; and in place of using centrally produced primers disseminating top-down knowledge, learners and facilitators generate their own context-derived literacy materials based on local concerns. Critical literacy, then, is a process in which learners read not only the 'word', but also the 'world' (Freire & Macedo, 1987), with the aim of bringing about empowerment for social, political and economic transformation.

Extending these broader political perspectives to ELT, Tollefson (2000) refers to proposals put forward by Giroux (1988) for teachers and learners to become transformative intellectuals, concerned with moral and ethical issues and the impact of English language teaching on socioeconomic stratification, rather than merely technicians who apply a set curriculum to learners. These concepts of social transformation have influenced the development of dialogic, negotiated teaching practices which ground language education in the everyday challenges and political concerns affecting the lives of students (see, for example, Auerbach, 2000).

An example of how critical approaches to literacy and development have been brought together is demonstrated in a pedagogical model of participatory adult education known as REFLECT (Regenerated Freirean Literacy through Empowering Community Techniques). At its inception in the mid-1990s, this approach aimed to combine Freirean philosophy with practical tools developed for Participatory Rural Appraisal to draw on the knowledge of participants in the planning and management of development programmes. *Reflect* is a collaborative process designed to systematise the knowledge of participants, analyse topics of local concern, and promote empowerment towards individual or collective action (Archer & Cottingham, 1997; Cottingham *et al.*, 1998). From its beginnings in pilot programmes in Uganda, Bangladesh and El Salvador, *Reflect* has diversified and spread to over 70 countries and 500 programmes that encompass a range of social and political aims, and promote the development of multiple languages and literacies integral to the achievement of political change (www.actionaid.org; Archer & Newman, 2003).

What *Reflect* and other Freirean-inspired programmes emphasise is the importance of plans for action that are derived from an ethnographic understanding of contextual constraints that limit the opportunities of marginalised communities, rather than a technicist approach that determines project goals and then measures success according to predetermined targets (Mosse, 2004; Robinson-Pant, 2010). In this regard, Archer (2003) emphasises that *Reflect* is not a quick fix approach to social and political change. Also, of particular importance in relation to promoting the concerns of marginalised communities, the facilitator should ideally 'come from within the same community as the participants and from the same socio-economic condition' (Archer, 2003: 199), a principle that would rarely be realised in the case of First World teachers deployed in development projects.

Questioning critical pedagogy in development

Realising the broad aims of critical and participatory pedagogy inspired by Freirean philosophy has proved to be challenging, and literacy development projects based on these ideals have been subject to acute critical scrutiny. Critical evaluations assert that the technologies employed in participatory development programmes merely enable 'new and more subtle forms of manipulation' by 'specially trained change agents' (Rahnema, 1992: 125–127) and overlook the practical challenges faced by individual learners and facilitators. On a systemic level, Tabulawa (2003) holds that participatory pedagogy has been enthusiastically embraced and prescribed by donor institutions as a value-neutral, one-size-fits-all approach, but in practice is designed to install Western education (via the teaching of modern literacies) and to 'facilitate the penetration of capitalist ideology in periphery states . . . under the guise of democratisation'. In this sense, a focus on participation merely serves to incorporate individual learners into the broader trajectory of mainstream development, while obscuring the agency and power that continues to reside in the institutional position of the facilitator.

At the project level, a range of problems is faced; for example, when participatory ideals and messy social processes meet prescriptive measurable aims; when an essentialised, depoliticised focus on 'the local' obscures analysis of wider structures of oppression; or when participation is deployed as a technique to recruit, produce and domesticate 'proper' beneficiaries who conform to the modernising or civilising norms of development organisations (Bartlett, 2005, 2008; Mohan & Stokke, 2000; Mosse, 2004). Caught between ideals and realities, Bartlett (2005) observes that teachers, in particular, face immense difficulties in translating Freirean concepts into practice, and seldom have sufficient time and opportunity to engage in praxis, that is, to reflect, problematise, rethink and revise their teaching. On an individual level, Fiedrich and Jellema (2003) point to the impossible expectations that surround participatory projects and their exaggerated faith in the power of human agency to effect change. They argue that the 'triumphalism of participatory orthodoxy' has meant the struggles of participants, and their contradictory alignments in the discourses of language, literacy and empowerment tend to be silenced (2003: 21). Unable to carry forward Freirean ideals of deploying literacy in the service of class struggle, development practitioners retain participatory techniques and literacy methods as part of a depoliticised and professionalised programme, while notions of social critique and transformation are abandoned. Thus, although participatory approaches are 'usually presented as a fundamental break with "top-down", ethnocentric paradigms of development', their reported achievements in producing 'modern rational selves' ironically mirror 'the very same attitudes and practices long championed by the [mainstream] development community' (Fiedrich & Jellema, 2003: vii).

Dominant languages and critical pedagogy

Discussions of both functional and critical approaches to language and literacy have largely been oriented towards first-language contexts, and require some rethinking when transferred to other (foreign language) teaching situations, particularly those mediated by dominant languages and unequal economic and political forces. In particular, the powerful forces surrounding notions of English as an international language significantly affect the ways in which critical or participatory approaches are realised in development projects (see, for example, Abbott, 1992, 2000; Appleby *et al.*, 2002; Taylor-Leech, 2009; Watson, 2007). In globally diverse sites of English language teaching, transformative agendas are associated with the shift from 'appropriate pedagogies' that adapt dominant ELT practices to periphery contexts, to 'pedagogies of appropriation' that take the local context (with its social, political and economic contingencies) as a starting point for teaching, and focus on the ways that English language can be taken up and transformed at the micro level of the classroom, and used as a form of disruption and resistance to globalising norms (Canagarajah, 1999, 2002). Such proposals attempt to move beyond dichotomous views of power as residing solely in institutions or in human agency and focus on the negotiation of a discourse that traverses these polarities. However, as we have seen in the critiques of participatory pedagogies, the seeming simplicity of this shift can obscure the contradictory demands that come into play in the development classroom when both functional and transformative aims are focused on the foreign teacher and his/her role in the classroom.

In summary, English language teaching projects in international development appear to be caught between conflicting demands, expectations and desires, shaped by an ambiguous mix of instrumental, centre-prescribed, modernising aims, combined with principles of 'bottom-up' empowerment and social transformation. Although there has recently been a shift in interest towards critical, political understandings in this field (see, for example, the *TESOL Quarterly* 2002 special issue on Language in Development; and later accounts of practice in the 'Language and Development' series, such as Copley *et al.*, 2005), there appear to be few studies of how foreign English language teachers in periphery development projects negotiate these conflicting demands. The challenges of

enacting critical, participatory pedagogies through the teaching of a dominant language, while meeting the instrumental demands of donor-funded
projects, are rarely discussed.

The need for a new slant on language in development

The various discourses of international development and the spread
of English as an international language outlined in this chapter provide a setting for the discussion of issues related to ELT and gender
throughout this book. Where these domains overlap, in language and
development programmes, the prevailing mainstream institutional and
pedagogical practices tend to reflect liberal Western models of progress,
favouring donor-approved aims of upgrading vocational skills through
the application of functional approaches designed to enhance economic
growth. The problem here is that these approaches risk reinscribing the
sedimented social and economic inequalities of international development. In contrast, alternative approaches to development have emphasised the importance of participation, collaboration, social justice and
gender equity in processes of societal change. Although these principles
have in recent decades been incorporated into the rhetoric of mainstream
development policies, such incorporation has too often left intact the hierarchies of knowledge and power inherent in mainstream development
practices.

In the field of education, alternative approaches such as those adopted
in explicitly political projects like *Reflect* have stressed the importance
of developing a critical stance in relation to processes of economic, cultural and political oppression. Yet these political strategies have received
relatively little attention in studies of English language education in development. Indeed, the potential for practicing alternative pedagogies that
attend to social and political dimensions of given development contexts
appears to be constrained, in part, by the very nature of the development enterprise: it would seem contradictory to expect donor-sponsored
English language projects to mobilise opposition towards the fundamental orthodoxies of the development enterprise. Thus, it may seem logical
that Centre-trained English language teachers have been better equipped
to implement the instrumental and functional aims of language and
gender equity in development, than the transformative aims imagined
in critical analyses of these domains. What is needed, as Eversole (2003:
793) has pointed out, is 'a new slant' that 'acknowledges in detail the
complex social landscapes in which [development] change is conceived,
implemented, and resisted'.

The differing perspectives and attendant ambiguities outlined in this chapter inform my consideration of the discourse and practices of English language teaching in the development contexts of East Timor and Indonesia. They point to a range of challenges that face those involved in English language teaching as they struggle to meet the contradictory demands of development projects. In the next chapter I will outline a theoretical framework of time and space that seeks to bring a new slant to the complex social, cultural and political landscape of development and English language teaching.

Notes

1. The 1990 World Conference on Education for All (WCEFA) was organised by international agencies, including UN organisations and the World Bank, and resulted in a framework of goals for education to be achieved in the coming decade.
2. A notion of *trans*local works with the assumption that *all* places and cultures are crisscrossed with paths of external influence. This is further discussed in Chapter 2.

Chapter 2

Time and Space in English Language Teaching, Gender and Development

> *. . . there is no knowledge of the Other which is not also a temporal,*
> *historical, a political act.*
> Fabian, 1983: 11

In the previous chapter I outlined various ways of understanding English language teaching and gender in the context of international development, and pointed to some of the challenges for taking up critical approaches to language and literacy education in contemporary development projects. I suggested that mainstream notions of development are structured according to discourses of modernisation that assume a logical, developmental progress through the intervention of First World expertise and the application of certain 'universal' principles. Critical analyses suggest that development perpetuates global inequalities inherited from an earlier colonial era, inequalities that are also associated with the spread of English as an international language. In educational domains, critical and alternative pedagogies have been proposed that value local knowledges, and rely on principles of participation and collaboration as a means of challenging those inequalities. However, on the whole, while critical approaches have been taken up in various literacy programmes, they have received limited attention in studies of English language teaching in development. It seems that the potential for practicing alternative pedagogies that attend to social and political dimensions of context appears to be constrained, in part, by the nature of the development enterprise.

In this chapter, I suggest that an underlying discursive framework, operating through regimes of time and space, serves to maintain certain prevailing Western notions of development, education and gender relations. The framework introduced in this chapter draws on insights from postcolonial, postmodern and feminist cultural geographies, and provides a hermeneutic tool for understanding the relationship between teachers' everyday experiences and the broader geopolitical forces that come into play in international development. An analysis based on time and space illustrates on how modernisation narratives impose a limited template of progress on practices of development, gender and English language teaching, and hinder an engagement with the specific gendered and racialised contexts in which development and language teaching projects occur.

Modernity and the Control of Time and Space

Over recent decades, scholars in diverse disciplines have discussed the various ways in which naturalised understandings of time and space shape our understandings of the world. In what follows, I discuss several key interrelated aspects of time and space in modernity: the conception of time as historical progress, the mechanical control of time, the spatialised construction of disciplinary knowledge, the separation of time and space in the processes of globalisation, and the implications of all these for globalised development, education, and the production of modern, gendered and racialised subjectivites.

Modernisation theories of development, referred to in the previous chapter, proposed a shift from traditional to modern social and institutional forms. In turn, theories of modernisation are underpinned by particular notions of modernity as an advanced form of society that represents a radical break with the constraints of tradition. Whereas traditional societies and individuals were seen as mired in fatalism, custom, indiscipline and stagnation, the transition to modernity was associated with the adoption of rationality, efficiency, and the idea that the world was open to change through human intervention; with economic institutions such as industrial capitalism and the market economy; and with political institutions such as the nation state and mass democracy. For traditional societies, a shift towards universal education, literacy, and a reliance on discipline and individual self-improvement were seen as central to the achievement of modernity, and a metaphor for the maturation from childhood to maturity.

Regulating time and space

Time as progress

The primary notion of time underlying modernity is one of an unfolding, historical progress towards a predetermined end. 'Traditional' history, according to Foucault (1984a: 88), presents itself as objective and universal, and traces the past as an 'ideal continuity . . . a teleological movement or natural process'. Belief in universal progress and historical destiny was the 'great obsession of the nineteenth century' (Foucault, 1986: 22) and, as a result, time was associated with agency, action, will, development and progress, played out as a human drama against a static background of space. This notion of an advancing history, grounded in an Enlightenment story of rational progress, draws together many other disciplines and systems of knowledge into a modernist metanarrative that describes a unifying sense of direction within historical time (Lyotard, 1984), and rationalises the continuation of a select sociopolitical system into the future. Time, the privileged signifier, 'equals change/movement', and with time are aligned 'History, Progress, Civilization, Science, Politics and Reason' (Massey, 1994: 257). The metanarrative of rational progress can be seen in examples as wide ranging as religious stories of destiny and God's will, scientific stories of evolution, Marxist stories of class conflict and revolution, colonial stories of taking up white man's burden, and development stories about the transformation from traditional societies to modern states.

The persistent influence of 19th-century historicism, or the view of history as a natural succession of predictable stages, is also evident in education. Understandings of the 'natural stages' of evolutionary biology were evident in early approaches to population management through compulsory schooling, which was designed to ensure a 'natural path of development, the best kind of civilising process ... a correct progress from animal infant to civilized adult' (Walkerdine, 1992: 17). In the 20th century, developmental psychology leant scientific weight to theories of child development towards scientific rationality, and supported the rise of child-centred pedagogy as means of securing within the individual the broader societal aims of modernisation and progress (Walkerdine, 1984). These underlying metaphors of development have meant that modern educational theory is dominated by considerations of time: 'by historically oriented theories, by temporal metaphors, by notions of change and progress exemplified, for instance in "stages of development", whether conceived in terms of individual psychology ... or of modernisation theory' (Peters, 1996: 93). In this way, time becomes implicated in the formation of modern subjectivities through its organisation of the developing individual.

Clock time

The advent of modernity has also been associated with a growing awareness and ordering of abstract, mechanical time as an adjunct to capitalism, industrialisation and the control of labour. In premodern agrarian cultures, time reckoning was tied to the seasonal, diurnal and bodily rhythms for tending animals and the cultivation of crops, but the diffusion of the mechanical clock from the late 18th century allowed the construction of a universal, 'empty time', and the separation of time from space (Giddens, 1990). An abstract, quantifiable time detached from context could, as Marx demonstrated, be commodified and used as a basis for industrial development, and 'saving time' to maximise efficiency and profit became integral to life in capitalist society (Adam, 2002, 2003, 2004). In the European project of taking industrialisation to other countries, the ordering of time facilitated the structuring of a labour force, minimised individual and organised rebellion, and provided a regulated world view (Thompson, 1967): to be modern, progressive, even civilised meant to adopt the industrial approach to time. Temporal regulation was an integral element in the project of modernity to construct order out of chaos, and continues as a crucial dimension of the time politics that underpin the processes of globalisation and development (Adam, 2002, 2003).

Spatial regulation

The hegemony of historicism has, until recently, tended to 'occlude a comparable critical sensibility to the spatiality of social life' (Soja, 1989: 11), yet spaces and places are central to the social construction and management of normality and difference in the modern nation state. For Foucault, spatial politics is 'fundamental in any form of communal life; space is fundamental in any exercise of power' (1984b: 252), at all levels 'from the great strategies of geopolitics to the little tactics of the habitat' (1980: 149). Across the territory of the modern nation state, society is constructed as the object of systematic sustained political observation and intervention through the functioning of administrative apparatuses, institutions and the organisation of bodies in space. Epitomised in the panopticon, spatial control brings together knowledge and power to regulate individual subjects in a process of normalisation: through observation, examination, judgement, classification and separation (Foucault, 1977). Enfolding this spatial control into individual subjectivities produces a 'spatialization of being' that can be seen in the different behaviours we take on according to our location in different spaces (N. Rose, 1996).

Temporal and spatial regulation of society has had significant implications for teaching and learning, and the rise of mass education in the 19th century provides an illustration of institutional reliance on the mechanical ordering of time and space. On the one hand, the spatial enclosure and separation of education from community life helped to promote the sense of its independence from political and economic interests, thereby fostering, in Bourdieu and Passeron's terms (1970), its own 'misrecognised existence' as a disinterested system of knowledge and practices, activities and resources. Then within the school, the ordering of time and space has been crucial in establishing the surveillance and micro-control of activities designed to produce docile subjects in accordance with developmental regimes, such as may be found in psychology or theories of second language acquisition (SLA).[1] Spatial segregations and timetabling are integral to the successful introduction of an invisible disciplinary power, evident in the processes of grading and streaming, classification and examination which, in turn, regulate both the teacher and the progress of students through designated stages of achievement.

Spatialised disciplinary knowledge
Spatial regulation is also implicated in the formation of modern disciplinary knowledges. Through the 'spatialization of knowledge' (Foucault, 1984b: 254), disciplines such as education, linguistics and English language teaching are constituted as scientific knowledge systems, sometimes broken down into a set of atomised skills, and presented as autonomous and objective, context-free and released from historical specificity (Thorne & Lantolf, 2007). The development of disciplinary knowledge as science was associated with the production of a static, systematic order from the chaos of nature: the classification of objects according to observable characteristics, and their organisation into spatial taxonomies and hierarchies, which had the effect of establishing power relationships between objects, both non-human and human, positioned in accordance with the taxonomic system.

A crude example of spatial taxonomies at work could be seen in the colonial production of racial characteristics fixed into abstract spatial and temporal taxonomies that justified white European supremacy; a more recent example might be seen in the concentric circles model of World Englishes (Kachru, 1996) that constructs and categorises language varieties, speaker types and geographic locations according to implicit hierarchies. Within language-related disciplines, fixed knowledge systems have, in turn, effected the constitution of particular identities for participants by ascribing characteristics to particular groups of language learners according to their geographic origin, gender and so on. English language teaching, in its own separated existence, operates as a specific educational discipline, in both senses of the word. Nested within the academic disciplines of applied linguistics, SLA and education, English language teaching has been described as a practice that 'classifies, docilizes, and disciplines the disenfranchised into their place within the larger social system' (Grinberg & Saavedra, 2000: 435), one that is organised through a politics of both space and time.

With the development of modern disciplinary knowledge, other systems of knowledge fell away, relegated to the field of unscientific superstitions; and the production of knowledge in the form of abstract, mobile technologies meant that the resultant 'scientific truths' could be disconnected from their original contexts and applied universally in distant locations. The mobilisation of disciplinary and institutional knowledge through spatial technologies of communication (writing, maps, textbooks and now digital media) helps to explain how centres, nation states and empires 'reproduce their influence by establishing cultural, as well as economic monopolies, over time and space' (Heyer, 1993: 103).

Separation of time and space

It is the abstraction, separation and recombination of empty time and space that provided the globalising scope of European modernity. The production of an 'empty' clock time, its lifting out from specific places and its consequent spread across 'empty' space, forms the basis of territorial control and fosters 'relations between "absent" others' (Giddens, 1990: 18). In this process of 'time-space distanciation', modernity 'tears space away from place', and so that 'what structures the locale is not simply that which is present on the scene; the "visible form" of the locale conceals the distanciated relations which determine its nature' (1990: 18–19). So, for example, the construction of standardised units of empty time and space enabled European explorers' discovery and mapping of remote regions of the world, without reference to privileged local knowledges; and in more recent times has facilitated the global spread of modern institutions which, disembedded from the 'particularities of contexts' and the 'restraints of local habits and practices', greatly extended their scope (1990: 63). In this way, particular social, cultural, institutional and disciplinary practices were deterritorialised as 'universal', mobilised in the form of multivalent technologies (N. Rose, 1996) and reterritorialised as norms and ideals in new places.

In summary, the abstraction and ordering of time, its valorisation as historical progress, and its regulation and separation from space can be seen as hallmarks of modernity. The location of nations along a chronological spectrum of development and the global spread of time, through a conjunction of capitalism, modernity and colonialism, have given rise to the assertion of temporal agency over an inert geography, or space. Taken together, these concepts and practices of control over both time and space provide a basis for interrogating the institutional interventions and disciplinary practices of international development, whereby First World disciplinary experts are dispatched to Third World countries positioned as less advanced in the march of progress. This dispersal does not, however, ensure a wholly deterministic outcome, since in each specific site or locale the intersection of various global and local practices and discourses can give rise to conflict, opposition and resistance to regimes of institutionalisation, development and regulation.

In the current era of globalisation, an intensified stretching of time–space distanciation continues to link 'distant localities in such a way that local happenings are shaped by events occurring many miles away and vice versa' (Giddens, 1990: 64). Thus, one of the key features of contemporary cultural analyses is the 'push and pull' between globalising, hegemonic tendencies, and the simultaneous trend towards localisation and difference. What emerges is a paradoxical spatial relation that highlights the extremes of contemporary modernity which 'has acquired a relentlessly uneven and contradictory character: material abundance here, producing poverty and immiseration there; . . . The rich "West" – and the famine-stricken South' (Hall, 1989: 124). It is this paradoxical space that is evident in the particular locations of international development, and in the relationship between donor and recipient communities.

Rethinking modernist space and time

Recent decades have marked a turn from a universal, temporal narrative in favour of an interest in the particularities and politics of spaces, places and geographies. The reappraisal of Western historicism, associated with the decline of Marxism and the ascendancy of a poststructuralist episteme, has been associated with a transdisciplinary 'spatial turn' which has highlighted the impact of spatialisation in political, economic and social life. Influenced by the pioneering work of Henri Lefebvre (1991/1974) on the social construction of space and the role of spatial organisation in the reproduction of capitalism, the spatial turn has been signalled in social and cultural theory by the emergence of spatial metaphors indicating relations of power: position, location, margins, third space, centre–periphery, border crossings, liminal space, contact zone and so on. These concepts of space are not merely passive, abstract backgrounds, but imply an active, complex 'spatialized politics of identity' (Keith & Pile, 1993: 2), and may encompass real, imaginary, symbolic or metaphoric aspects of space. In order to engage with this more complex realisation of space, the term spatiality has been used to indicate the ways in which the social, political and spatial 'are inextricably realized one in the other' (Keith & Pile, 1993: 6). Despite this interest in the social politics of space, and the integral role of space and place in the cultural politics of education, Gulson and Syme (2007: 100) observe that these remain largely 'under-examined and under-theorized components of educational studies, development and critique'.

The development of a spatial hermeneutic is concerned with rethinking the relationship between time and space, and examining the implications of spatial politics for the construction of identity and difference (Soja, 1989). A spatial ontology proposes a way of understanding our being-in-the-world on many different scales, from being in the body, in the locales and networks of human contact and settlement, and in the flows of people and cultures in a globalised world. Here, the inseparability of social and spatial form is critical: just as social relations (of gender, ethnicity or class) constitute particular forms and arrangements in physical space, so spatial patterns (architecture and institutions, global corporate networks, classrooms or ghettos) constitute particular social relations. Being created out of social relations, space is 'full of power and symbolism, a complex web of relations of domination and subordination, of solidarity and co-operation' (Massey, 1994: 265). Rather than being understood as an ordered, Euclidean frame in which events occur, space then becomes the articulation of social relations which necessarily have a spatial form.

An emphasis on spatial interpretations is not meant to replace historical, time-based interpretations, thereby reinscribing a binary opposition between the two, nor does a spatialisation need to promote a simplistic anti-history. Rather, spatial interpretations attend to the intersection of time and space in order to disrupt a range of associated binary distinctions, insisting that although temporality and spatiality are different from each other, 'neither can be conceptualised as the absence of the other' (Massey, 1994: 264). Similarly, for Soja (1996: 71), drawing on Henri Lefebvre (1991), spatiality, sociality and historicality are inseparable, forming a 'trialectics of being'. Thus, while space is not a static backdrop to the march of time, it is nevertheless implicated in the production of events and histories, as can be seen in the geopolitical development of industrialisation or capitalism, and the rise and fall of empires. In a further blurring of binary distinctions, Massey brings together various meanings of space as both order *and* chaos: the order of physical, discursive and symbolic spatial systems, arrangements, networks; and also, most importantly for the realisation of a transformative development, the chaos of happenstance, juxtapositions, paradoxical mixtures and unintended consequences.

Spatiality and development

Spatiality is a key theme in the reinterpretation of development as a historical discourse (Soja & Hooper, 1993). Within the dominant temporal narrative, development is seen as a time-lagged diffusion of capitalist modernity to the 'undeveloped, traditional, not yet fully modernized parts of the world' (Soja, 1989: 33). A spatial theorisation, on the other hand, suggests that uneven development is actively produced through the geography of modernity, and in the maintenance of a spatial hierarchy resulting from the rise of hegemonic European imperialism and the internationalisation of capital. From a spatial perspective, uneven development might thus be understood as the 'spatio-temporal patterning of socially constructed differences at many different scales from local to global' (Soja & Hooper, 1993: 185). Uneven development in this sense is evident in the disparate economic conditions that exist within a household, across the nation state, or between distant countries, and results from the workings of hegemonic power as it produces and reproduces difference to create and maintain advantageous social and spatial divisions.

To forward an understanding of what spatiality might entail, and how it might be relevant to thinking about language teaching, development and gender, in the following sections I take up some ideas that have emerged to destabilise fixed, modernist notions of time-as-progress, and its binary opposition to space. These ideas have emerged from various transdisciplinary locations, grouped here under postcolonialism, postmodernism and feminist geography, and are intertwined with images of flows, movement and travel, and with experiences of place as a contact zone of engagements with difference.

Postcolonial Conceptions of Time and Space

Considering the colonial heritage of both ELT and development, as outlined in the previous chapter, it is useful to look more closely at how colonial legacies can be understood through the concepts of space and time in postcolonial scholarship. In terms of a spatial geopolitics, Young (1990) has observed that the temporal narrative of European history mirrors the territorial (spatial) absorption of the non-European world into a totalising 'world history'. Historicist forms of knowledge, epitomised in European knowledge of Other societies, enabled and legitimised the power of European imperialism, bringing together the Occident and the Orient in a chronological relationship of modern and not-yet-modern, of domination and hegemony. In anthropology, the effect of this '*chronopolitics*' was the 'denial of coevalness', that is, a denial of radical difference amongst spatially separated societies (Fabian, 1983: 31). From the European perspective, 'global *space* appeared transformed into a *time* sequence, with Europeans...the sole inhabitants of modernity' (Neverdeen Pieterse, 2001: 19). Spatial distance between different societies was converted into a single chronological sequence; differences between coloniser and colonised were relocated along a linear teleology of progressive time according to the 'one and only narrative it is possible to tell' (Massey, 2005: 5; see also Mignolo, 2000). As Massey (2005: 5) explains, 'that cosmology of "only one narrative" obliterates the multiplicities, the contemporaneous heterogeneities of space. It reduces simultaneous coexistence to place in the historical queue', and dulls the appreciation of difference. In response, the struggle *against* colonialism challenged not only the order and direction of Western history, but also the very idea of time as a linear story of progress (Bhabha, 1994).

Postcolonialism, then, is not so much a temporal progression from colonialism, as a deconstruction of forms of knowledge and power, realised in a multitude of textual practices that work to construct and inscribe imperial discourse on colonised land and people, and that persist in present-day global relations of international development. Taken together, these textual practices produce a colonial discourse (Said, 1978) that served the historical and territorial processes of colonisation, and is evident still in the neocolonial spaces of development.

Exploration and mapping of space and the Other

Colonial discourse is enabled by the illusion that space is transparent, so that the world and the Other can be recognised or examined (by an implied imperial presence) as knowable objects (Blunt & Rose, 1994; Mills, 1994). With literal and metaphoric practices of exploration, mapping and naming, the imperial gaze of European colonisers emptied newly discovered landscapes and people of their earlier meanings and produced 'new knowledge, meaning and history' (Mohanram, 1999: 76). By integrating epistemic and spatial practices, the spread of imperialism thus became 'an act of geographical violence through which every space in the world is explored, charted, and finally, brought under control' (Said, 1994: 271): colonised space was re-presented in textual form as a place open to European presence and control, 'an object of study, an area for development, a field of action' (Spurr, 1993: 25–26). Combining practices of surveillance and measurement (observation, judgment, evaluation, comment), enabled the mapper to maintain an objective distance, to master the environment from a secure, superior position, and at the same time erase his own physicality. From the explorer's (governor's, soldier's or peacekeeper's) visual sweep over the geographic landscape, and the administrator's (or professional development worker's) panoptic surveillance of institutional spaces, to the academic or scientific gaze constructing objects of knowledge, visual authority acts as a concrete sign of power derived from a larger political sphere.

The propensity of colonial discourse to construct, situate and represent the Other as a geographical entity within the context of European imperialism persists into the present day in both international education and development, reinscribing the relationship between the 'West and the rest', and confirming the West as the primary source of rational progress and enlightenment (Corbidge, 1995). Just as the discourses of colonialism set out a relation between two cultures that justified the imperial project, in a similar way the disparity between developed and underdeveloped nations provides a rationale for international development intervention. One culture is 'fast-moving, technologically advanced, and economically powerful; the other slow-moving and without advanced technology or a complex economy' (Spurr, 1993: 6), warranting the introduction of regulated, modern temporalities (Adam, 2002), and providing a path for progress that has outlived its colonial origin and continues as an organising principle in the present-day project of development. In this project, spatial variation or difference is thus rendered as a temporal sequence: the dominant spatial imaginary of territorial expansion has given way to an alternative imaginary dominated by time as the essence of modernity (Mignolo, 2000). In development we see both space and time come together, in the temporal narrative of modernity legitimising the 'spatial reach of power and the control and management of other peoples, territories, environments, and places' (Crush, 1995: 7).

The rhetorical moves of colonial discourse, described by Spurr (1993), have also outlived an earlier imperialism. 'Classification' and 'debasement' fix negative characteristics onto a physical space and people, producing chaotic, weak or failed states existing beyond the limit of order and stability, democracy and modernisation. 'Negation' establishes a place of absence, lack or deficiency, of darkness and undevelopment, while 'insubstantialisation' of the colonised space constructs a disorientating, confusing backdrop to the coloniser's action. On the other hand, seemingly more positive 'romantic' representations, such as 'naturalisation' and 'idealisation' that present the noble savage dwelling in paradise, also produce a deficiency when contrasted with ideas of human progress. In contrast, an affirmation of the coloniser's superiority legitimises the authority of those in control of the discourse, and justifies interventions that introduce modern methods and civilised values.

In development, then, it is the conflation of progress, modernisation and Westernisation in colonial discourse that has produced a Third World, where people are defined and measured by deficiencies and lack, thus perpetuating colonial images of the Other as backward and ignorant (Escobar, 1995). Economic growth models of development which aim to correct such deficiencies in recipient communities tend to reinforce rather than address sources of inequity and marginalisation by viewing poor people as objects of someone else's externally imposed policy, rather than active participants in the shaping of a better future (Mayo, 1997; Zachariah, 1997). At the same time, notions of First World superiority are maintained with the import of professional 'experts' from other cultures who, in response to perceived deficiencies, can prescribe and implement an appropriate solution based on Western scientific, technical, cultural or pedagogical models. Development discourse thereby establishes hierarchical relations between these two, determining 'who can speak, from what points of view, with what authority, and according to what criteria of expertise' (Escobar, 1995: 45), and establishing the rules for how problems are identified and what solutions are proposed.

Disrupting colonial discourse by deconstructing colonial space

However, imperialism is always an incomplete endeavour, and in postcolonial theory we see the unitary, monologic meaning of colonial discourse disrupted by various means which will be taken up in my discussion of ELT experiences in development contexts. These disruptive practices may be seen as ways of moving from a temporal to a more spatial understanding of engagements in a postcolonial, globalised world. Adopting Foucault's 'spatializing metaphor', Spurr (1993) proposes a spatial interrogation of the boundaries and limits that inscribe established systems of representation and separate the Western Self from the non-Western Other. Such an interrogation would be aimed at exposing the underlying linear logic of colonial discourse and positing, in its place, 'a perpetual openness to the unexpected' (1993: 195).

An intriguing form of spatial interrogation is illustrated in Kirby's (1996b) analogy of the lost colonial explorer. Armed with the representational system of Cartesian cartography, the colonial explorer constructed a secure, rational mapping subject detached from a stable organised environment and an objectified Other. However, when the master subject becomes lost in new surroundings, the position of separation and mastery is difficult to maintain, the land 'appears chaotic and unstable, moving in its own unpredictable logic' (p. 48) and the 'individual who seeks to negotiate this landscape suffers defeat, anxiety, and confusion' (p. 51). Despite the sense of chaos, Kirby claims that this experience affords the subject 'an opportunity for a substantial interaction and personal transformation' (p. 52). Through an awareness of conscious embodiment, and a disruption of the hierarchical spatial boundaries between Self and environment, Self and Other, the ordered spatiality of our culture and our selves is reconceived in terms of porousness and fluidity (see also Pratt, 1992: 222).

The disruption of a smooth colonial space of consciousness and society is also apparent in Bhabha's (1994) analyses (drawing on Fanon) of the instability and ambivalence of the master subject. Ambivalence, uncertainty and internal resistance are seen to disturb the relationship between coloniser and colonised, and unsettle the unified authority of colonial domination. Although this may result in cultural confusion and the disabling dissolution of a knowing position, it can also lend impetus to a strategy of political subversion, and facilitate a more productive engagement with difference and alterity 'that never resolves itself into a stable, unified structure' (Spurr, 1993: 185). Undermining a rational, unified logic by offering alternative ways to think and act outside the boundaries of the self thus becomes a precondition for dialogue, or engagement with others.

The idea of imperial or development space as a contact zone of contested meanings (Pratt, 1992) also raises possibilities for disrupting colonial discourse. Transcultural engagements in the contact zone can generate productive ideas for working in development and ELT because they focus on relationships and forms that emerge in the movements across difference. So, for example, Somerville and Perkins (2003: 253) suggest that working in the 'discomfort zone' of cultural contact can be precarious and risky, but can also give rise to a range of productive outcomes. For Carter (1992), the space between participants, the space between discourses, can be maintained as an interval of difference, enabling a performative act of moving back and forth that unhinges unified authority and produces new understandings. By contrast, the in-between space might be conceived as a 'third space' where constitutive histories and polarised politics are displaced to produce a form of hybridity as 'something different, new and unrecognizable, a new area of negotiation of meaning and representation' (Bhabha, 1990b: 211).

Carter (1987) proposes a further creative rethinking of colonial space in the writing of 'spatial history', which similarly unsettles the certainty of Western historicism and challenges the Eurocentric spatial practices of cartographic inscription. In contrast to a teleological history that envisages place and context as the empty space in which history is enacted, spatial history examines the entwining of events, place and cultural identity through the motif of the palimpsest. The palimpsest traces successive inscriptions that constitute the complex experience of place through an accretion of textuality; in mapping, naming, fictional and non-fictional narratives and so on, spatial history sees 'space' becomes 'place' through language. The experiences of precolonial, colonial and postcolonial societies' evolving, contested cultural identities are deeply implicated in the constitution of place as palimpsest, and form the basis of a spatial history.

Postmodernity, Postmodernism and Proliferation of Space and Time

Reconsiderations of time and space have also arisen in contemporary social and cultural theories of postmodernity (the material changes of late capitalism, globalisation and the information age), and postmodernism (the philosophical questioning of a modernist, Eurocentric worldview). Analyses of postmodernity frequently focus on the intensification of space–time compression, and the apparent disappearance of space and time in an age of instantaneous electronic communication and cultural flows (Castells, 1999; Crang & Thrift, 2000; Harvey, 1989). Valuing the speed and excitement of cyberspace, these analyses tend to figure an engagement with the material specificities of space and place as a conservative force, grounded in a politics of location, identity and security, and the slow motion, cyclical, generational time of culture and tradition (Castells, 1999; Edwards & Usher, 2000; Virilio, 1991). However, drawing on feminist and postcolonial theories, Massey (1994) argues that these inert notions of place as stasis originate in a dichotomous, First World construction that links place with home and the feminine, in opposition to masculine, notions of time and agentive action. Rejecting celebratory explanations of the new space–time compression as apolitical hyperbole, Massey points out that the uneven distribution of technological and economic changes across the globe has led to new forms of inequality, rather than increasing homogeny and harmony. In the information age, flows of knowledge, capital, power and surveillance have followed 'very deeply worn channels' (Nespor, 1994: 15), and so exacerbate existing gulfs between rich and poor, both between and within countries, while enabling widespread control and governmentality (Deleuze, 1992: 3).

Retrieving place from its correlation with fixity and opposition by emphasising its heterogeneity has been central to more complex, political understandings of the relationship between time and space, and between global and local. Seen in its complexity, place can be understood as always already translocal, full of internal conflicts and connections to spaces and social movements from beyond. Of course, places in the colonised periphery have for centuries been complex locations where numerous different communities intersected, not only across vast distances, but in encounters that are immediate and intense. In this sense, the notion that flux, fragmentation and flows are only recent characteristics of late capitalism is a peculiarly elite First World view that ignores the intersecting flow of cultures in specific places across the globe over preceding centuries. In the present day, this sense of interaction between global (flows) and local (places) is evident in Appadurai's (1996) vision of cultural and symbolic resources, in the form of languages, knowledges, ideologies, capital and so on, whose complex and irregular movement is inflected by specific historical, linguistic and political conditions, contexts and peoples. Crisscrossed by these flows, the identity of a particular place does not derive from a coherent internalised history which stands in opposition to global flows, but from interactions with the outside, meeting and weaving together at a particular locus, with uneven and unpredictable effects.

Metaphors of travel, incorporating these ideas of flow and movement, have also been adopted to problematise fixed notions of space and place. Rather than viewing travel and contact as necessarily resulting in deterministic patterns of domination and subordination, Pratt (1992) associates travel with transculturation, to invoke the interactional and improvisational relations brought about by the movement of people and cultures. In a similar vein, Clifford (1997) looks to images of movement, travel and change as a more productive means of understanding and representing complex 'local/global encounters, co-productions, dominations and resistances' (p. 24), a way of engaging with 'the transcultural, transnational and translocal' (Pennycook, 2007). Despite its imperialist and colonial connections, then, travel – of the type undertaken by English language teachers – can be an impetus to reflexivity that 'unsettles the confidence of authority' that lingers in the encounters of international development (Thomas, 1994: 5).

For de Certeau (1984), travel on a small scale, in spatial practices like walking, are posed as fleeting, non-systemic interventions, bringing with them memories and experiences of other times, places and knowledges that can unsettle the authorised, representational meanings of places. This mode of 'knowledge as travel' presents a way to think through spatially linked narratives consisting of 'verbal relics', juxtaposed in a collage of relationships rather than an ordered symbolic whole (de Certeau, 1984: 143). The intervention of verbal relics points to the importance of memory as an inspiration for practical knowledges of places and the transformation of authorised space. Memory, de Certeau suggests, is a transgressive concept, not limited to the past but instead present in the form of a more practical knowledge of spaces, places and paths; it carries not only events, but the remains of different knowledges. Thus, no matter what place we are in, connections are made by thinking about other times and places, thereby destabilising an ordered temporal and spatial logic. And from the spatial stories so constructed emerge, however fleetingly, palimpsestic sites and subjectivities, reminding us that 'being-in-the-world consists of linking incommensurable space-times' (Bingham & Thrift, 2000: 291).

Notions of time have also become more complex and relational in postmodern theorisation. A modernist reduction of time to history, teleology and causality has been opened up to concepts of chance, randomness, openendedness, and becoming (Grosz, 1999). In contrast to notions of a linear, predictable time that envisage a future contained by the past or present, these notions of time suggest a more positive, active force, operating with the concept of chance as *excess*. Importantly, for international development, they signal 'the openness of the future, its relative connection to but also freedom from the past, the possibilities of paths of development, temporal trajectories uncontained by the present' (Grosz, 1999: 4). From a different angle, and undermining our reliance on naturalised clock time, Serres and Latour (1995) point to the way our experience of time does not flow in a linear fashion, but is turbulent and disordered: stopping, slowing, recycling, rushing, rupturing in processes of entropy, ageing, memory, permanence and mutations. For the individual then, a proliferation of times in experience and memory, can converge in a 'temporary knot', so that an organism might be considered as a 'sheaf of times' (Serres, 1982: 75). Both these approaches to time help us see its proliferation, to move beyond an obsession with historical progress, and to engage with possibilities for new, different futures.

Feminist Conceptions of Time and Space

From the standpoint of feminist geography, Massey (1994) argues that the models of space and time in both modernism and postmodernism are profoundly patriarchal and have enabled the endurance and flexibility of sexism. It is the continuing effects of patriarchy in the spatial experience of women that are of central concern in this section. In writing on this subject, I acknowledge the debates concerning the category of 'woman', and recognise that neither gender nor sex are natural, pregiven conditions but rather the performative reiteration and materialisation of regulatory cultural norms that constitute our embodied experiences and dictate aspects of women's social, economic and political treatment (Butler, 1993). And although I am interested in exploring how these regulatory norms and reiterations organise the lived experience of women in the development context, these effects need to be understood in relation to other hierarchies of racial, national and economic status. The intersection and interaction of these hierarchies is notoriously difficult to theorise, yet postcolonial and feminist theories of space point to certain parallels: imperialism and patriarchy 'exert analogous forms of domination over those they render subordinate' (Ashcroft *et al.*, 1998: 101); and in terms of challenging this subordination, similarities have been drawn between 'writing place' in postcolonialism, and 'writing the body' in feminism. Nevertheless, postcolonialism has also presented a challenge to Western feminism, which has been accused of complicity in imperialism and of failing to account for the racialised and gendered experiences of non-Western and Third World women (see, for example, Mohanty, 1988; Spivak, 1999). Since my focus is on providing a basis for understanding the spatial experiences of women as foreign aid workers in development, who are also defined by multiple axes of difference including colour, class and nationality, this section brings these diverse categories into dialogue.

Time as male, space as female

A concept that is central to a feminist understanding of patriarchy in development concerns the way in which, in the West, 'time is conceived as masculine (proper to subject, a being with an interior) and space is associated with femininity (femininity being a form of externality to men)' (Grosz, 1995: 99). Time is the projection of the subject's interior, the mind, and is conceptual, introspective, while space becomes the exterior object of knowledge: passive, observed, measured, and controlled. Moreover, masculinist, universalist, abstract models of space–time (Euclid, Newton, Einstein), based in the prestigious hard sciences, correlate to particular representations of gendered subjectivity, and confirm the 'fundamental masculinity of the knower' as the active agent in Western thought (Grosz, 1995: 100).

The binary logic of space–time organises knowledge around 'the masculine knowing subject' and a 'feminized world-object' (Lee, 1996: 206), with particular implications for the structuring of social life from parliaments to pubs, from boardrooms to beaches. The mastery of space and freedom of movement afforded the autonomous masculine subject, detached from the contextual specificities of place/space, unencumbered by emotions and corporeality, ignores the significant restrictions on mobility experienced by others. For women, restricted mobility results from the gendered messages inherent in particular spaces and places that reflect and affect the ways in which gender is constructed, understood and experienced. Gendered messages signal the control of spaces and places by an active, dominant male subject and support the exclusion of unwanted bodies through the threat of violence.

Besides functioning as a pervasive means of mastering the environment, the male gaze serves as a potent means of conveying these gendered messages. As a consequence, a common female experience of traversing public space is one of bodily awareness and threat that has parallels in Althusser's concept of hailing:

> [i]t takes little more than a hoot, a whistle, a 'Hey, you!' or the noticed gaze (hostile or admiring) of another to force us to contract into a much more limited space, one that correlates more or less with the body, that is marked by cultural divisions coinciding with those in discourses of race, class, gender, and nation. [...] I know when I am the one intended. I *take my place*. (Kirby, 1996a: 15)

Exclusion from particular spaces and places is not targeted solely at women, but is also enacted through violence against a range of others marked by embodied differences. Control of individual bodies and, by extension, the body politic is governed by fears of such unruly and dangerous elements entering places where they do not belong, and translate into the practice of enclosing unruly elements within carefully guarded spaces. In times of social instability, such as might be experienced in certain development contexts, a politics of difference, operating through spatial segregation and separation, becomes especially significant. Contestation of spaces or transgression of borders is seen as a threat to order, and so hegemonic power acts to reinforce control: the boundaries around spatial entities at all levels, from the house and the street to the nation, and around groups bound by nationality, ethnicity and gender, are brought into focus and vigorously policed.

Public and private space

The restriction of women's mobility in Western culture has also been traced to the coding and separation of public and private space in ancient Greece, and to Enlightenment ideologies of nationalism and individualism, in which the realm of public and political life was constructed as one of 'rationality, individuality, self-control and hence masculinity'

(Rose, 1993: 363). Binary logic presents the master subject of the public realm as not only masculine, but also white, bourgeois and heterosexual; however, reduced to a neutral container of rationality, the master subject remains ironically untainted by the bodily specificities that mark others by sex or skin colour. The exclusion of women from the public, political domain was justified by the representation of females as natural, maternal creatures, compelled to remain in the private domestic sphere, the world of unreason, thereby limiting both mobility and identity by binding women to the biology of a disordered, weak and unreliable body. The rejection of bodily specificity thus underpins both the separation of male reason from female body, and the construction of the civil body politic (Pateman, 1989). In response, an important aspect of the feminist challenge to dualist thinking has therefore entailed retheorising the material and discursive body as 'the most intimate of personal-and-political spaces, an affective microcosm for all other spatialities' (Soja, 1996: 112).

The neat binary division of public and private space, claimed to be mostly relevant to white, middle-class feminism (Blunt & Rose, 1994), becomes blurred and complexified when other axes of difference come into play. Moreover, the intrusive reach of governmentality into private domestic space has ensured its subjection to the normalizing techniques of modern power and policing, in a displacement that confuses the borders between home and the world, between the private and the public. Conversely, as women *do* enter public space in their many private and public roles, any conception of the public domain as being solely the preserve of masculine activity is challenged.

The empire as public space

Gendered understandings of imperial space are also underpinned by the division between public and private domains. The empire, as the projection of the public sphere, was a place where gender roles were more polarised than in the home country: the coding of imperial masculinity was 'hardened, militarized, physical games-oriented' (Pennycook, 1998: 63), and the imperial context was 'a place of masculine endeavour, where heroic individual males behave in adventurous ways, exploring undiscovered lands and subduing the inhabitants' (Mills, 1994: 36–37). The entry of white man as hero and monarch-of-all-I-survey simultaneously reinforced imperial representations of a passive, feminised colonial landscape (Pratt, 1992). Vividly illustrated in Freud's description of woman as the 'dark continent', the symbolic correlation between land and the female body signals the concept of colonisation as sexual domination, and of the colonies as places that offered sexual experiences unobtainable in civilised Europe (Nandy, 1983; Said, 1978). In this masculine domain, females were viewed as unnecessary, unruly or at the service of male desire that silences female desire through labelling and denigration (Ramazanoglu, 1993; see also Charlton, 1997; Fox, 1999). The colonised female, variously depicted as veiled and mysterious, immoral and libidinous, or the victim of Oriental male barbarity, represented feminised colonies that were to be 'penetrated, raped, silenced and (dis)possessed' in a yoking together of racial and sexual violence (Loomba, 1998; Stoler, 1995: 174).

The representation of feminised colonial lands as the domain for male colonial action had significant implications for the management of sexual practices in the colonies. In the colonial context, the management of sex was clearly linked to colonial politics, patriotic priorities and the legitimisation of territorial possession. The discourses on sexuality simultaneously regulated the behaviour of gender, ethnicity and class to secure the privileges of individual whites and a white body politic. In the case of the Dutch East Indies (colonial Indonesia), the supposed self-restraint of the bourgeois European male was challenged by the 'passions that the tropics unleashed' and, in consequence, the availability of native women became part of the wages of whiteness (Stoler, 1995: 177). The continuation of this particular discourse in the contemporary phenomenon of sex tourism (Jeffrey, 2002) or in institutionalised prostitution that accompanies military occupation or UN peacekeeping (Bowcott, 2005; Jolliffe, 2001; Murdoch, 2006; Wax, 2005) testifies to the persistence of colonial relations of sexualised power in situations of First World spatial domination that have been reproduced over succeeding centuries. In response, feminists have called for solidarity against the rise of an increasing masculine militarisation of the globe which has come about as an adjunct to global capitalism (Mohanty, 2003), and as an aspect of the new wars of humanitarian intervention (Mazurana, 2005).

White women in other lands

White women occupied an ambiguous position in the imperial project, as both insiders and outsiders, part of the centre and yet marginalised, a positioning that is significant in white teachers' experience of international development. Through the combined effects of male territorial and sexual dominance in the imperial context, the naturalised place for white women was in the nurturing roles of the private sphere, as wives and mothers, teachers and nurses (Mills, 1994). Given these conventions, the unattached status of the Lady Traveller aroused suspicion, since legitimate travel to further scientific enquiry and exploration was traditionally the preserve of men (Clifford, 1997: 32). Although white women could, like the imperial masculine subject, exercise power in relation to colonised subjects, feelings of racial superiority were tempered by vulnerability, since white women were also 'mythologized as the desired objects of colonized men' (Stoler, 1995: 183). The call to guard virtuous, white womanhood from the sexual threat of the colonised Other unified the transplanted community, necessitated the redrawing of racial boundaries, and reaffirmed the need to confine women within secure physical spaces. As Loomba (1998: 162) points out, both black *and* white women became 'the terrain on which men move and enact their battles with each other'.

In the post decolonisation era, stereotypes of white female chastity and native female license continue to shift and multiply. In contemporary Southeast Asia, Western women may be cast as promiscuous and local women as modest and restrained, reproducing the traditional division between 'damned whores' and 'God's police' (Summers, 1975) across a division of bodies distinguished by ethnicity, gender and economic privilege. Images of the modern Western liberated woman might be read as a sign of Western depravity that threatens conservative Asian values, or alternatively as a sign of the subject's desire to engage with alterity. Meanwhile, lingering masculine colonial fears of the sexually alluring black/Asian men perpetuate images of white women as vulnerable and in need of protection.

* * *

In this chapter I have outlined particular notions of time and space that underpin the projects of modernity, colonialism and patriarchy, and form a critical base for understanding English language teaching, gender and development discourses. First, a metanarrative of time as historical progress has occupied a privileged position in Eurocentric social, political and economic theory, shaping mainstream discourses of international development and education through a hierarchical categorisation of nations that sees the West leading the rest in the process of modernisation. In international development, this focus on a singular path of temporal progress can perpetuate inequitable relations between an imperial Self and colonised Other, and limit engagement with the particularity, multiplicity and alterity of spaces, places and times. Second, modern institutions and disciplinary knowledge have been constituted as advanced, mobile technologies detached from a context of origin, thus enabling their application across distant spaces with little regard for the specificities of context upon which they are imposed, or for the consequent devaluing of social, cultural and disciplinary practices in the periphery. Third, the regulation of time and space within sequestered modern institutions facilitates the introduction of disciplinary power, the production of docile subjects, and the inculcation of norms by which individuals constitute and take their place in the larger social system. In effect, *chronopolitics* sits as a foundation not only for a *geopolitics* of international development, but also for Western practices of English language teaching when presented as a means of progress and advancement for non-Western societies and individuals.

Feminist analyses considered in this chapter suggest that time and space have also been mobilised in specific ways to support the perpetuation of patriarchal regimes. On the one hand, the privileging of time over space has been aligned with the domination of masculine agency over a passive, feminised world-object; at the same time, the division between public and private space has inhibited women's full participation in public life on the basis of embodied differences. In contemporary development contexts, particularly those accompanied by military intervention, lingering colonial discourses that constitute the public realm as the domain of heroic masculine endeavour sustain patriarchal regimes that marginalise the participation of unruly others marked by gender and race.

In summary, my argument is that these naturalised concepts of time and space underpin orthodox discourses of English language teaching in development, produce a particular view of communities in receipt of development aid as backward and lagging behind a progressive West, and thereby justify the introduction of modern disciplinary texts and methods at the expense of a critical engagement with radical difference and a differently imagined future. In order to challenge the modernist regimes of time and space that underpin language education, gender and development, a range of approaches is available. Some of the key approaches I will adopt throughout this book involve, first, a focus on the interaction of *time, space and an active social politics*; second, a focus on *ambivalence* as a form of disorientation and a means of undermining the detachment of the rational subject from a spatial context; and third, an exploration of *alternate experiences of time and space* that emerge in specific contexts. My discussion will also engage with an awareness of *spatial history* as a means of rearticulating the relation between subjectivity, knowledge and local spaces, places and times, and an awareness of *spatial practices* that signal different ways of being in the development context. Taken together, these approaches aim to make available a more critical notion of context for language teaching and gender in development that challenges entrenched social, economic and political hierarchies.

These concepts will be taken up in Chapter 4, where I consider teachers' observations of development contexts and discuss the ways in which temporal hierarchies and spatial detachments are seen to organise the contact zone. They also inform my discussion in Chapters 5 and 6 of the ways in which temporal and spatial regimes organise teachers' work, and suppress or enable dialogue between ELT and the alternative spaces and times of the world outside the classroom.

Note

1. As Zuengler and Miller's (2006) review of SLA demonstrates, both traditional cognitive theories and more recent sociocultural theories of SLA rely on models of developmental progress, whether this occurs primarily through individual cognition or social interaction.

Chapter 3
Spatial Context: East Timor, Indonesia and Australia

Contact history is spatial history
Carter, 1992: 179

Moving on from the more theoretical discussion of time and space, this chapter outlines the intertwined colonial and linguistic history of East Timor and Indonesia, and considers the geopolitical relationship between those nations and Australia. I discuss accounts of the United Nations mission to establish the independent nation of East Timor following the popular consultation in 1999, and include my own observations of daily life in the interim period prior to the achievement of full independence. The complex set of political, historical and linguistic relationships explored in this chapter situates the experiences of foreign language teachers and their narrative accounts of living and working in East Timor and Indonesia.

Colonial History in East Timor and Indonesia

The first concerted European incursions in the Southeast Asian region came about with Portuguese attempts to secure the spice trade in the Indonesian archipelago during the early 16th century. Portuguese influence across the islands was gradually extended through military and missionary activities, negotiated alliances and trade, but from the early 17th century the Portuguese were losing control to Dutch commercial, military and missionary conquests. The island of Timor had officially become a Portuguese colony early in the 18th century, but the Dutch formally took over the Western half of Timor in 1859 in their process of expanding territorial and governmental control across the archipelago during the 19th century. However, just as Portuguese attempts to rule the island of Timor were marked by rebellion and chronic insurrection so, too, Dutch control over Indonesia remained tenuous in the face of indigenous resistance.

During the Second World War Japan invaded and occupied the archipelago, prompted in part by the stationing of Allied troops on islands such as Ambon and Timor as a forward base in the defence of Australia. The harsh regime of Japanese control fostered a growing nationalist movement and, at the end of the war, Sukarno declared independence for Indonesia. Although it took several more years of struggle to finally defeat Dutch attempts to regain colonial control, the Netherlands eventually acknowledged Indonesian independence in 1949. In Timor, the Portuguese had also returned after the Japanese surrender, ruthlessly reasserted control and, with forced labour, rebuilt the economy's limited infrastructure. However, Timorese society had, according to Taylor (1999), continued to resist colonial incorporation by maintaining strong indigenous social, economic and judicial structures, which were later to be harnessed in the coming struggle for independence in the 1970s. Moves towards decolonisation in East Timor finally began in 1974 with Portuguese concessions to democracy, the establishment of political parties and strong support for independence being shown in elections held in early 1975.

In Indonesia, with the backing of Western interests, the Sukarno government was overthrown in a military coup, ushering in the New Order rule of the Suharto regime (1966–1998). Giving prominence to the aim of rapid development and modernisation through an authoritarian 'governmentality' (Philpott, 2000), the New Order regime simultaneously extended the Dutch colonial mission of unifying a geographically fragmented and linguistically and culturally diverse population (Anderson, 1991). It was, in part, the desire for unity that underpinned Indonesia's response to moves towards decolonisation and democracy in East Timor in 1974. Fearful that an independent East Timor might motivate other independence movements across the archipelago, and aware of rich oil reserves in the seas between East Timor and Australia, Indonesia launched a full invasion of East Timor in December 1975. In the aftermath of the invasion, napalm bombs were used over a wide area resulting in the loss of homes, crops and fields, and at least 200,000 East Timorese, a quarter of the population, were killed in the early years of the occupation (UNDP, 2002: 12).

In the following decades there were reports from the closed colony of violent military repression and human rights violations, but in the face of this oppression the independence movement led by the Revolutionary Front for an Independent East Timor (FRETILIN), the most radical, pro-independence and left leaning of the three Timorese political parties, maintained its opposition to the Indonesian regime. Once again, attempts at integration through Indonesianisation over succeeding decades were resisted by the resilience and persistence of Timorese society, and East Timor remained implacably 'Other' to the concerted project of Indonesian nationalism (Anderson, 1993). In response to Indonesia's anti-Communist demand that all citizens belong to one of five major religions, many East Timorese chose to align themselves with the Catholic Church, marking a further differentiation from a predominantly Islamic Indonesia. As a place of refuge and possible contact with the outside world, the Catholic Church, its power thus consolidated, also became a vital institution for political struggle (Arenas, 1998).

Meanwhile, the USA, Australia and other major Western powers tacitly approved of Indonesia's invasion and occupation as a bulwark against FRETILIN's leftist politics, seen as symptomatic of potential regional instability, and supplied military and economic aid in support of Indonesian control (Glassman, 2003; Wheeler & Ddunne, 2001). Nevertheless, in the 1990s transformations in the global geo-political economy, the end of the Cold War, the drive for economic liberalisation and the Asian financial crisis of 1997 helped to create the conditions for an end to Indonesian control. Following the fall of the Suharto regime, in 1999 East Timorese voted overwhelmingly against the offer of special autonomy within Indonesia, thus laying the path to independence. Violence escalated following the announcement of the referendum results, with massacres and large-scale destruction of properties and infrastructure as Indonesian troops and supporters withdrew. By September 1999 thousands of East Timorese had been killed and three quarters of the population displaced in the chaos that engulfed the country. Society was in a state of collapse with the destruction of 70% of the physical infrastructure and 90% of housing, and the cessation of all civil, government, legal and administrative functions (Chopra, 2002).

In order to quell the violence, Indonesia eventually approved the intervention of an Australian-led multinational peacekeeping force whose strength ultimately reached 11,500 troops (Chopra, 2000: 28). The International Force East Timor (INTERFET) was charged with restoring security, and in 2000 formally handed over military command to a genuine UN peacekeeping operation, under the auspice of the United Nations Transitional Administration in East Timor (UNTAET). Supported by a military strength of 8950 troops, 200 military observers and a civilian police force of 1640, UNTAET assumed its mandate to maintain law and order, rebuild the structure of government and public administration, develop civil and social services and coordinate humanitarian assistance during East Timor's transition to independence. In addition to the Australian troops, a vast number of Australian government and non-government organisations took a major role in the reconstruction of East Timor through the mobilisation of emergency relief efforts and the channelling of Australian aid funds and expertise into a huge array of assistance programmes in housing, health, education, welfare, public administration, business and industry. Supporting these endeavours, Australian television and mobile telephone services were prominent in the national communications network.

Linguistic Flows in Indonesia and East Timor

The region covered by Indonesia is remarkable for its linguistic diversity, with several hundred languages and associated dialects spoken across the wider Indonesia archipelago (Hajek, 2006). Pasar (bazaar) Malay, an important early trading language throughout the islands, remained as a lingua franca under Dutch colonial rule, with Dutch being used as the language of European administrators, settlers, and a small educated elite who acted as intermediaries. Dutch was the medium of instruction for a select few in the tiered colonial school system established in the East Indies in the mid-19th century, and not until the early 20th century was elementary education offered in local languages or Malay for the indigenous population (Bertrand, 2003: 270). With the Dutch controlling access to education as a means of maintaining a racial hierarchy, Dardjowidjojo (2000) reports that by 1930, only some 6% of the colonised population were literate.

In the struggle for independence from Dutch colonial rule, a guiding ethos of 'one homeland, one people, one language' promoted the role of Pasar Malay in the national imaginary. Renamed Bahasa Indonesia, it was adopted as the sole official language for the newly independent Indonesia in 1945 and was endorsed, through an expanding education system across the Indonesian archipelago, as a key element in the national project of advancing unity, order, modernity and development. Although it was promoted as more democratic than either Javanese or Dutch, Bahasa Indonesia was also seen as a 'relatively undeveloped language' in need of lexical and grammatical standardisation (Bertrand, 2003: 274). In this process of standardisation, the Indonesian language and the unified nation were mutually constituted, and the nation's goals of development were aligned with a global project of capitalist modernisation and progress: learning Bahasa Indonesia was seen as essential to becoming a modern Indonesian (Bertrand, 2003; Errington, 1998; Heryanto, 2007). Bahasa Indonesia has remained the sole official language of internal communication, although it is spoken as a first language by only a minority of the population. Several hundred vernacular languages remain in use (Gordon, 2005), and have been particularly favoured by communities in areas of greater resistance to centralised state control. Since independence, English has been the first foreign language for international communication, and is taught compulsorily in high schools and universities (Dardjowidjojo, 2000). With education as a key component of national unity and development goals, the literacy rate in Indonesia has risen to 90% (UNDP, 2008).

In East Timor, a variety of Tetum was used as the lingua franca between the Portuguese colonisers and the 15 to 30 indigenous language groups (Hajek, 2000), and as such it absorbed many elements of the Portuguese language. The creolised form of the language that evolved was given the name Tetum Praça and it was a combination of this form with Tetum Terik (a standardised form of the language based on a regional dialect) that the Catholic missionaries spread throughout the colony in the last quarter of the 19th century. While Tetum was a convenient common language, the language of instruction, reading and writing in the few colonial schools was Portuguese. However, Taylor (1999: 10) has argued that in line with a deeply rooted resistance to colonisation, the Timorese learned the customs and language of the Portuguese simply 'in order to be able to outwit them more effectively'.

From the 1950s Portugal commenced a more concerted programme of social development in East Timor through education and the activities of the Catholic Church in order to 'civilise the local population' towards becoming 'true Portuguese citizens' (Hajek, 2000: 402). As part of this process, mass primary education was used as a way of achieving 'linguistic acculturation in favour of Portuguese in all contexts' (p. 403). This 'civilising' process entailed acceptance of the Portuguese way of life, commitment to the Catholic faith and rigorous enforcement of the Portuguese language in the classroom, and was accompanied, from the early 1970s, by an oppressive clampdown on indigenous cultural expression using Tetum as a written language in secular life, 'which was perceived to be a sign of potentially uncontrollable indigenous nationalism and possible competition to the Portuguese ideal' (p. 402). The use of Portuguese as the medium of instruction, combined with the effects of an alienating colonial content and the provision of inadequate resources for oppressive linguistic assimilation policies, meant that some 95% of the population remained illiterate by the end of Portuguese rule (UNDP, 2002).

While the postwar era of decolonisation heralded the rise of modern postcolonial literary languages such as Bahasa Indonesia in the former Dutch East Indies, Hull (2000) claims that former French and Portuguese colonial subjects, affected by the Catholic missionary zeal and 'civilising' practices of cultural assimilation, were reluctant to relinquish their colonial linguistic heritage. However, Taylor suggests that the place of Portuguese in the postcolonial period was secured under the influence of the Timorese Portuguese-speaking elite who had been allowed entry into tertiary education in Portugal and returned to take up posts in government administration whilst Portugal maintained ultimate control of the territory. In these positions, the elites faced the harsh realities of colonial neglect that had fuelled resistance to Portugal's 'rigid political control, colonial hierarchies' and 'propaganda masquerading as education in sparely resourced schools' (Taylor, 1991: 18). They eventually formed the foundation of the democratic parties at the time of decolonisation and in 1974, when the Portuguese withdrew, FRETILIN declared that Portuguese would be retained as the official language. At the same time FRETILIN moved to increase its connection to the Timorese populace through the use of Tetum, spoken bilingually with a local language by at least two thirds of the population, and 'successfully elevated a culture despised by the Portuguese into a new language of independence' (Taylor, 1999: 42). To develop the status of the indigenous language they encouraged local level literacy campaigns in Tetum, on a Freirean model in the brief period from 1974 to 1976 (Cabral & Martin-Jones, 2008). These approaches have been revisited in literacy programmes sponsored by national and international NGOs in the transition to independence between 1999 and 2002 (Boughton, 2008; Merrell, 2001).

During the years of Indonesian occupation, the Indonesian government's concerted campaign of development and integration led to a flurry of school building in East Timor far exceeding the efforts made by Portugal in education of the population. In accordance with the aggressive spread of Indonesian language, both Portuguese and Tetum were banned in schools outside the Catholic system, and a whole generation of Timorese grew up with a systematic education in Indonesian ideology, culture and language with Bahasa Indonesia as the medium of instruction (Arenas, 1998; Cabral & Martin-Jones, 2008). Language and education were thus integrally tied to the maintenance of law and order in a pattern of social and political domination, yielding a system in which official estimates claim over 50% of adults remained illiterate (Nicolai, 2004). In this political milieu, Portuguese and Tetum represented secret languages of resistance, opaque to the Indonesian administrators, and range of literacies – associated with both clandestine and official texts – played a key role in resistance activities (Cabral & Martin-Jones, 2008). Despite their small numbers, the Portuguese-speaking elite emerged as the major protagonists and spokesmen for a postcolonial East Timor and played an important role as either leaders of the resistance or key intermediaries within the Indonesian regime. The Catholic Church also resisted integration by adopting Tetum, rather than Bahasa Indonesia, assisting its further spread and development and tying the Church even more closely to the community in its opposition to Indonesian domination.

Following vigorous debates over the national language policy, in 2002 the constitution of the newly independent East Timor granted Portuguese and Tetum equal status as official languages, with Bahasa Indonesia and English identified as non-official utilities. A key problem remained for a younger generation who had played a vital role in the struggle for national liberation, and critics lamented the fate of a 'lost generation' of youth educated in Bahasa Indonesia and excluded from 'symbolic and cultural identity in an independent East Timor' (Leach, 2002: 46). Despite resistance in some quarters to the perceived imperialist and linguicidal tendencies of English (as argued by Hull, 2000), the wave of international agencies arriving during the nation's transition to independence strengthened popular demand for the language and portended the possible *de facto* establishment of English as the majority foreign language regardless of internal policies. A demand for foreign English language teachers was created by the postreferendum destruction of the education system and the disappearance of Indonesian teachers who had been integral to that system. Because of the large-scale foreign, English-speaking presence, and the pace and complexity of change in the many domains affected by language choice, the linguistic situation in East Timor during the transitional period was described by Hajek (2000: 409) as 'nothing less than chaotic'. Nevertheless, in this time of reinvention, one of the new nation's great strengths is the underlying translingual agility of the population, who continue to use not only Portuguese and Tetum, but also Indonesian, English and the diverse varieties of local languages 'in many domains, activities and relationships' (Taylor-Leech, 2007: 250).

Emerging from centuries of colonial domination, and with a long history of resistance to colonial control, East Timor in the early years of the 21st century was struggling to establish itself within a new global context inextricably linked with English language and Lusophone interests. Indonesia, too, was in transition, with major shifts towards democracy on the one hand, and ongoing sectarian and separatist tensions on the other. A complex web of strategic, military and economic interests connected both East Timor and Indonesia to Australia, and to influential international political forces. While Indonesia has experienced extreme periods of rapid development and economic crisis, East Timor has had to balance the dynamics of emerging nationhood and independence with the confines of governmental and economic reliance on the United Nations and the international community. The paradox of national independence in an era of globalisation has required of both nations a delicate balancing act to acknowledge reliance on external engagement, while fostering an internal unity that encompasses the unique, historic and culturally diverse identities of their people.

Australia: Between History and Geography

Australia's relationship with its northern neighbours has long been marked by a 'chronic ambivalence', underpinned by the clash between historic ties to a predominantly white Western cultural heritage and a geographic proximity to Asia (D'Cruz & Steele, 2003: 34). Although the pressures of globalisation towards the end of the 20th century encouraged greater economic and strategic ties with the Asian region, Australia's conservative government from the mid-1990s rejected the rhetoric of 'Asian integration', with the claim that 'Australia did not in fact need to choose between its history and its geography' (Goldsworthy, 2003: 81): the Australian Prime Minister at that time claimed that a unique Australian identity had been forged in its positioning as 'a Western nation next to Asia with strong links to the United States and Europe', and declared that 'We have stopped worrying about whether we are Asian, in Asia, enmeshed in Asia or part of the mythical East-Asian hemisphere. We have got on with the job of being ourselves in the region' (Howard, 1999).

Despite such assertions, critics of Australian foreign policy have argued that the supposed 'superiority-of-being-us' (D'Cruz & Steele, 2003) has masked an ongoing fear of Asia as Other and opposite, and fuelled an 'invasion anxiety' that pervades relations, perceptions and policies towards Asia, and in particular Indonesia (Burke, 2001). Philpott (2001: 371) refers to a 'historical web of anxieties and fears' generated by politicians, journalists and academics in 'seemingly routine and benign descriptions' of 'Indonesia's 200 million plus population, its low levels of political and economic development and its status as the world's largest Muslim nation' which 'all play deeply on white Australian fears of Asia'. One key concern for Australian anxieties over its relationship with Southeast Asia, and with Indonesia in particular, was the invasion and occupation of East Timor. Fear of disintegration and separatism across Indonesia, and the spectre of having an unstable and possibly communist East Timor on our border, had prompted the Australian government to 'sacrifice' the rights of the people of East Timor and accept Indonesian annexation (Wheeler &

Ddunne, 2001: 805). Nevertheless, following the 1999 referendum, the Australian government's contribution to military intervention and reconstruction in East Timor, and ongoing economic and military support of Indonesia, was justified in terms of protecting Australia's own interests in fostering regional security (Howard, 1999).

The decision to lead the international peacekeeping force into East Timor in 1999 represented the biggest Australian military commitment in over 30 years, but ushered in a period of instability in Australia's relationship with Indonesia. Over succeeding years, relationships between the three nations have been tested through various conflicts around natural resources and terrorism, yet Australia's development aid programme has maintained a strong focus on both Indonesia and East Timor. The priorities for Australian development funds have been in governance and education, areas that would have a long-term effect in the stability and structuring of East Timorese and Indonesian societies. In East Timor, educational support during the transition to independence centred on higher education institutions and the provision of advanced or specialist training essential for positions in government, business and the professions. English language skills training was provided in conjunction with aid efforts in government administration and in vocational and higher education. Australia's military and aid activities across the region, and the rhetoric which surrounds them, have been shaped by constructions of Australian identity and, in turn, affect the identity of Australians working in the region.

International Aid in Transitional East Timor

In the volatile conditions that followed the withdrawal of Indonesia, East Timor had suffered significant upheaval and was mistakenly imagined in some quarters as a governmental *tabula rasa* or *terra-nullius* (Chopra, 2002), a space where only 'barbarity, excess and irrationality' remained in the wake of violence and societal collapse (Duffield, 2002: 1051). Such imaginings were highly problematic, but served the interests of intervening agencies. As Spurr has argued in relation to a colonial rhetoric of negation, such representations conceive of 'the Other as absence, emptiness, nothingness', and create 'a space for colonial imagination and the pursuit of desire' (Spurr, 1993: 92). In the case of East Timor, the imagined 'vacuum' that lay in the wake of Indonesia's withdrawal opened the way for donor governments, UN agencies, NGOs and commercial interests to gain economic, social and political influence in the guise of aid, and allowed 'monitoring, interventions and regulation unprecedented since the colonial period' (Duffield, 2002: 1066). Through the activities of these agencies, the United Nations and the international community provided assistance in establishing both an interim and eventually a permanent government, maintaining law and order, protecting national security, rebuilding all infrastructure, including the education system, and providing food, shelter and health care.

Assessments of the intervention and aid effort were mixed, with the United Nations and donor governments claiming success for their respective operations. In Australia, the military intervention was reported favourably with Australian soldiers 'constructed as "the good guys" helping out a neighbouring country in trouble', though in Southeast Asia they were 'the "bad guys" of the region' (Woods, 2001: 1). Australians were exhorted to be proud of their aid effort (AusAID, 2000: 1), but while some analyses acknowledged broad success in terms of basic rehabilitation, others warned of problems arising from dependence on development aid that, in the long run, was designed to serve foreign interests. Critical analyses also suggested that there were significant problems associated with the UN bureaucracy and an international aid community that had effected a territorial invasion, occupying all the best houses, taking over the best administrative buildings, and crossing the land in hundreds of white four-wheel-drive vehicles (O'Kane, 2001). With the Timorese 'being treated like guests in their own land', local leaders in the National Council of Timorese Resistance (CNRT) were obliged to 'go cap in hand to the UN to request permission to make use of public property' (Sword Gusmao, 2003: 282). On the streets, simmering tensions and frustrations were exacerbated with rumours and fears that insurgency from militia and disaffected elements of the Indonesian armed forces would at any time erupt to destroy the fragile peace and order (Hill, 2001: 1).

A key focus for dissatisfaction in some quarters was the huge income disparity apparent between local staff and international consultants, the resultant emergence of a 'dual economy', and the entry of profiteering Australian business entrepreneurs in a money-hungry 'race without rules' (Tooth, 2000: 1). Despite real improvements to living conditions, most of the Timorese population continued to live in poverty and suffer from poor health, lack of access to education and limited prospects for employment. The few jobs that were available to Timorese, working as drivers, security guards and interpreters were paid at a meagre daily rate, while the United Nations paid 'New York salaries' for its own staff in an administration dominated by foreign experts (O'Kane, 2001: 21). On the streets of Dili, the juxtaposition of ruined houses sheltering Timorese families alongside the shiny cafes catering to the international cappuccino set came to represent a nation divided into two worlds (C. Taylor, 2000). In some ways, as Traub (2000: 84) observes, 'the new colonialism looks and feels powerfully like the old', with an 'omnipresent and well-nigh omnipotent' UNTAET replacing the militias as 'the most logical target of resentment'.

My observations: Daily life in Dili 2000

The streets of Dili still have rows and rows of destroyed houses and shops, many just burnt out piles of brick and tin, although small shops and cafes are opening up amidst the rubble and tarpaulins every day. Arrangements of bamboo poles and rusty corrugated iron constituted shops selling an assortment of goods ranging from warm Australian beer to plastic coat hangers, toothpaste and dried fish. There are no road rules and no road signs. There is no organised financial system, no credit card facilities, ATMs, and money for all daily needs must be carried in cash, in the three currencies in use: Australian dollars, US dollars and Indonesian rupiah. The electricity supply is intermittent and the water reticulation system incomplete. There is no postal service and no conventional telephone service, communications being dependent on the Telstra mobile network established for the Australian PKF. The network is only available in the centre of Dili and a couple of the other major towns across the country, and is frequently subject to interruptions and failure. My only contact with my family is by a mobile phone that works, inter-mittently, if I stand out in the little street in front of our house away from the overhanging tin roof.

'News by rumor' flourishes, and aid workers circulate unsourced reports about impending militia attacks. There is scant communi-cation from any official sources, apart from a recently established local newspaper that publishes in several languages. The only radio news in English we hear is a 10-minute bulletin on the UN radio station at 6 a.m. It seems the only other radio station is FALINTIL which broadcasts in local languages. The one television station is a broadcast of Sydney's Channel 7 or, occasionally, BBC World News, neither of which contain much information about Timor unless there are recent killings to report.

Daily life in Dili is dominated by the ever-present sight of armed soldiers: in groups, in battle fatigues and carrying large, menacing automatic weapons at all times. The traffic in Dili is mostly UN and PKF vehicles: 4WDs clearly marked with the logos of the United Nations or one of the numerous other aid, diplomatic, police or military organizations, troop carriers and armoured personnel carriers adorned with flak jackets, a soldier standing on top with machine gun at the ready. Overhead there is the drone of military aircraft and at dusk and in the evenings helicopters search low over the ground with large spotlight beams swooping over beaches and palm jungles that fringe the city.

Just before our arrival a soldier was killed by an exploding landmine on a beach to the east of Dili. In the first weeks after our stay, nightly clashes between the PKF and militia result in a number of fatal shootings on the border to the west. At the time of our arrival, tension is mounting with preparations for the first congress of the National Council of Timorese Resistance (CNRT) to be held at the end of August, coinciding with the anniversary commemorations of the popular consultation and remembrance of the slaughter and destruction that followed. There are fears that militia may try to destabilise the CNRT congress, rumours spread of militia infiltrating Dili on suicide missions, and reports that the United Nations have raised the security rating to the level of 'prepare for evacuation'. Security is tightened with tanks and sand bags on many intersections, road blocks and car searchings along the roads leading into the town centre. As the anniversary is commemorated there are celebrations in the streets during the day but at night the unlit streets are lined with candles as a silent vigil remembers those whose lives were lost.

At the beginning of our second month in Dili we hear of the horrific massacre of UN aid workers dragged from their offices in Atambua, just on the western side of the border. Militia unrest in the border region and in Kupang is high as negotiations continue over disarming militia gangs, identifying those responsible for the post-consultation slaughter, and repatriating refugees who have fled to West Timor in the wake of the fighting. All remaining aid workers there are airlifted to Dili, and my only consolation in the face of the madness is the logic that Dili must therefore be safe.

In security briefings we are advised not to travel outside Dili, not to walk alone in Dili at night, to stay away from the markets and any

Continued

other place where Timorese gather, lock doors and windows when driving, keep emergency numbers stored in our mobile phones and with us at all times. Our bus drivers to and from the University are to be equipped with two-way radios and our houses to be assigned 24-hour security guards. We are advised to register our passport details and addresses with the Australian Mission in Timor so they will know our whereabouts in case of evacuation, no easy task in the total absence of street names and numbers in the location where we reside. After the benign repose of Sydney, this really feels like a war zone.

A sense of social alienation, fuelled by the economic divide and colonial-style behaviour, characterised the international aid effort. In response to the level of physical and governmental destruction, unprecedented powers were conferred on the United Nations and other international organisations, which in turn 'attracted the very type of individual who would be intoxicated by that thought' (Chopra, 2002: 981). Foreign experts, flown in 'fresh from the post-conflict zones of Kosovo and Bosnia', were on short-term contracts that afforded little time to develop an understanding of the complexities of East Timor's situation (Sword Gusmao, 2003: 302). Under these conditions, 'the mission itself was corrupting', and produced a 'whole state-building enterprise that skidded on the surface of the country' (Chopra, 2002: 998). Despite their rhetoric of participation, the poorly coordinated international aid agencies failed to recognise the value of Timorese sociopolitical processes: under pressure to achieve predetermined, measurable outcomes and a return on investment within limited time frames, aid organisations were accused of imposing a development agenda according to external norms with 'standardised solutions and approaches reflecting a top-down Western attitude to development' (Brunnstrom, 2003: 314). More time, rather than more money, was required in order to develop a more equitable, fully consultative process that could meet the needs and priorities of Timorese communities.

In its peacekeeping and development operations, UNTAET was to have a focus on 'mainstreaming' gender perspectives. The notion that East Timor is a patriarchal society, and that women have suffered disproportionately under waves of occupation, is widespread amongst both Western and Timorese scholars, with some claiming that customary tribal practices, Portuguese colonialism and Catholicism have contributed to women's oppression. However, despite the establishment of a Gender Affairs Unit in UNTAET, staffed mostly by foreign nationals, achievements in improving gender equality were limited by poor planning, limited funding and hostility from male officials within the UN mission (Charlesworth, 2008). Moreover, Joshi (2007) claims that UNTAET was itself militarised and masculinised, and under the control of a male-dominated Department of Peace Keeping Operations, the UN mission failed to protect civilian women from sexual violence perpetrated by international military and police personnel. Only 2.4% of the peacekeeping forces and 4% of the international civilian police were female and although 33% of the civilians in UNTAET were women, almost all the key positions were held by men (Charlesworth, 2008).

The millennial wave of foreign influence in Timor was also accompanied by an increase in the use of English as a common language of communication, though its ultimate role was poorly defined and hotly debated. Not only had the United Nations adopted English as its official language, to the dismay of many East Timorese hopeful of employment, but aid agencies preferred to employ English-speaking local staff, often in junior positions, rather than attempt direct collaboration with local organizations (Brunnstrom, 2003; Hajek, 2000). This reinforced a perception that English, as the new language of necessity, could provide access to economic and cultural rewards, and generated a demand for English language training despite the designation of Portuguese as the official language.

*   *   *

By the end of the 20th century, successive waves of colonialism had already formed a palimpsest of inscription and reinscription across the Indonesian archipelago, and in East Timor the latest territorial invasion by a large foreign community of military forces, UN agencies and international aid workers had produced yet another disruption and reorganisation of physical, social and discursive relations. The meanings embedded in the geography of Indonesia and East Timor, inscribed in places, landscapes and territories through the struggles over territorial and linguistic occupation and possession, are integral to the circulation of power and knowledge: the struggle over geography is 'not only about soldiers and cannons but also about ideas, about forms, about images and imaginings' (Said, 1993: 7). The discursive construction of external engagement and development in Indonesia, and an imagined societal and governmental *tabula rasa* in East Timor, opened the potential for a reterritorialisation in the image of the West, through the processes of aid as the 'will to govern' (Duffield, 2002: 1049). The resultant asymmetrical relations of economic, social and political power between the international and local communities in these contact zones of development produced a particular set of spatial configurations, and it is within this spatiality that we can read the experiences of Western teachers in the following chapters.

Part 2

Teachers' Narrative Accounts

In previous chapters I have discussed the theoretical and contextual dimensions that inform my understanding of language teaching in development. Chapter 4 marks the beginning of Part 2, which comprises an exploration of English language teachers' narratives of experience in East Timor and Indonesia. In the following three chapters, I discuss the way teachers perceived the context of their teaching, and their role within that context. Chapter 4 is located outside the classroom, and Chapters 5 and 6 inside the classroom, although the worlds 'inside' and 'outside' the classroom wall do not represent a neat differentiation. The nature of the discursive and material flow across the boundary of the classroom, and its effects on teachers and students, forms part of the discussion in Chapters 5 and 6. In each chapter I consider the ways in which social and spatial relations were mutually constituted, and affected the teachers' sense of place in the development context.

A major task of these three chapters is to extend the understanding of English language teaching 'in context', through a theoretical framework of time and space. Discussion in previous chapters has suggested that modernist binaries produce a division of time and space in which time, as the privileged term, is aligned with the active drive of history, change and progress, while space provides a passive, unchanging background, or context, in which the change occurs. In the era of European imperialism, geographical context, the space of different lands and different peoples, was transformed into a chronological sequence, a historical queue: Europe as modern, Other lands and peoples as not-yet-modern. In this process, 'human differences in space', as Mignolo (2000: 288) explains, were converted to 'human differences in time'. By association, naturalised modernist paradigms of development and gender share in a metanarrative that privileges time, in its guise as teleological history and progress, over space, and its alignments with the particularities of place and context. This 'temporal narrative' establishes a hierarchy of nations according to their level of achievement or progress, legitimates donor nations' intervention in the development enterprise, and dulls an understanding of context as a space of social multiplicity, contestation and difference.

An underlying temporal narrative can also be identified in approaches to the spread of English as a language of progress, and in the status accorded to professional practices of ELT derived from English-speaking donor countries. With a focus on the 'improved' methods of ELT offered by foreign teachers, less attention has been paid to developing a complex understanding of the social and political contexts in which teaching and learning is located. Using a lens of time and space offers a means of interrogating the complex relations between English language teaching and development, and opens possibilities for different ways of thinking and working in particular domains.

Central to this study is the notion that space must be conceptualised integrally with time, to disrupt the dualism that underpins much development and language practice. Since English language teaching and development depend on a constructed, stable sense of time and space, a consideration of diverse temporal and spatial experiences is intended to highlight the inherent ambivalence and contradictions of development contexts and development classrooms. Thus, in Chapter 4, I examine aspects of space, place and time in terms of the social, economic and political relations that constitute the development context, including the spatial relation between foreign and local cultures. I will argue that teachers have a complex and ambivalent relation to context, and to the communities that coexist in development. Chapter 4 also demonstrates the way this problematic relationship of space and time involves particular social constructions of gender. Chapter 5 looks at how a temporal paradigm shapes understandings of ELT, and affects spatial flows from outside the classroom. The analysis suggests that the policies and practices of ELT in development, premised on notions of advancement, can work against the incorporation of local spatial and temporal contexts into language teaching, and can replicate spatial inequalities identified in between development communities. Chapter 6 focuses on the complex ways in which gendered spatiality emerges within the classroom, and explores how gendered subjectivity affects the teaching role.

Chapter 4
Being There: Teachers' Spatial Engagements with Development Contexts

> *No one lives in the world in general*
> Geertz, 1996: 262

This chapter begins an exploration of English language teachers' experiences in the world of international development. Focusing on teachers' narratives of life outside the classroom, it examines the social, political and gendered relations that constitute the spatial patterns of development. Working from the premise that context is fundamental to language meaning and language teaching, I consider how the teachers position themselves in relation to their sense of similarity to, or difference from, the various communities that comprise the context in which they find themselves. These relationships constitute teachers' subjectivity through a series of identifications and disidentifications that, in turn, suggest a spatial pattern of social, political, economic and cultural life in which it was often difficult for the teachers to find a 'place'. The teachers' narratives, discussed in the light of insights emerging from previous chapters, point to a range of contradictions and tensions between the principles and practices of international development and illustrate the divisions and hierarchies that reproduce relations of power in the contact zones of development.

The first section of the chapter revisits key themes concerning the temporal and spatial organisation of development, and indicates the contradictions and ambivalence that may disturb participants working in development enterprises. The second section engages with teachers' narratives and explores the motivations and challenges related to development work in Indonesia and East Timor. It discusses themes of alienation, whiteness and masculinity that emerge in Indonesia, and considers how teachers working in East Timor position themselves within the development context through their dis/identification with a number of loosely defined groups: the development community, the Australian community, the teaching community and the Timorese community. The third section focuses on teachers' perceptions of gendered relations amongst the foreign community in East Timor, and shows how teachers disidentified with the gendered subject positions available to them in the development context. This section also considers teachers' perceptions of gender relations between foreign women and Timorese men, where a complex array of factors, including age, perceptions of Western sexuality, economic and professional status, affected the women's sense of place. In the final section, I explore teachers' accounts that signal the emergence of a different way of 'being here', and a more productive engagement with a localised sense of place.

The Temporality and Spatiality of Development

As a means of understanding teachers' relation to the complex social and political interactions of the development context, and contesting the dominant temporal narrative, I have proposed the use of a 'spatial hermeneutic' (Soja, 1989: 2). This perspective assumes that the experience of social life and power in any context is integrally dependent on the organisation of space and time (Foucault, 1984b: 252), that social relations are necessarily spatially constituted, and that spatial configurations are socially produced (Massey, 1994: 254–255). The interaction of social power, space and time is captured in the terms 'spatiality' and 'temporality'. A spatial perspective does not simply invert the dominance of time indicated in the mainstream development narrative, but rather aims to 'think in terms of all the dimensions of space-time' since both interact in the formation of complex events (Massey, 1994: 264).

Foregrounding spatiality, then, is intended as a means of interrogating the particular social and political relationships in the development context. If we look at development from a spatial perspective, we might see that social life, in all its historic, economic, political and cultural dimensions, produces particular spatial patterns. This is evident, for example, in the geographically uneven distribution of wealth and privilege that underscores the development enterprise; in the spatially gendered division of labour; in the spatial divisions between public and private life; in spatial distributions according to ethnicity or nationality; and in the spatial segregations and controls operating through modern institutions such as schools. In turn, those particular spatial organisations and exclusions work to reproduce the social hierarchies and divisions inherent in the development context. When the privilege of the West is transposed onto 'developing countries', the production and maintenance of macro-level, geopolitical spaces of privilege can be reflected in the everyday practices of development, producing an 'ever shifting geometry of power' (Massey, 1994: 3).

Several aspects of spatiality emerge in teachers' accounts of the development context. First, the context of development is represented as a contact zone, a space 'where disparate cultures meet, clash, and grapple with each other, often in highly asymmetrical relations of domination and subordination' (Pratt, 1992: 4). The contact zone of development is a physical and social space that is interactional, and constituted not only in particular relations of power between 'us' and 'them', but also amongst 'us'. Second, teachers situate themselves in the contact zone through multiple and conflicted dis/identifications with the social groups and spaces that constitute 'us' and 'them'. Third, teachers perceive the contact zone as a space where patriarchal and sexist regimes served to control the spatial mobility of females, and to reinforce racial boundaries. On the whole, teachers resisted identification with exclusionary spaces and practices that they saw as reproducing colonial hierarchies of gender, ethnicity and class in a contemporary form; however, teachers also struggled to understand their own contradictory presence in the development context, and recognised a certain complicity with the relations of power that facilitated their participation in the development enterprise. Finally, other ways of being-in-the-world, of connecting to local places and people, emerge in teachers' accounts of spatial practices and constructions of spatial history (Carter, 1987). Spatial history produced partial and situated knowledges of place, and involved teachers in a process of relating to the spaces and places of the contact zone in ways that resisted the most overt expressions of power, distance and detachment.

Ambivalence and the disruption of development context as transparent space

In earlier chapters, I have argued that the mainstream development paradigm conforms to a universalising 'temporal narrative': an idea of progress in which developing countries would achieve economic growth and development by following a model established by wealthy Western nations. The narrative of progress that shapes the development enterprise grants superior status to advanced or 'developed' nations and to the knowledge imported by foreign experts working in development, thereby supporting the maintenance of hierarchical relations in the contact zone. Hierarchical relations also figure in the construction of a dominant, detached subject position that separates the foreigner from a local context perceived as a passive, surveyable space that is transparent and knowable (Rose, 1993). Described by Pratt (1992) as the 'monarch-of-all-I-survey', this is a subject position produced in colonial relations, and identified in contemporary contact situations, including international tourism, journalism and development. As a means of problematising the dual production of a dominant, Western identity and a passive, transparent space of context, my focus in the teachers' accounts is on ambivalence and on the disruption of naturalised concepts of time and space.

Two key contradictions that underscore ambivalence and undermine the unified subject position in development emerge in the teachers' narratives. The first refers to the inherent contradiction in development between self-interest and altruism (Rist, 2002) which can coexist in development practices. Self-interest can be interpreted as contributing to development enterprises in a way that serves to preserve a position of economic privilege and enhance strategic interests, while maintaining a safe distance from contextual entanglements. Altruism is perhaps a more slippery term, and is sometimes seen as having overtones of moral superiority, missionary zeal or Western beneficence used to assuage guilt. These positions also suggest a maintenance of spatial distance and privilege. Other meanings of altruism might better be described as encompassing a spirit of generosity, or a commitment to social justice, and could be imagined as a way of being-in-the-world that opens a space for the possibility of a more democratic, negotiated connection with context and with difference. This type of spatiality suggests a way for Western teachers to more productively engage with otherness.

A second important contradiction relates to the positioning of the female subject as development worker. The gendered narratives themselves represent a position of 'complex ambivalence', since they are both inside and outside the 'imperial' subject (Blunt & Rose, 1994: 14); and the specific experiences of the female body as the smallest space of political expression relate, in complex ways, to a broader geospatial politics. By disrupting the rational, unified subject, this remapping of colonialism-in-development posits a complex, fluid subject with the potential to resist the detached objectivity implied in official accounts of donor activity in the development context.

Aliens in Indonesia: Whiteness and Gender

For both Bree and Ann, motivations to take up two-year contracts as volunteer teachers in Indonesia were shaped by a complex set of factors that align teachers with a desire to make a positive connection with a different context and people, while offering a means of personal and professional fulfilment. Their desires reflected the contradictory forces of self-interest and altruism that Rist (2002) recognises at the core of the development enterprise. On the one hand, both teachers identified with the opportunities for the realisation of personal aspirations that development work promised: adventure and travel, an escape from the commodification and marginalisation of ELT work in Australia, and the chance to find meaning in their professional lives. For Bree, a two-year sojourn meant *'the experience of living in a different culture, and learning another language'*, and for Ann the chance to *'stay in a place and really get to know the people rather than just travelling through'*. At the same time, volunteering, for Ann, meant an opportunity to fulfil more altruistic desires to *'give something back'* in return *'to all those people who were good to me and generous to me as a backpacker, I want to give something of mine'*. Yet, in both sets of desires there is also a common thread, a yearning for connection, for identification, with something different and other is evident.

Neither Bree nor Ann had much foreknowledge of the places to which they were assigned, which added to a sense of adventure into the 'unknown'. However, their most often expressed recollections of their two-year appointments concerned sensations of intense isolation and alienation, feelings that were realised in images of remoteness, and in the stark spatial segregations of ethnicity and gender. Bree's years as a volunteer in Ambon were in a location she described as *'off the beaten track, it was a wild place'*, where she learned about *'crossing new frontiers of boredom and isolation'*. The few foreign professionals she saw departed within the first year, and the remaining group of Western missionaries stationed nearby were *'a complete breed apart, I couldn't relate to them at all'*. Her sense of dislocation from place was palpable: *'It was a really odd place for me. Sometimes I'd walk down the street and I'd feel really alone, I'd just think, there's nothing I can relate to.'* Ann, in similar circumstances, saw *'no other white people'* for many months in the vicinity of her small Sulawesi village. Although *'in the last couple of months there'* she found *'some [white male] geologists'*, they also seemed to lead a separated existence, and *'spent a lot of time out in the jungle looking for gold'*, returning briefly to separate quarters where *'they had their own cook and everything in town, so you didn't see them around'*. Like Bree, in this situation Ann *'drew on every inner resource [. . .] to keep balanced, because it was so lonely. [. . .] I had no one from my culture who could understand my jokes or understand how I felt'*.

For both Ann and Bree, feelings of alienation were complicated by an intense othering they experienced in relation to their host communities.

For Ann, this alienation was experienced as an elevation above the local community and context, which she felt was a result of her privileged professional status. With some pride, she identified with her image as '*the first and only ever English native speaker they'd had, as a lecturer, so I arrived there adored before I even got there, you know, this was something really precious*'. But this adoration was gradually experienced as objectification, and became a source of irritation and resentment.

> *They would all say "Oh, you're so beautiful and so gorgeous!" and I know I'm not beautiful, I'm old enough to know myself, and so I think that was a bit of reverse racism really, because I was white, you're beautiful and clever and all the rest.*

Treasured as a '*novelty*', she was regularly invited to public events, where she eventually found the watchful gaze that constructed her otherness '*very tiresome*'. At weddings she '*felt like a souvenir doll*', an imposed identity she refused, if only in silent repudiations:

> *Dressed up in traditional costume, they would wheel me up the front to take a photo with the bride and groom, and sometimes I didn't even know them. Hauled up like a puppet. I remember once, I had the fork to my mouth and I saw every pairs of eyes on me, watching every mouthful. And the mother of the bride said to the bride, "Does she eat rice?" and I thought, well I've been here for months, if I didn't eat rice I'd starve, and besides that I could speak for myself. I had enough Indonesian to speak for myself.*

Nevertheless, her conspicuous embodied differences, and the religious tenets she ascribed to the host community, did afford Ann particular privileges. As a lone female, gender was '*never a problem*' when she stepped out in public: '*As a native English speaker I was worth my weight in gold, so I felt very protected. When I was on my way to college, walking, people on bikes would stop and ask did I want a lift, everyone knew me and also they were all good Muslims so [as a woman] I felt very safe.*' On the streets, in the public domain, the high regard accorded to her whiteness and English-speaking status was taken up as a welcome form of separation that offered particular benefits.

In contrast, Bree felt her relationships with her host community were compromised, in part, by expectations of white privilege and spatial segregation generated by the long-term presence of a white male supervisor. One of '*five blokes*' administering an ELT project across Indonesia, her supervisor '*lived in a kind of marble mausoleum, and had a driver and a live-in maid and air-conditioning all through this massive house and a big high fence with barbed wire on it'*. Bree distanced herself from the neocolonial hierarchy represented in the 'marble mausoleum': she *'lived in the village'*, and was struggling to manage financially on a local salary; yet she was isolated from the infrastructure of community support, and subject to an informal *'skin tax'* that inflated the cost of *'everything'* sold to white Westerners on the assumption that all were well paid. *'People thought that I'd be earning the same money as the advisor, you know, they were quite perplexed about why I was walking to the bus stop or being canoed across the harbour, and I didn't have a driver and all the rest of it.'*

These contradictory positions of whiteness were further complicated by the effects of gender, and reflected the awkward and ambiguous positioning of Western women in the neocolonial relations of development:

> *Um, it was a difficult place to live, because as the head of the project said within the first 5 minutes of my landing, "It's a man's world Bree", and I thought, "Oh, here's trouble!" [. . .] It was a blokes' project. Just, it- it's hard to explain, um, well there were no women in the same position [as my supervisor], and they did tend to be a bit blokey about it all. My bloke, he was in his 50s but he was married to a young local girl and, I don't know, that was a bit odd.*

Again, Bree distanced herself from the taint of sexual exploitation that she saw in the white male relationship with a 'young local girl', and positioned herself as also potentially exploitable as a female professional in a patriarchal education domain. The Indonesian educational institution in which she worked was also perceived as patriarchal, and the male headmasters were *'flirtatious'*, although in deference to her professional status and her connections as a foreign teacher they were more cautious and wouldn't *'step out of line'* by making physical advances. Away from the institutional domain, however, any privileges attached to her professional status disappeared, and she became an unplaceable outsider: *'If they tried to fit me in they couldn't, so what they did was went "she's a Westerner, she's got a completely different thing, she's an alien"'*.

In the public domain of the streets, where Ann had felt adored and protected, Bree *'stuck out like a sore thumb'* and was troubled by the *'aggressive'* attention she received as one of the few white women: *'all the verbal stuff, and being stared at a lot, [. . .] in the street you get this funny hassling all the time'*; *'you knew every time you walked past a group of men, someone was going to say something'*. Bree suspected the hassling was a consequence of an enforced idleness, and perhaps frustration, amongst Ambonese men, which contrasted with the interventionary activity and agency of missionaries and development experts: *'so there were lots of unemployed young men sitting around in the street and they just hassle you for fun really'*. When walking in public she was continually stared at, hissed, hassled and had stones thrown at her feet by men and boys. She became particularly angry and frustrated at continual male shouts of *'"Hey fuck you!" I don't think they knew it was as bad- you know, how incendiary saying that is to somebody. And when it happens to you all the time, you just get really annoyed.'* In public spaces, she became an unruly body in the wrong place, an object of *'chauvinistic'* attention, subject to the scrutiny and surveillance of the male gaze as a crucial means of organising the spatial field, and the female body, as an object of control.

Bree reasoned that a female Ambonese teacher of the same age *'would have been accorded a lot more respect'*, so was ethnicity a factor in these events? Certainly, some harassment did appear to be targeted more directly to her whiteness, such as being followed with chants of *'Orang barat'*, meaning 'Westerner', or *'bule'*, a *'semi insulting'* equivalent of *'albino'* in English: *'it's a bit like being called the "white nigger" sort of thing. Sort of like, you'd hear this word and you'd feel [wary], and they'd go "orang barat, orang barat"'*. But positioning according to ethnicity was not the only factor in play: Bree observed that white men were treated differently to white women, they were *'harangued in a different way, they got lots of offers for marriage and that sort of thing'*. Harassment of white men appeared to be more focused on the potential economic benefits of marriage to a Western man. In contrast, Bree's presence seemed to evoke a reading of Western women shaped by fantasy images of sexual availability and *'loose and easy'* morals. She had observed these pervasive fantasy images in readily available Western media, from soft porn videos to television soap operas, and despite the intrigue they generated, she posited a clash between these representations and the *'moral kind of code of conduct and everything'* in Ambonese culture. Reflecting on her positioning, then, Bree guessed that it was in fact a combination of her differences – her skin colour, her sex, her unmarried status and (therefore) suspect sexuality – that marked her as an *'alien'* and a target of masculine policing in the public sphere.

Walking out in public as a white female, Bree seemed to suffer the 'clearly punitive consequences' aimed at 'those who fail to do their gender right' in terms of the spatial rules that apply in a given context (Butler, 1990: 139). One set of responses to the discomfort of being so visible, so aware of being reduced to a sexed body, was therefore a desire to become *in*visible, to blend into the background, by complying with a more restrictive, and less sexual, gender code. In this sense she attempted to comply with the imposed restrictions that governed her body. Her painful self-consciousness about *'being a woman, a European woman'* made her *'want to* *cover up, you start, you know, getting very modest'*. She portrayed her performative response as a comic caricature in *'my bun, my kind of frumpy cotton dress, and missionary sandals'*, changing much of her own bodily behaviour and attire in an attempt to do her gender right: *'I just wore something that was really conservative, no trousers [. . .] On the surface you had to appear to be completely pure and well behaved.'* However, enforced compliance became extremely wearing: *'It really depressed me at times, just getting up the energy to go outside, and I used to pull my umbrella down so people couldn't see my face. It was terrible.'* This attempt to keep her other, Western self hidden, entailed not only taming and camouflaging the physical appearance of her body, but also hiding past and present bodily practices she thought would be unacceptable, in the belief that *'it was going to be far less complicated if I took [a new] role than if I was the real me!'* Yet this projection of a different, appropriate self ironically underscored her detachment from the community: like Ann, she felt she *'couldn't tell my friends everything that I'd ever done in my life, because they would have been absolutely appalled, as I am sometimes!'* In this way her adjustment to spatially defined cultural norms not only produced a different sense of self, but also formed a barrier against a fuller engagement with Ambonese friends.

In time, an increasing sense of resistance to these gendered spatial regimes led Bree to challenge the harassment she experienced in the public domain. By identifying with the agency offered in her professional identity, she was able to refuse a sexualised positioning, and assert a more powerful representation of her self. Drawing on her status as an English teacher with implicit connections to Indonesian institutional authorities, she retaliated with vigorous and unexpected opposition to vocal harassment that centred on her sexual identity: *'they didn't expect me to turn around and go charging back and say, in Indonesian "I'm going to take you to court for sexual harassment!"'*. At other times she practiced an insistent silent retaliation: *'I got so sick of it after two years of people saying "Fuck you Mister!" I thought, "Fuck me? Fuck you!"'* Unable to openly voice these words, she translated them with a twist, pointing to the ironic confusion of linguistic labels and gendered identity, she shouted back: *'Don't call me <u>Mister</u>!'*

Through Bree's and Ann's accounts, we can begin to see the ways in which development, as a mode of progress facilitated by foreign aid workers, and as a meeting of different cultures ascribed with diverse meanings, produces complex, shifting social and spatial arrangements. Hierarchical social relations, underpinned by notions of advancement, and accompanied by embodied differences of economic, racial, professional and native-speaker status, can constitute a spatiality of segregation that divides participants in the contact zone of development. For some, it is the notion of development as a form of progress from tradition to modernity, a temporal narrative that holds the promise of economic wealth, that appears to be carried in the body of the white, professional English language teacher. But the temporal narrative is never quite settled, and different readings of the body come into play in the public arena. As they entered the public domain, conflicting readings of the teachers' gender echoed the ambiguous positioning of white women in an earlier colonial era, and served to isolate the teachers, singling them out either for adoration or depredation. Otherness, isolation and alienation produced, for both teachers, a sense of separation from a situated engagement with place and people. In their initial desires for development work they pursued an engagement with otherness, but resisted the isolating effects of becoming Other themselves. As we shall see in the following section, these dislocating sociospatial relations shifted again in the experiences of teachers working in larger development programmes in East Timor.

Out of Place in East Timor: Colonialism Revisited

Identification with a view of development work as an altruistic humanitarian gesture, rather than an opportunity for personal gain, was prevalent amongst the teachers going to work in East Timor during the nation's transition to independence. Before their departures from Australia, many of the teachers' understandings of East Timor had been shaped by an interest in the province's long struggle for freedom, and by more recent pleas for international assistance to construct a new nation from the destruction that followed the separation from Indonesia. Some, like Elly, had previously been involved *'in rallies and stuff in support of Timorese independence'* and others, including Fay, identified with a commitment to *'the last of the colonial type struggles'*, while Dana was *'interested from a social justice point of view'* to be involved in what seemed *'like a wonderful opportunity to help out and do something meaningful'*. Some teachers made an effort to distance themselves from notions of self-interest. Carol, made a point of explaining that her *'motivation was to help'* in some way, and insisted that her involvement *'certainly wasn't for financial reasons – that was just a bonus'*. Nevertheless, Dana conceded that *'the money also helped, I couldn't have afforded to go as a volunteer, and I had already done my time at volunteering and being poor'*. While such identifications are never simple, most accounts align teachers with a desire to make a positive connection with a different context and people, and to engage in *'something meaningful'* through their professional practice as English language teachers.

On their arrival they were met with unexpected circumstances that were often at odds with these desires. Initially, it was the shock of material destruction resulting from recent political upheavals that provoked in some a visceral, embodied response, and a sense of dislocation (see Figure 4.1). Ann *'looked at all the burnt out houses and all the schools and it felt like being kicked in the stomach'*; while for Dana the physical destruction carried meanings of a haunting social tragedy, *'the reminders of what had occurred in the streets before we arrived, such as the rubble and the burnt out buildings. There was an eerie feeling about the place at times perhaps because of this.'* Elly *'felt like there was a lot of bad energy in Timor [...] the actual atmosphere felt bad, like bad things had happened or were going to happen, you know, there was this sense of doom'*. The spatial evidence of violence was exacerbated, in Elly's recollection, by the phenomenal domination of the place by the military (see Figure 4.2): *'You know down at Café Dili, you know how they used to walk in there and clunk, clunk all their guns on the ground. That freaked me out. I found the violence and the war stuff quite distressing.'* Rumours and warnings about the risk of attack by local militia intensified teachers' sense of alarm and alienation, and official briefings that detailed

Figure 4.1 Burnt buildings in Dili

Figure 4.2 Military roadblock in Dili

emergency and evacuation procedures did little to diminish the mood of fear and imminent danger.

Social and spatial privilege in East Timor

Alienation from a physical spatiality was then replicated in a sense of social dislocation, as teachers' expectations of *'helping'* were seriously challenged by their perceptions of the development community they had joined. In contrast to the teachers in Indonesia who saw very few other white people, teachers in East Timor were part of a vast international presence: government and non-government organisations, international agencies, multinational peacekeeping forces, an assortment of construction workers, solidarity activists, journalists, volunteers and a rush of Australian business entrepreneurs had all arrived to build the new nation. The teachers' overall impressions were of a wealthy, Western and white community of foreigners that constructed exclusive spaces for living, working and transport, reproducing economic, social and racial relations of distance and detachment from a complex, local physical and cultural context of development. The physical spaces occupied by the United Nations, in particular, seemed to reflect the conditions of a modern Western consumerist lifestyle, a mobile 'home', transported around the globe to service the needs of the elite expatriate development community. Teachers disidentified with these detached spatial practices, and in their accounts we glimpse a desire for a more meaningful engagement with local spaces and places.

The development community was also perceived by teachers to be competitive, inward turning, and socially, economically and politically fragmented by judgements and conflicting hierarchies. These hierarchies were seen to fix people into defined places in a series of inclusions and exclusions according to different measures of status. The most salient measure of status appeared to be economic, although other markers associated with difference, including gender and ethnicity, were also apparent and were seen to position teachers in various negative ways. Having distanced themselves from the social spaces marked by wealth and elitism, most teachers saw themselves as more closely aligned with what they understood to be the social and political commitments and values of the volunteer and NGO sector. However, teachers on paid contracts felt excluded from this group because of their supposedly 'privileged' economic position, and some expressed ambivalence about their own complicity and location within a hierarchy that separated them from local conditions.

Observing the range of activities and tensions across the various groups in the development context of East Timor, Dana recalled the feeling that the teachers had *'walked into a development minefield'* where they negotiated *'a difficult position'* between competing discourses and practices, and struggled to find their place through identification with or separation from the various groups.

Amidst this crowd of foreign workers, where Fay had expected to find a *'highly politicised group of activists'*, she saw instead *'a group of misfits who weren't really interested in the local situation'*, a multitude of uncoordinated groups who were each *'unaware of what other organisations were doing'*. Despite an avowed commitment *'to involving the Timorese people, and empowering them'*, Elly felt the various sectors of the development community were engaged in a *'massive in-fight'*:

> *It was what I call turf war, they were there, they had their own agendas and they had their area that they were trying to protect, and they had their ideas about who the good people to work with were, and I mean they were really politicised.*

In this *'development minefield'*, Dana distinguished several social categories, each with its problematic, dislocated relationship with the Timorese community: globe-trotting UN careerists, opportunistic business entrepreneurs *'exploiting what was there to be had'*, professionals *'just there to do a job [...] and making money'* and a mixed bag of *'more sensitive'* NGO volunteers. As a whole, the foreign workers appeared as a separate entity functioning autonomously from, or overlaid onto the local space. Adding to this sense of autonomy, a sudden influx of development wealth had produced, in Helen's words, a *'post-war fake economy'* that connected transnational communities to a flow of commodities and services way beyond the reach of the local population, and supported social relations of distance and detachment from the specific physical and cultural context of Timor.

Within the inwardly focused development community, social and professional hierarchies often operated through a comparison of salaries and conditions, a primary sign of status and invariably the subject of conjecture, envy, disapproval or pity. Elly was urged by those on lucrative contracts and higher salaries to *'get out of the [teaching] project I was on and get into the UN and get on the gravy train: "get on the gravy train love, it won't last forever!"'* In other sectors, any attachment to the financial rewards available in development work was looked on with contempt. Money, in this sense, signified the inherent contradiction in the concept of development between altruism and self-interest, and many teachers were deeply ambivalent about the salaries they received. In this regard, the distinction between teachers on paid contracts and volunteer workers was crucial, with teachers often feeling despised by both of these groups: while they identified more with the commitment ascribed to the volunteer sector, their own contract salaries aroused *'resentment'* amongst development workers on lower incomes. As Dana explained, there was *'a difference between a teacher who goes in and works for a local salary and a teacher who goes in and works for AusAID and is paid a lot more'*. Being on a paid contract, she felt volunteers viewed her with disdain as *'a white Westerner, who had a lot of privileges and who was being paid well to be over there'*. The resulting *'black mark against our names'* was seen as another cause of social exclusion experienced by the teachers. In this way, teachers struggled with their own complicity in competing hierarchies that operated to fix people in place, and in which high status could be marked either by a lucrative contract or by recognition of the moral commitment and solidarity associated with volunteering.

With their desires to align with discourses of commitment and solidarity, most teachers vigorously disidentified with those elements of the development community who displayed the more obvious signs of wealth. The most widely criticised were those described by Dana as *'the brash UN workers who drove round in their Land Rovers and went to Hello Mister'*, the only Western-style supermarket, and who *'didn't seem to be very respectful of their position, or that other people were in, you know, lot more difficult positions'*. The UN community was singled out, by Fay and others, for scorn as

> a travelling circus who don't actually engage with the local context, a group of traumatised people travelling around from one traumatised place to another, having very little knowledge of the place that they're in, and getting duty free beer and cigarettes.

In the capital Dili, Helen observed the *'big machine'* of the United Nations had *'rebuilt the government buildings on the wharf and moved in'* (see Figure 4.3), producing a 'hermeneutic office world increasingly disconnected from life on the streets' (Chopra, 2000: 33). And since most of Dili's housing had been destroyed, a large residential ship, the *Hotel Olympia* (see Figure 4.4), *'all lit up with fairy lights'*, was moored in Dili harbour to provide accommodation: *'it has a swimming pool, hairdresser, beauty parlour, bars and restaurants etc. they have an entertainment complex with cinemas and God knows what else floating nearby. Meanwhile the locals live in bombed out squalor'* (see Figure 4.5). Access by Timorese was restricted, 'except to serve drinks and food' (Chopra, 2000: 33). Adamantly disidentifying with this

Figure 4.3 UNTAET offices in Portuguese Colonial Governor's building, Dili

Figure 4.4 Hotel Olympia in Dili harbour

Figure 4.5 Makeshift shacks and market stalls adjacent to Dili harbour

site of privilege, she felt *'embarrassed to think I might be associated with it all'*. From the teachers' perspective, the self-sufficient physical spaces carved out by the elite UN development community constituted 'separate spaces for separate races' (Gunn, 2001, in Benwell & Stokoe, 2006: 206).

Similarly privileged administrative and domestic spaces occupied by non-UN staff were also the object of criticism. Ann described, in dismissive terms, the sequestered lifestyle of two non-teaching acquaintances *'on huge salaries and amazing conditions'* in a government-funded aid project: *'I was just unnerved at the amount of money they were getting, a free house, with servants, they led a life of- in their air-conditioned office, back in their air-conditioned car, and off to the beach on the weekend'*. The exclusive, hermetic spaces they inhabited contrasted with the way teachers regarded their own lifestyles in Timor, and Ann believed these privileged foreign workers *'could leave here after two years and they won't see a fraction of what I've seen'*. In comparison, Ann felt *'very fortunate'* in living with a Timorese family and regarded this as an opportunity to learn: *'I just thought, because [the Timorese] were lovely people, I just thought how very lucky I am that I'm not living like [those colleagues] because I've learnt so much'*.

The spatial separation described in living conditions was replicated in teachers' perceptions of segregated leisure activities. Some teachers reported positive experiences of mixing socially with a diverse and dynamic international community, but once again disidentified with the social hierarchies they perceived, and the alienation that these activities evoked. One of the recreational spaces established by the United Nations was the '*UN HQ "happy hour"*', initially attended by Helen shortly after her arrival in Dili:

> *That evening was like something out of a movie. There were the journalist types in chinos and pressed white shirts; the volunteer types in jeans and thongs with long hair and baggy T-shirts; the UN types in designer casuals; a selection of fabulous looking women all very fit and tanned and people of every race, creed and colour.*

But for Helen, the excitement of international glamour in this particular place soon faded, and two weeks later she described UN happy hour as '*an evening of pissed, patronising idiots and glamour secretaries slumming it from Geneva*'.

In similar depictions of the international scene in Dili, Ann described exclusive cafes and restaurants serving cliques of elite international staff, and expressed an explicit rejection of those exclusive spatial practices:

> *I found myself- I don't know if I was slightly snobbish, I just chose really not to associate with people who were there on very much larger incomes than me. I didn't really want to go to the UN parties and I didn't really want to go to the very wealthy places with the other malais [foreigners] who were very blatantly- it irked me, it really did, a lot about the UN made me really furious, angry and frustrated.*

Like Helen, Ann was concerned that she might be identified by the Timorese community as part of this malai lifestyle:

> *I suppose about being white, I thought: do they all think I'm rich like the UN? And you almost have to say, "No, I'm <u>not</u> on a UN salary", you know, informing people that you're not one of them. There were assumptions about those people, and so about being white.*

This self-imposed separation from a wealthy expatriate lifestyle was typical of the spatial positioning adopted by many teachers within the development context. But while economic status was the most salient marker of spatial separation, a sense of moral spatiality was also in operation. In this case, Ann's political and moral preferences were set in opposition to the prevailing economic hierarchy, yet her supposed complicity through a shared whiteness required ongoing refusal and separation.

If the UN social spaces appeared to be marked by wealth and glamour, other social spaces for foreign workers were delineated by celebratory rituals such as *'barbecues, parties', 'hard drinking'*, and exaggerated displays of stereotyped, male-dominated cultural practices. Here again, teachers expressed mixed responses of pleasure and approbation in relation to these spatial practices. Dislocation from the conditions and restraints of daily life at home seemed to provide a carnivalesque mood, and promote behavioural extremes that Helen found *'absurd! Everyone's out of their normal routines'* and *'pushing the boundaries'*. In scenes similar to the UN happy hour, these translocated and dislocated cultural practices concretised in specific places, such as the hotel frequented by foreign workers:

> *I mean everybody drank. And that was part of the problem I think, but the heavy drinking I think contributed to a lot of the back-biting, the gossip, the talk, you know, and just some of the plain bad behaviour. They loved to tear everybody apart, it wasn't just the teachers, I mean I would sit there in the hotel and just listen to them sometimes, it was everyone, everyone: this particular journalist, or that particular aid worker, or that particular teacher or this or that, it was very destructive, and common [...] the rumours and everything, it was very, very common.*

Helen's observations evoke the particular spatiality of the development community. The hotel space was marked physically, but was also constituted through social relations and habitual activities: drinking, back-biting and gossiping were actions that required constant repetition to bind a transitory group. The place of the hotel was seen by the teacher to form a viewing position from which the development community 'out there' was obsessively scrutinised and judged. By sharing gossip about various individuals, each was continually under surveillance to determine exclusions and inclusions, distinguishing insiders and outsiders in a process of group consolidation and border maintenance.

Helen observed that this 'balcony view' from the hotel offered opportunities to pass judgement on teachers, who saw themselves as outsiders in relation to the hotel scene. Helen suspected *'professional jealousy'* was at the heart of the criticisms and exclusions directed at teachers, who were *'easy targets, because people seem to imagine that we have a light job'*. Such 'light jobs' could be contrasted to the masculinised, physical work undertaken in development sites, such as Timor, characterised by danger and designated for emergency relief. In related recollections, Fay suggested that in the eyes of male aid workers, *'we were this sort of bunch of middle-class teachers from Australia with no commitment'*, cast as outsiders in a masculinist hierarchy.

Teachers also perceived the inward turning aid community to be directing criticisms outward towards the Timorese. Placing themselves in opposition to these criticisms, teachers continued to distance themselves from groups with whom they might otherwise be identified. Elly was particularly critical of what she interpreted as a masculine mode of relating to people and context through the authority expected of an *'emergency scenario'*, an action-oriented performance that *'didn't even connect with what was happening on the ground, to local people'*. In contrast to her own political allegiances, she noted an *'overall lack of sympathy or solidarity with the Timorese people'*, which was evident in *'the comments by Australians about how lazy all the Timorese are, and how dumb, and how they just kind of follow instructions'*. Similar comments were condemned by Helen as *'patronising, arrogant and often downright racist'*, and led to a more general criticism, particularly of Australian male aid workers: *'I detest the way they used the term "locals". I loathed their xenophobic attitudes.'*

Being Australian: Finding place between past and present

As Australians, teachers in development contexts reflected on their location within a broader picture of the complex geopolitical relationship between Australia, East Timor and Indonesia. Shaped by conflicting historical and geographic discourses, Australia's development enterprises reflect the underlying tensions between a fear of and a desire for engagement with Asia. In accounts of development work in East Timor, we can see teachers' ambivalent identifications as Australian subjects, struggling within conflicting discourses. Although this ambivalent identification potentially offers different ways to connect with the context of their work, by 'open[ing] up the possibility of other narratives' (Bhabha, 1990a: 300), the teachers' reflections also demonstrate the difficulty of constructing a narrative that could satisfactorily account for their own complicit presence in the development mission as a self-interested endeavour.

I will focus here on two aspects of ambivalence that emerged in the teachers' accounts. The first relates to teachers' growing discomfort with official benevolent versions of Australia's historical relations with East Timor and Indonesia. A second aspect of ambivalence emerged from teachers' perception that, in the contemporary period, Australia's development presence opened a space for potentially exploitative foreign government and commercial enterprises. The degree to which teachers saw their role in development as complicit with these political and economic interventions varied. Some distanced themselves from past and present 'betrayal', and some saw the aid effort as producing positive effects in East

Timor, while others realised they were inevitably part of a more complex and contradictory space of intervention.

While the intervention in East Timor represented Australia's largest ever response to an international emergency (AusAID, 2001), many of the teachers, like Fay, recognised that *'apart from this last ditch effort, Australia's actually betrayed Timor'* through years of neglect. In this recognition, the teachers observed a latent self-interest in Australia's latest altruistic endeavour. For Elly, the aid effort, disguised in *'that 1950s idea of helping your neighbours'*, masked moves to secure Australia's economic and strategic interests in the region by *'constructing the sort of state that they felt was needed'*, and *'economically it was smart, Australia wants to keep its finger in the pie, they're after all that oil'*. Responsibility for betrayal and exploitation was attributed to politicians, and their patrician visits to development projects on which teachers worked were viewed with contempt: *'Politicians doing their swanning in and out, politicians being politicians, they wanted to see a nice functioning program, that Australia was something. It was politics, it wasn't actually meaningful I don't think in any way.'* In the light of this self-interested performance, for teachers to position their own activities as Australians was no easy matter. Resisting identification with official narratives, Carol acknowledged that *'politicians did awful things in the past, Australia had let [the Timorese] down'*, and that now *'we owed them a lot'*. But she extracted herself from the larger political picture, by refusing *'to be blamed for what our Prime Ministers have done in the past, I'd rather people judge me, personally'*.

For several teachers, ambivalent feelings about being Australian related not only to their views of the past, but also to their doubts about the benefit to the Timorese of Australia's current territorial intervention. Teachers like Ann distanced themselves relatively easily from what they saw as commercial exploitation by *'business people from Darwin coming in and making a huge financial killing'*, *'working the local people under atrocious conditions'* and *'betraying them still'*. By contrast, participating in educational projects was construed by Elly as a means of fulfilling the *'genuine wishes'* of the *'general population'* in Australia to offer support and maintain a historical *'tradition of connection'* between the two countries:

> *Because we were there in a skilling and education capacity I didn't feel that the teaching role, the project we had, was so detrimental. I felt kind of okay about that, because it was a short term project, because it was about getting in there and skilling people and then getting out, because it wasn't about setting up infrastructure that then we were going to hold positions in for the next 3 years and make good salaries.*

Elly relied on the illusion of a quick fix English language project being politically neutral and harmlessly beneficial, yet she was also *'aware of being part of a Western intervention'* that had darker consequences in the construction of a *'cultural and social space'* for Australian occupation:

> *I felt that we were kind of part of that whole system of- well we were, indirectly, part of a system that was about setting up certain markets and cultural and social space for Australian/Western/neo-colonial businesses, values, ideals, and culture. So I did feel that we were we were part of making sure that Timor was tied into that.*

The contrast between an awareness of these territorial encroachments and the popular image of Australians as liberators was a source of disquiet, and made teachers uncomfortable about the way they felt they were seen by the Timorese. Fay recalled *'the attitude to Australians was quite positive generally at the time we were there'*, and was *'amazed at how forgiving [Timorese] people are'*. Reactions to Australians were, however, spatially dependent and Elly noted that they differed between rural areas and Dili, the capital city where the vast majority of aid workers were located:

> *If you were in the country, the people just loved you because they associated you with the Australian army that had gone through and that were truly liberators, that had actually gone through and saved them from being massacred in their villages. But in Dili, as an Australian you were associated with the whole UN barrage of fairly parasitic kind of organisations, all those structures and things.*

Even within the streets of the capital, Elly experienced different responses to her presence according to whether she was viewed as a teacher, or simply another Australian: *'I felt, although you could walk down the street and all the students would love you, but I think even when we were there, there was hostility towards Westerners and there was hostility towards Australians'*.

Indeed, being seen as Australian in Dili became increasingly problematic for British-born Helen, whose *'biggest problems were with other Australians, some of whom I felt behaved very badly towards the Timorese, worse than many Brits can be. By the end of my stay I had stopped identifying as Australian and was seeing myself as English again.'* While Helen took the opportunity to distance herself from complicity in the negative social and political aspects of Australia's development enterprise, Australian-born teachers could not. The challenge for Australian teachers was to somehow come to terms with the past and the present, to hold together the contradictions and ambivalence inherent in their national identity, rather than avoid the dilemma by a total repudiation of their heritage.

The teachers' community: 'We started out with good intentions'

Just as teachers struggled to locate themselves amid what they saw as the disjointed and ambivalent aid community, they also had difficulty in finding a place within their perceptions of a fragmented, unhinged and transient professional community. Helen described teachers suffering severe *'culture shock'*, while Elly expressed surprise at the *'extent to which pressures'* of the context could make *'people a bit loopy'*. Amongst teachers working in teams Helen recalled *'terrible fights, terrible conflicts'*, and Fay insisted she had *'never seen anything like it before, the effects of the environment on the teachers, having tantrums, there were a lot of strange people there'*.

In the professional domain, the social and the spatial experiences were in conflict, as teachers were, in Ann's words, *'thrown together, all in the same environment, with people who back home would probably not be friends'*. Helen saw her fellow teachers as an *'odd group of people who were expected to suddenly become a team'*, but *'just couldn't and wouldn't act together'*. The teaching teams comprised a disparate group of *'people without a shared professional base, so some of the people have got more of a backpacker mentality, other people are maybe finding a way to make a bit of money quickly or, like me, they're a bit sort of lefty in their views and into development politics, other people are religious'*. As a consequence, although the teachers *'started out with good intentions'*, very soon the *'personality clashes did become very, very harmful to the performance of the project'*.

Adding to these professional tensions was an even greater concern about the lack of free, private time and space, uncolonised by the weight of timetabled classes and professional duties. In some projects, excessively long teaching hours in harsh physical conditions left teachers emotionally exhausted, yet unable to find respite after hours. Dana found, *'the conditions that we were living and working in didn't enable us to have enough time or space to ensure that we got what we needed to look after ourselves, [...] to have time when you just got out and forgot about everything'*. Faced with an unresolvable *'situation of people living on top of each other'*, Elly also found lack of space became critical: *'people don't cope psychologically without certain things that they're used to. Bottom line things, and I think personal space is probably the key one'*. For many, including Kate, this spatial crowding became the most unbearable aspect of life in East Timor: *'My only challenges were with the living arrangements I think, and expectations, yeah, my concerns were not with "us" and "them" [Timorese], but it was amongst ourselves.'*

Between us and them

Spatial juxtaposition between 'us' and 'them' was also a challenge for teachers. Like volunteers discomforting experiences of being the 'other' in Indonesia, teachers often felt exposed and watched in social spaces, as their desire to connect conflicted with a discomforting self-consciousness. This tension was expressed in Helen's written account of social engagements with Timorese:

> *I love meeting people and chatting to them. I can use a combination of English and the odd Portuguese borrowed word in Tetum. But I find it a strain being on show all the time. Every single thing the Malai do is keenly observed.*

While teachers' sense of otherness was apparent in public spaces, a more acute and dislocating sense of exposure and alienation arose from the blurring of public and private space when teachers lived amongst the Timorese community. Dana, Elly and Fay had been initially housed in a makeshift container hotel at the centre of Dili (see Figure 4.6), but were relocated to a suburban house, within a Timorese neighbourhood and with Timorese domestic staff. This move had been arranged by project management in order to encourage a greater sense of engagement between teachers and the Timorese community; however, in this situation, proximity ironically intensified teachers' sense of alienation. Living and working amongst a community so different from her own, Fay felt

Figure 4.6 Teachers' accommodation – container hotel in Dili surrounded by barbed wire

herself to be on display: she was *'from another world'* and *'very, very cut off from the culture'*. The desire for a reprieve from the demands of negotiating cultural and linguistic differences at work was evident in teachers' longing for a private space outside the classroom, but because public spaces of work and private spaces of domestic life overlapped, there was no place for Fay to be herself, unobserved:

> *I felt alienated from the culture both inside and outside the classroom. Living in the community, we should have interacted more, but we were working so hard that the last thing we wanted to do at the end of the day was to make conversation in broken English. In Australia [. . .] I could go home at the end of the day to my own place. We didn't have that, we were living in their community.*

For Fay, alienation was related to her sense of being read as Western in both public and private:

> *There wasn't any privacy so they saw everything we did. We'd come home and drink and smoke and go off in couples and, you know, it was all there. [. . .] Morally we do actually operate differently, you know, we divorce, we have affairs, we drink, we smoke, all of those are quite common parts of Western culture.*

Making the self appropriate in a different context thus became a spatial dilemma. By being housed in a Timorese neighbourhood, and spatially separated from the centre of the development community, the teachers' otherness was obtrusive. Fay wondered how this sense of cultural and spatial otherness could be ameliorated:

> *What do you do as a Westerner going into a Third World country? We couldn't even keep the Western stuff- I don't know whether it should be hidden, but you couldn't keep it hidden like you can perhaps on a holiday, where you can actually just shut yourself in your room at night with a book and a boyfriend or whatever. There everything is on display [. . .] So what do you do? Do you shut people off so no one knows how we live? [. . .] But this whole thing about keeping this whole other side of yourself hidden- because you did feel like it was disapproved, it was disapproved of.*

The presence of Timorese domestic staff, employed to cook and clean in the small houses, intensified this sense of being inappropriate and under scrutiny. On the one hand, Jane justified the employment of Timorese staff as an effective means of *'creating employment, without it necessarily being a handout'*, and Fay recognised that domestic staff offered a possibility *'to interact with Timorese, to find out about their culture'*. However, the presence of Timorese staff was also a discomforting reminder for Fay of the colonial relations that structured the domestic space and mirrored the inequalities that inhered in development: *'Even the people in the houses who were working, our servants* [laughs]. *I cringe, I cringe, I cringe. [...] It's so easy to turn into a colonial, that's the horrible thing. Yeah, we were very much colonials there. That whole sort of set up worked to support it, we had our servants.'*

Domestic spatiality echoed with the hierarchies of an earlier colonial era in a way that was discomforting for a group of foreign women who had come to East Timor with an expectation of solidarity. Although the women may have disidentified with the colonial heritage of development, at the same time they felt caught in a spatial dilemma that structured their experience of and relationships with the Timorese community. Just as echoes of colonialism were evident in domestic spatiality, they were also apparent in gendered spatiality, as we shall see in the following exploration of gender relations in the contact zone in international development.

Gendered Space in East Timor

Amongst the foreign community in East Timor males greatly outnumbered females: muscular pursuits in the military, diplomatic, business and construction industries were male dominated. As noted previously, over 95% of the peacekeeping forces and international civilian police were male, and although 33% of the civilians in UNTAET were women, almost all the key positions were held by men (Charlesworth, 2008). Amongst aid agencies, women were represented in the traditional areas of health and education, yet administrators in those programmes also tended to be male, so while female teachers outnumbered males by four to one, each of the women teachers in this study had a male boss. Most of the women residing in Dili, the location of the greatest number of foreign workers, experienced the public social space to be intensely patriarchal, and assessed much of the behaviour of men as *'incredibly sexist'*. This behaviour was seen to be doubly inappropriate: the gendered performances were seen as historically dislocated, reflecting outdated norms that would be unacceptable at home, and geographically inappropriate in being transposed into another cultural space where different norms may need to be considered. In this way, the development community was seen to produce a space in which women were out of place, and the male gaze was perceived to have constituted the teachers as sexed bodies, positioning them as passive and in need of regulation.

This section focuses on the recollections of two women who, while not atypical in their observations, were particularly expressive in their anger about the perceived sexism of the social space defined by a privileged foreign community. Both enjoyed social interaction on their own terms but vigorously resisted the scrutiny of an objectifying gaze; they bristled at perceived gender hierarchies in an overarching patriarchal regime; and they lamented the gendering of particular places through practices that they experienced as hostile to women. For these women, many social spaces were perceived as reproducing and enabling an exaggerated masculinity: from their perspective, this too was a 'blokes' world'.

War games

Elly conservatively estimated the gender ratio within the community of foreign workers in Dili at the time as *'nine men to one woman'*, and observed that the degree of active military presence seemed to establish a *'patriarchal'* mood, even influencing NGO workers and journalists to don *'little military outfits: there was something very "war-games-y" '*, something *'very male, about the whole scene'*. The emergency scenario and war games, the expectation and evidence of violence and conflict, constructed a particular type of gendered space, attracting the sort of men who, in Elly's opinion, *'would just never get jobs with that sort of authority or money or sense of importance at home, and they can do it all in these situations'*. Neither foreign nor Timorese women were obviously visible in the public domain, and the gendered construction of public space was felt to contain a specific message to women: *'Watch out, it's males that operate here!'* As in an earlier colonial context, mainstream development in this case was male territory, and the position of white women was essentialised and yet inherently contradictory: Elly recognised that they were an *'anomaly'*, caught between a professional and sexual identity.

Elly's strongest complaints concerned being identified by men as a *'sex object'*, constituted through the effect of the male gaze, in a way that was reminiscent of Australia in a different era. As we saw in the opening chapter, from Elly's perspective:

> *As a woman it was probably one of the freakiest experiences of my life [. . .] Oh my god, yeah, look that was full on. The whole bar scene, the pick up in the bars, like those World War II movies. And men, those truckloads of soldiers looking like predators, looking at us like predators. They'd drive past and I'd just look at them and think, when I was by myself and I'd think, thank god I'm not in one of the villages that you're liberating! [. . .] I just looked them and I thought- the way they look at you!*

In social situations, Elly felt some of the men she met *'were able to acknowl-edge the value of the person they were speaking to'*, but her specific criticism concerned the reduction of interaction to a sexual exchange, and therefore the exclusion of other possible ways of interacting on the basis of profes-sional or social interest and respect. Social behaviour amongst the foreign community was described as *'predatory'* and *'people were out to score in a real kind of meat market'*:

> *Why was it so bad? Because there was no attempt for people to make friends, people didn't even bother to have a conversation about who I really was, and then thought "oh, this woman's interesting", [...] that's not what it was. They bloody looked at the room, looked at women as bloody sex objects, and they came over with the intention of inviting you somewhere, I guess on the basis of looks or something. No, I don't even think it was on the basis of looks, I think it was on the basis of being a new female that had arrived, that you happened to be female, that's what I think it was. And I hated it, I just think it was so gross. I got so tired of expat type people.*

Elly described her own experience of being observed, discussed and reduced to a sexed body in one of the bars frequented by foreign workers:

> *There were a couple of UN guys there, at that army bar, [...] a black UN guy, and I was chatting to him, and I left and he came out and said, 'oh well, I've got her in the bag!' And basically he had this running thing about how long it would take to get me into bed, and I just died.*

This *'incredibly sexist'* regime was felt to be far more primitive than in Australia, and Elly reasoned that by travelling overseas, normal social expectations were removed, allowing some men to enter a time warp and *'revert to that type of behaviour'*:

> *It was bizarre. I just felt I was kind of flipped back into some spy novel of the 1930s or 40s, I felt like I was in Biggles, 'cause there's no girls in Biggles, because it's like that old British foreign service stuff that has this overlay of politeness but has the seedy underworld, and it kind of felt like the old politeness has gone, it's just the seedy underworld in Timor.*

With the veneer of politeness stripped away, the *'incredibly archaic, double standard'* operated as a means of surveillance and control. Elly observed men *'having a wife at home and sleeping [their] way around the world as well'*, but believed such men judged the behaviour of women by a different standard:

> *I don't have any problems with casual sex for christ's sake, but the parame-*
> *ters, the way it was set up, it was set up as a boy's game, not as a mutual*
> *kind of- put it this way, if [a woman] went off for casual sex, you'd get a*
> *reputation as being a slacker, a slut, and it would go round and you'd pay*
> *the price. Would [a man] pay the price? No, he'd be the hero because he's*
> *the king bonker and he's out there wheeling and dealing, it's kind of like they*
> *were entrepreneurs. It was bizarre.*

An archaic double standard had produced a male territory, where females were constructed as either unnecessary, unruly, or at the service of a male desire that silences female desire through labelling and denigration (Ramazanoglu, 1993).

Helen's description of a gendered social space was remarkably similar to Elly's: being in a male domain, where at times she felt relatively power-less, provoked ambivalent reactions of enjoyment, disgust and fear. While her letters expressed pleasure in the company of a range of workers from various locations, particularly those from Europe and South America, she found the enforced company of some men to be tedious:

> *There are about six of us women at the [residential] hotel and we're sick of*
> *being patronised by men droning on at us as if we have never travelled in our*
> *lives, never asking us about ourselves [. . .] There are so many men here, some*
> *of whom have difficulty recognising boundaries or accepting that we might*
> *not be that desperate for their company.*

Such hotels, frequented by foreigners, were places for men to '*scoff at the trough, drink beer and watch violent, noisy videos night after night*'. These were hostile places for women, where they were subject to '*groping*' and harassment:

> *The biggest threat came from predatory Australian men. There were some*
> *real sexist creeps who just couldn't seem to understand that we had not come*
> *to Timor to get laid. It was quite fun as this hasn't happened to me in years.*
> *But one man in particular started to harass me and I got really freaked by*
> *this. I am no supermodel, believe me. I think it was a case of anything in a*
> *skirt!*

Helen's fear was partly a result of her sense of disorientation in a strange place: '*I had lost my sense of perspective, I mean, here I am this middle aged woman, I'm saying "wah-wah-wah, he scares me"*'. Her unease was intensi-fied when incidents of harassment would occur in places where members of the Timorese community were present. In these events, Helen's obser-vation highlighted the behaviour of foreign men as doubly inappropriate, both in terms of what would be acceptable in an Australian cultural space, and perhaps even more so in a Timorese cultural space:

> *You know, touching me in the wrong way, and bothering me, winding me up in front of Timorese or, you know, grabbing me in the wrong- you know, if anything like that happens in front of the Timorese it's ten times worse. He did it to me at a party and I just nearly died. Awful.*

In their accounts, both Elly and Helen articulated the feelings of many of the foreign women teachers in East Timor. They found pleasure in male company, with Fay even expressing initial delight that they'd arrived in an environment where *'It's raining men!'* But they soon saw foreign men in the development context taking on the unwelcome, extreme masculine behaviours identified in feminist analyses of the colonial era, and producing public spaces that were hostile to women. In these spaces, personal boundaries that protected the body from unwanted visual or tactile intrusions were breached and women felt themselves disempowered, reduced to the objectified space of the sexed body, kept under surveillance, monitored and controlled. Thus, despite the progressive rhetoric of social justice and gender equity espoused in development rhetoric, spaces constructed by the foreign aid community were characterised by social discord and temporal regression that marginalised women and reinforced their anomalous positioning.

Gendered interactions with translocal space in East Timor

Just as the gendering of aid enclaves served to secure control over women, it also further entrenched the divisions between foreigner and Timorese communities. Reports of Timorese political instability and rumours of impending violence consolidated the position of a militarised, masculinised foreign community, charged with exerting control. In the complex patterns of gendered behaviour in this space, we can see Stoler's point that 'sexual desire in colonial and postcolonial contexts has been a crucial transfer point of power, tangled with racial exclusions in complicated ways' (1995: 190). From the teachers' perspective, the potential dangers were construed as a threat to women's safety, and added to their sense of being monitored and controlled.

With troops and armoured vehicles patrolling the streets, helicopters swooping over the beaches, and the US and Indonesian warships appearing in the harbour, teachers were warned of the potential danger of attack by local militia, and advised on emergency and evacuation procedures. Helen recalled Ramos Horta's observation that *'if this country could export rumours, we'd be wealthy'*, and noted the response of donor organisations who were *'paranoid and put the fear of God into us'*: there with briefings on current threat levels (yellow, orange, red for evacuation); instructions about avoiding unsafe public areas; exhortations *'to keep our mobiles with us at all times'* (see Figure 4.7). Escalating reports of street and beach attacks on white women meant that *'the whole place was completely paranoid, absolutely paranoid'*. *'Oh my god! We weren't allowed to leave the hotel just about, we were told to stay away from any meeting, any gathering of people, you know, don't go out at night, don't go to the beach alone, be careful of people in the street.'*

PERSONAL SECURITY NOTES FOR STAFF.

Following are some points on personal security. They should be read in conjunction with the attached booklet "A Guide to Personal Safety Measures"

The security situation in Dili is stable but sensible security practices need to be followed at all times:

- Always be alert to events in your immediate vicinity. Stay away from crowds. If you are caught up in an incident move away as quickly and calmly as possible. If shots are fired take cover and remain there until the incident is resolved. Inform the Mission Security Officer (DHM or Consul) of your whereabouts and circumstances.

In an emergency call the CIVPOL headquarters on 04___ if that does not work ring 04___ which is the UNTAET security number. They will assist in passing an urgent message to CIVPOL. Program both numbers into your mobile.

- Take particular care when driving. Keep your doors and windows locked, particularly at night and, if possible, park the vehicle in a well-lit spot close to your venue. **Drive slowly** (UNTAET has set the speed limit in Dili as 45kms) particularly at night when pedestrians and bicycle riders can be difficult to see.
- Familiarise yourself with Dili's street plan and the principal restaurants/venues. Do not search for a venue in the dark but confirm your destination in daylight. Do not linger in the street at night but walk quickly to your vehicle with your keys in your hand. Do not wander around Dili at night.
- Do not carry or display significant sums of money or valuables and stay in the company of friends wherever possible.
- Officers travelling outside Dili are required to inform the Mission Security Officer of their destination and to take a satellite phone. Officers should inform the Security Officer if there is a delay in their expected time of return to Dili.
- Your mobile is your constant companion in Dili but do not discuss classified matters on the mobiles or landline. Mobiles can easily be intercepted. Do not discuss sensitive matters in front of LES. Go outside or to the secure area if a discussion is highly sensitive.
- Staff are required to report all security incidents to the Security Officer.
- Staff are required to familiarise themselves with emergency procedures and the Mission Contingency Plan (circulated separately). Procedures related to security practice in the Chancery are cirulated separately.

Figure 4.7 Security instructions for development workers in East Timor

Despite early feelings of alarm, over time teachers began to realise that many of the reputed dangers were inflated. Helen suspected both government and non-government agencies made '*the threat and the risk much worse than it actually is*', '*exaggerat[ing] the security issues to suit their own purposes, and in [the NGO's] case, to control our movements*'. '*Our every move was vetted and watched [by the NGO], and I think it was because maybe we were high priority, because we were with- from AusAID. They wanted nothing going wrong, you know, as far as AusAID was concerned.*' The warnings were indeed effective in restricting women's mobility, and secured a patronising, protective role for men, who were '*hectoring us about how to keep safe. They all do it.*' The result was spatial confinement, and Helen lamented: '*I feel a bit marooned in the expatriate enclave and I miss [my] freedom of movement*'. With white women implicitly 'mythologized as the desired objects of colonized men' (Stoler, 1995: 183), a discourse of fear was mobilised by masculinist claims to know what the dangers were and how to avoid them. Those claims for territorial control necessitated the redrawing of racial boundaries, and reaffirmed the need to monitor and confine women within secure physical space.

Spatial adaptations

These spatial controls were never quite complete, however, and while some women did feel threatened by Timorese men in their negotiation of public spaces, these fears were not experienced equally by all the women teachers. The effects of spatial control were moderated by other markers of identity, and resisted by the exercise of teachers' agency. Some older women, like Kate, suspected that '*the grey hair earns a lot of respect*', and expressed a greater sense of freedom or confidence in their use of public space. Similarly unfazed by the hassling that upset other women teachers, Carol explained that when eyed and approached by men during her walks on the beach, she had simply to announce that she was an '*English teacher*', and '*to say in Indonesian, quite firmly, to go away*'.

Of the women who *were* discomforted by the amount of attention they received from Timorese men in public spaces, several recounted incidents of being watched, followed or confronted, and were at times fearful for their safety. Encounters on the beach suggested that this was a particularly challenging site where gender representations came into play. Teachers who wanted to escape the claustrophobic space of a shared house, or the enclosed space of the classroom, often expressed a desire to walk along the beach at the end of a long day teaching inside in extreme heat; however, Elly described walking in this contested public space as '*horrific*', and Dana recalled being targeted as *'the centre of attention'* by the male gaze:

> *People looking at you because you're a woman, on the beach, [. . .] Yeah, just getting hassled. I remember there were incidents where people followed me and Elly, where I had somebody waiting on the beach for me if I went in for a swim. That kind of thing, it was a bit intimidating.*

Although Fay didn't believe that these encounters were *'going to go over into anything more than perhaps a bit of a grope'*, the awareness of being watched and confronted was discomforting, and brought about changes in the women's spatial behaviour and feelings about themselves. Heeding official warnings, most rarely went walking by themselves, and even when in pairs, changed their route for walking after work. Elly recalled:

> *There seemed to be a bit of a difference between which way you went, if you went right or left, from our houses. We went left [to the beach] once, and we got harassed, and then we went right after that [along the streets], and we hardly ever went left even though it's much nicer down the other way cause that's where the water was and everything, nice places for swimming and stuff, but so, we kind of just went the other way which is a lot more public.*

In this account, the public space of the streets was distinguished from the public space of the beach, indicating again the geographic contingency of the regulatory regime.

On the beach, an increased sensitivity to being identified as Western, and associated with an immoral code of behaviour, began to shift teachers' images of what was appropriate in this context. Fay was puzzled by

> *those episodes on the beach and the whole thing about Western women and sex and- oh dear! I didn't know where all that came from there, whether it was having some Westerners behave like Westerners, be publicly affectionate, have sex and that, in a traditional context being misinterpreted. But you end up feeling that you're blaming yourself for not being a good Catholic girl and all that, there's all sorts of things about behaving appropriately in someone else's culture, but how much you actually can change yourself- we're probably all inappropriate in the culture to some extent.*

Being outsiders, the women could only make assumptions about the way they were identified by Timorese men, and whether they were seen as more of a threat or an intrigue. Nevertheless, the women's contrasting reaction to the behaviour of Western men and Timorese men is of interest: whereas the attempted regulation by Western men was perceived by the women as doubly inappropriate, the women's reflexive, ambivalent response to Timorese men suggested a greater inclination to see Western women, including themselves, as being inappropriate in that space.

The incidents of harassment by Timorese men caused the women to change their behaviour in an effort to become less conspicuous in this space. The sense of finding an appropriate way to behave was of concern to most teachers, and apart from curtailing their mobility, also affected their bodily performance and attire, with an awareness that their clothing needed to be concealing despite the heat. Taking on these attempts to bridge the gap between different embodied discourses, to be spatially inconspicuous, and therefore acceptable, many teachers changed their mode of dress and, like Bree in Indonesia, some even swam in full clothing. For her part, working together with the students as cultural mediators, Fay submitted to a form of spatial veiling as a mode of embodied accommodation: *'The veneer is there, you know the students would actually say, "you must wear sleeves", they knew what was socially acceptable and what wasn't. I did wear the blue sack [a large, shapeless blue dress]. That was my concession to Timor.'* As with Bree's frumpy frock disguise in Indonesia, Fay's concession implied an acknowledgement that her dress served as a veneer, a mask, a means of passing unnoticed in the public domain.

Threat or intrigue

Teachers attributed the attention they received from Timorese men to a complex set of factors relating to cultural and gendered identities. For a start, racial and economic divisions were exacerbated as local levels of unemployment remained high despite the large international workforce being fully employed (re)constructing the country. Helen observed that the streets had become the public domain of a privileged, masculine, *'UN junket'*, while groups of *'bored and frustrated young men feeling like second class citizens'*, were robbed of their agency in the face of external intervention.

> *There were a lot of foreigners going running and stuff like that, with their wallets and what have you, early in the morning or at dusk, and making themselves vulnerable really, just not understanding that there would be that rather odd reaction to them. But there was also a lot of hostility on the street, the brutalised atmosphere and a lot of frustrated young people around. There's no money and that massive UN gravy train where people-the place was really, really full of foreigners living very affluent lifestyles, driving around and throwing money about, so I think at that point, those contradictions were really intense.*

Dana felt that the teachers were complicit in this contradictory activity, *'being over there and having money and having jobs and a lot of people not, you know, another occupier coming in, an unofficial one'*, and that female teachers were therefore a target of disenfranchised masculine Timorese hostility.

Teachers also saw themselves as positioned in relation to a complex game of sexuality, played out within these conditions of territorial invasion and displacement, economic disparity and hostility. Dana wondered whether the anger provoked by Western affluence and agency was perhaps more easily expressed as an exercise of power over Western women rather than Western men: *'if you're not feeling very powerful, then sexually harassing someone can make you feel pretty powerful, if that person is seen as pretty frightened and pretty vulnerable'*. But Western women may also be implicated in discourses of sex tourism, and implicated in the uses of economic power for the pursuit of sexual relations in Third World countries (Jeffrey, 2002; Ryan & Hall, 2001). Thus, Elly believed the approaches by Timorese men were influenced by expectations that *'wealthy, single women go to Indonesia [to] pick up a toy-boy'*, or by hopes that a wealthy Western woman might be able to give *'a golden handshake out of some situation'*. As Dana explained:

> Well if you're a Westerner you've got wealth, and if you're a woman then— and if you're a Western woman then that means you're promiscuous or, you know, possibly promiscuous. So, you're a bit of a target and a bit of an intrigue I guess, that's how it felt to me.

In these unresolved patterns of engagement, bringing together threat and desire, Fay sensed that white women were not only the target of *'hatred'*, but also of *'an underlying antagonism about Western sexuality'*.

Regardless of the harassment in the streets and on the beach, however, it never occurred in the grounds of the university, where the women appeared to be read not as sexed bodies, but in terms of a professional identity produced in a specific place. Elly demonstrated this spatial contrast succinctly: *'You couldn't lie on the beach, you did get completely harassed there. And certainly I got followed around in town a fair bit too. But not on campus: I was "the teacher" on campus.'* The particular space in which she appeared interacted with how she felt she was perceived and produced as a subject: the teaching space of the campus created a different meaning for the space of her body.

Relocating a Sense of Place and Self

Over time, the significant effects of dislocation, detachment and displacement experienced by foreign teachers in Indonesia and East Timor gave way to a variety of more productive spatial connections. In these accounts, we see more nuanced affective and corporeal engagements with the liveliness and multiplicity of place, with a sense of spatial history constituted through global flows and local meanings. These spatial engagements suggest a way of understanding the integration of place and self that destabilises the linear, ordered sense of time and spatial disconnection in development hierarchies, offering instead a way of 'being there' that moves beyond the limitations of visual mastery to a more embodied, phenomenological engagement with context.

For the volunteers in Indonesia, as Bree concluded, despite the challenges *'the really amazing things far outweighed'* the difficulties. With her increasing fluency in an Ambonese language, Bree had managed to develop threads of social connection, most importantly in the everyday domestic spatiality of the home with the *'woman who came to my house every day [to clean and cook], who lived in the village and who was very willing to share all the gossip with me, and she was my connection to real life'*. She also appreciated the incredible *'generosity of the [Indonesian] teachers who became my friends on certain levels'*.

An appreciation of spatial history also offered a means of connection, as Bree became entranced not only by *'the physical beauty of the place'*, but also by *'the place in terms of history'*. Diverse flows of French, British, Dutch colonial, scientific and missionary activities had left tokens and tracks in the landscape, and present still from beneath these, there were tangible traces of an older culture, *'a really strong belief in magic and spiritual power that was underneath everything else'*. In the social relations that criss-crossed this space, there were signs of more recent movements of transmigration, religious and political rivalry and exchange between the neighbouring islands, a movement of which she was now a part. Her connections with the context were represented in terms of her own experiences and social encounters interweaving with this geographical history, evoking a shift from dislocation to reinhabitation. From feeling isolated in a place flung out on the far margins, Bree had a chance to engage with somewhere that was its own centre: *'When you're actually in- on Ambon, it feels like the centre of the universe, it's quite a big bustley town, it's got a huge deep harbour. Lots of ships come in, and go out, and so, it's a very bustley sort of place, and it's got a fascinating history.'* In these recollections, Bree repositions herself within a living place, one constituted through juxtapositions, entanglements and configurations of multiple histories and multiple trajectories (Massey, 2005).

In East Timor, despite the limited time available on short-term contracts, teachers' initial experiences of discordant spatiality and apprehension also gave way to a variety of deeper, emotional and political connections. Circulating rumours of impending militia violence lost their edge, and teachers like Elly realised '*it actually wasn't that dangerous, you weren't going to get blown up or killed.*' What replaced the embodied feelings of panic, shock and dislocation were more complex relations to place, through spatial practices such as walking, listening, reflecting on local struggles inscribed in places traversed, and just being present in the moment.

Teachers' spatial explorations began to connect with the palimpsest of interventions already inscribed in the landscape. One site in which the palimpsest of transcultural engagement was most evident was the towering statue of 'Christ the King', set on a hilltop at the eastern end of Dili's broad bay (see Figure 4.8). Evoking Rio de Janeiro's 'Christ the Redeemer', it bears the implicit legacy of Portuguese colonial interventions, but because it was built by the Indonesians in an effort of appeasement, the statue was largely rejected by the Timorese (Chesterman, 2001). The influx of development agencies brought about another discursive framing of the place, as the site became a 'tourist' mark on the landscape visited by foreign aid workers. Many teachers followed the path up to the statue, adding further layerings to the spatial history of East Timor by their own presence, and marking them as particular types of participants, tourists or perhaps pilgrims, in that space. But beyond a participation in tourist discourses, Helen's visit to the site brought out harsher memories and meanings in the layers of connection between place, people, histories and cultures buried in the landscape:

> *Today on our walk up the hill to the Jesus statue we passed a pretty little beach. My companion told me it was 'Areia Branca' (White Sands) where the Indonesians massacred hundreds of women and children and their bones still lie there. Dili is at the end of a long peninsula and it is quite easy to see that there was nowhere for people to go. The Indonesians lined people along the wharf and shot them so that they would fall into the water. Then they sent the Timorese along to push the remaining bodies (in many cases their relatives) into the water.*

As Kingsbury (2002: 175) observes, travelling anywhere in East Timor brings one face to face with 'grim reminders of its bloody past'; but where there are no official plaques, statues or memorials, only the stories remain.

Listening to East Timorese people relating similar personal stories of their experiences during Indonesian occupation also deeply affected some of the teachers, whose earlier ambivalence and placelessness was partially erased by an evolving engagement with spatial history. Responding with admiration as much as sympathy, Helen recounted in her letters a story

Figure 4.8 View looking East from the ascent to 'Christ the Redeemer', with shadow of Christ on the beach

of one man's bravery in the face of militia brutality at the site of the hotel where she stayed:

> *I've just had a short chat with Senhor Jose, the hotel concierge, who gave me a quick account of his experiences with the Falintil. I will learn more later I hope. The hotel gardener, Senhor Marcos, came out when the Indonesians arrived in front of the hotel. He stood in front of them with all their weapons, Dili burning all around, and told them, 'You can take what you want but you cannot burn down the hotel'. They did not burn the hotel, [instead] they fired into a few rooms on the street front.*

Helen was subsequently warned by a *'cynical'* male aid worker, who had earlier been keen to impress with his own exploits and heroism that such Timorese accounts were *'mostly bullshit and everyone has a story to tell about the militia'*. Determined to listen and connect regardless, Helen insisted: *'I don't care what he [the expat] says. My students are now starting to tell me things and I don't think they're bullshitting.'* Listening to Timorese experiences opened a connection with difference not necessarily reducible to a hierarchical relationship and, for Helen, presented an understanding of her students that was more relevant than some external measurement of truth. For some teachers, then, an awareness of the struggles and challenges faced by Timorese in past and present conditions of colonial and neocolonial intervention produced more complex and affirming accounts of alterity, and served to further reinforce teachers' disidentification with the hierarchies and exclusions they perceived in the development community.

As opportunities arose for more personal and positive connections to the local context, some teachers sensed that these layerings of spatial history began to enfold into their sense of self, so that the spatial palimpsest became intertwined with an embodied, biographical palimpsest. Despite the difficulties of dislocation, this sense of presence and a desire to connect with something meaningful beyond small everyday concerns became part of a layered subjectivity through the mutual constitution of place and subject. *'With Timor'*, Fay explained, *'you think, it's the last of the colonial type struggles, to have just been there, at this juncture in history in this tiny country that had made such a stand [. . .] I feel like it's part of my life now'.*

Being there, in the moment

Alongside this affirming, enfolding sense of place and subjectivity was a sense, expressed by some teachers, of being left in in-between space, neither part of the local community, nor completely identified with the expatriate community. This sense of occupying a liminal space was articulated by Jane: *'With the East Timorese that I worked with, I was made to feel very welcome, but I'm not East Timorese, I didn't have the language, and I think the first step in any culture is to learn the language. And so yes, I didn't feel like an outsider, that it was lonely being an outsider, but I felt, I certainly wasn't an East Timorese.'* But far from being disabling, the uncertainty of this location also opened up new spatial and temporal possibilities.

In Jane's early days in East Timor, she and her colleagues had been warned about the perils of leaving the bounded enclaves of presumed safety, and entering the unknown territories of the Other. The beach and the markets were *'dangerous'* places where *'we were told not to go'*; the darkness of night was perilous and *'we were told as females'* to make sure *'we had somebody else with us, that it wasn't a good idea to go out at night alone, although we always were in twos'*. In response to these warnings, Jane had originally accepted that she should wait for a male driver to take her home at the end of each teaching day in a rural school: *'I used to just sit and wait for the car'*. This was the institutional four-wheel drive that signifies the Western aid worker as privileged foreigner: large, white and air-conditioned, they stand out from the Timorese landscape as the expat cocoon, just passing through. But by the end of her journey, something had shifted. Jane's way of being in the world, her sense of self had changed, as *'any fears that I had, had dropped away'*. After her teaching day at the village, instead of waiting as usual to be collected by the vehicle, she stepped out into a different sort of journey:

> *Towards the end of my time there, the time when I felt that I'd settled in, I started walking, and that was fine, I felt so comfortable, it was at sunset, everybody spoke to me: 'Where are you going?' uh, what was it- [I said], 'Bapasa Baucau'. And they looked at me like: 'You're walking to Baucau?! Is she off her head?!' They do it every day, but you know- and I had the pack full of books and stuff, and everybody was really friendly, and I felt very comfortable. I certainly didn't feel threatened at all.*

Conventional cartographic maps, had they survived in the violence and destruction that attended the emergence of a new nation, might have inscribed an official path through the landscape; but walking here became a different means of mapping, a 'spatial acting-out of the place' and 'a space of enunciation' (de Certeau, 1984: 98). Rather than being the passive object of distancing development discourses, and of masculine surveillance and control, confined to viewing the landscape from the imperial, impersonal safety of the four-wheel drive, Jane encountered a more practical, nocturnal, sensual knowledge of place, made up from fragments of conversation, and the rhythm of walking in the contact zone.

Fay: *Oh, being there changed me, [. . .] Yeah, I had never experienced that continual sense of being in the moment that I did towards the end. [. . .] I thought, my joy is being here, that is how I felt. [. . .] It was so sharp and so beautiful, but that experience I've only ever had like for seconds or for minutes or for a day, but I'd get up in the morning and it would be there, and you know, it would be there, the wonderment I think.*

Ros: So can you describe more about what it means, being in that moment?

Fay: *To be aware, to be conscious, to be content, to be happy, um, to be there. To not have conflict going on, um, as to- I suppose I had learnt to live in Timor time, and not have that conflict of rushing here, rushing there, and knowing things will get done. Yeah, so that slowing down to be in Timor time, and to be there. [. . .] I was very content, and everywhere I looked I thought, 'this is great, I am happy to be here'.*

If a regimented, commodified ordering of time, *'rushing here, rushing there'*, signalled a detachment from the phenomenal world, Jane's changing experience of time and space indicated a negotiation of spatial co-existence, and a closer sensate engagement with being-in-place in a way that influenced her classroom teaching, as we shall see in Chapter 5. Unlike the balcony view of the 'monarch-of-all-I-survey', her account suggests a sense of the permeable self being in, and part of, the social and physical encounters that constitute the environment: a shifting sense of time that stands in contrast to her normal experience of clock-time, a dissolution of self within the environment, and an enfolding of the environment into a new sense of self.

*   *   *

The experiential accounts of teachers in this chapter offer a spatial view of the development context as a fragmented discomfort zone that enabled the reproduction, and contestation, of colonial discourses and practices. Rather than a story of rational, orderly progress, or the realisation of humanitarian ideals, these accounts represent development as a complex pattern of sociospatial relations linked to the circulation of power in the contact zone. Spatial relations of power manifested in 'turf wars', in the marking of places and boundaries, and in practices of inclusion and exclusion that structured hierarchies within the development community and maintained cultural, economic and political inequalities between foreign and local communities. Seen from the perspective of teachers, these inequalities suggested a perpetuation of colonial superiority and power exercised through the construction and imposition of exclusive expatriate spaces that failed to connect with the local contexts. This is the picture of a development community at war with itself, a vision that corroborates Chopra's assessment of development as an enterprise in East Timor that 'skidded on the surface of the country' (2002: 998).

For most teachers in these development sites, negotiating conflicting social, cultural, economic, political and historical discourses and identifications produced a sense of extreme ambivalence that undermines a singular narrative of development as teleological progress, and troubles a vision of the development context as a stable, rational space. Ambivalence is demonstrated in the teachers' uncertainty about the authority of the development enterprise, and about their own complicity in the development process. On the one hand, teachers were often drawn to an identification with the humanitarian ideals of development, and yet they were repelled by cultural and spatial practices of 'being us' in development contexts; they disidentified with the display of economic excesses, but experienced the black mark of complicity in inequitable economic relations; were marooned in privileged enclaves, and felt positioned by various others as wealthy white Westerners. Although they started out with ideals of professional commitment, their intentions were tested by the erosion of spatial and temporal boundaries between work and personal life; they desired space and time of their own, and yet often felt personally and professionally isolated. Their original desires for solidarity and engagement with host communities and cultures were also challenged by feelings of dislocation and disconnection: in these contexts, they were the Other, occupying a liminal space, neither fully belonging to the community of wealthy foreigners nor integrated into Indonesian or East Timorese communities. Moreover, teachers' growing awareness of multiple, contradictory historical narratives of allegiance and betrayal worked to undermine the superiority-of-being-us, and the 'simple teleology of the one and only story' (Massey, 1999: 281), leaving teachers with a sense of doubt about Australians' presence in the region, and uncertainty about their own presence in the development context. These conflicts and dilemmas signalled the general ambivalence in which most teachers operated, and highlighted a complex network of sociospatial relations through which racial, economic, political and professional power circulated.

From this complex position of ambivalence, ambiguity and uncertainty, in some small ways, different spatial relations were able to emerge that affirmed diverse histories, perspectives and knowledges. As Kirby (1996b) observes, although ambivalence can be discomforting, it can also be productive: from the chaos of instability, comes the opportunity for new relationships between self, other and environment that do not necessarily rely on colonial and development hierarchies. In some circumstances, teachers' narrations constructed alternative ways of being-in-the-world that made an attempt to accommodate multiplicity and difference. These ways of being comprised spatial practices that tentatively wove together multiple stories and co-existing spatial histories, without reducing these to a singular narrative thread set against a static ground. They included productive, prolific shifts in time, understandings of place and self as palimpsests, modifications of the textual space of the body. Moving from the detached, balcony view of the master subject, these practices and experiences offered an engagement with place that 'abdicate[s] the *a priori* relation of dominance and distance between describer and described' (Pratt, 1992: 222). For these teachers, a sense of 'being there' and making connections with difference was part of a spatial experience of context that moved beyond the limitations and fixed boundaries they perceived in the social and spatial exclusions and detachments of the development industry.

Despite these tentative spatial connections, a sense of unresolved disquiet remained in relation to the gendered spatiality of the contact zone. The temporal narrative of development has, in recent decades, been expanded to incorporate progress towards supposedly universal goals of social justice and gender equality; nevertheless, the teachers' accounts suggest that gender remains a troublesome dimension of subjectivity in the development context, where complex geometries of power perpetuate patriarchal and sexist regimes, and where women's roles continue to be defined in relation to masculine desire. Just as public space has historically been constructed in the West as a masculine sphere so, too, can development contexts be read as public spaces that reproduce normative gender hierarchies, privileging First World masculine agency and control over a feminised world space and female bodies, and over disenfranchised/feminised non-Western male bodies. From the perspective of women teachers, this is a blokes' world, a domain for masculine intervention and agency, where men were positioned at the head of public institutions charged with the regulation and control of the development context as a public space. Development projects, international organisations, diplomatic missions and the military all served to sustain patriarchal regimes akin to those of the imperial explorers, mapping and surveying the landscape, producing plans and defending the territory against external threats. In this space, sexual and racial desire became sites for the transfer of power: women experienced the marginalising effects of being cast as an anomaly, found their mobility curtailed, and felt themselves subject, through the male gaze, to surveillance, monitoring and control. Returning the gaze, women saw the patriarchal and sexist regimes of Western men as doubly inappropriate, on the one hand exemplifying the archaic double standards of a different era, and on the other hand transgressing perceived gender boundaries of the local context. Emerging as they do from the teachers' narratives, these gendered, geopolitical relations demonstrate the weight of political meaning attached to personal and interpersonal space, and once again highlight the complexity of development that defies reduction to a singular temporal narrative.

Gender as a dimension of teachers' subjectivity was entwined with various axes of embodied difference that pertained in the contact zone, particularly those implicated in the colonial legacies attached to whiteness and English language. In certain circumstances, whiteness and native-English–speaking status appeared to override gender readings of the body, placing the teacher in a position of somewhat isolated superiority in relation to the host community. In other locations, the intersection of whiteness and the female body in the public domain appeared to be read in a negative way, giving rise to harassment, derision or resentment. In these public spaces, the gendered meanings attributed to the body became exaggerated and burdensome, so that the white female body had to be disguised if one was to enter public space. A physical disguise of the body was enacted by veiling in modest, missionary clothes to obscure femaleness, while a discursive disguise was enacted by invoking more powerful professional identities and connections; that is, the power vested in the native-speaking English language teacher. These disguises suggest attempts to androgynise or discipline the space of the unacceptable female body in order to enable women to appear, under the gaze of both local and foreign eyes, as appropriate participants in the public domain.

The discussion of teachers' accounts in this chapter has sought to assert a critical spatial thinking into dominant temporal understandings of development discourses and development as a context for English language teaching. My focus on ambivalent spatiality, territorial boundaries, hierarchies and juxtapositions aims to undermine development's story of itself as a model of rational progress, a story that legitimates a deterministic asymmetry between 'us' and 'them'. As we have seen, the anomalous situation of these Western women, as both insiders and outsiders to neocolonial discourses of authority and power, was in some situations strategically employed to resist being positioned solely through embodied signs of gender and ethnicity. By identifying themselves in their professional capacity as teachers, they were at times able to defend themselves from sexist harassment. In this way, the performance of the teaching body can be seen to modulate the performance and perception of gender.

The relations between gendered performance, pedagogy and institutional space, and the ways in which teachers address gender as an aspect of their pedagogical practice is the subject of Chapter 6. Before we return to gender in that chapter, I will explore in Chapter 5 the sociospatial organisation of the classroom as the domain of teachers' professional activities in English language teaching.

Chapter 5
It's a Bubble: English Language Teaching Practices in Development

> *How can we inhabit the present as if it were a place, a home rather than something we pass in a mad scramble to realise the future?*
> May and Thrift, 2001: 37

In the previous chapter I discussed teachers' experiences of the development context as a contact zone structured through social and spatial relations. In this chapter, I focus on teachers' experiences and practices inside the classroom, and consider the dimensions of, and constraints on, a contextualised practice of English language teaching in development. The teachers' narratives point to the ways in which spatial and political hierarchies evident in the development context can be reproduced or resisted in classroom practices.

As we have seen, many teachers going to work in development contexts had a desire to '*do something meaningful*', and were disturbed by the social, economic and political hierarchies and dislocations they observed between the foreign and local communities. Yet the narratives at the heart of this chapter suggest that, despite teachers' desires to overcome those barriers, to make connections with students and local contexts, the spatial and temporal construction of classrooms hindered their capacities to do so. Institutional, pedagogical and development discourses, together with the orthodoxies of ELT, on the whole served to maintain social and spatial boundaries that separate teachers from students, and divide the classroom from the world beyond the classroom wall.

To introduce the themes of the chapter, I begin with *Fay's story*, in which she describes the dilemmas faced in performing the conventional scripts of English language teaching. In the second section I discuss how classrooms and contexts might be understood in terms of their temporal and spatial organisations, and point to problematic effects in the scripting of language teaching practice. The third section presents a brief description of the specific educational contexts referred to by the teachers, then considers how the imagined power of English and tenets of ELT, particularly the reliance on Western method and texts, scripted teachers' performance, organised the spatiality of the classroom and regulated the flow across classroom walls.

The chapter then focuses on three patterns of teaching evident in teachers' narratives. In one group, teaching practices maintain boundaries by filling the 'empty space' of the classroom with familiar texts from elsewhere, and by refusing interference from the local context. In another group, teachers experience disorientation and disillusionment as their routines of practice fall apart, and the stability of classroom space is disrupted by the flow of influences from the world outside. In the final group, teachers mobilise a range of spatial and temporal practices to make connections between themselves and their students, and between the worlds outside and inside the classroom. The chapter concludes with a discussion of teaching and spatiality in development. The analysis suggests that despite the widely acknowledged necessity of relating language teaching to the context of language use, the principles and practices of ELT in development can work against the incorporation of local spatial and temporal contexts into language teaching.

Fay's Story

After the popular consultation which set East Timor on the path to independence, Fay had joined a development project bound for Timor with a desire to participate in *'the last of the colonial type struggles'*. This was an opportunity to redirect her professional life as an English language teacher, to *'teach in a situation that meant something more politically'*, a chance to escape from a soulless job in the *'8 week factory turn around'* of commercial English language schools in Sydney. But where Fay had expected to find a *'highly politicised group of activists'*, supporting the Timorese in the struggle to build a new nation, she instead found in the development enterprise a *'loony fringe'*, *'a group of misfits who weren't really interested in the local situation'*. With growing disillusionment, she also found herself on the wrong side of the colonial divide, an expatriate alienated from the Timorese community, the recipient of exclusive privileges in a household supplied with Timorese staff.

If the development enterprise at large was a disappointment, could Fay's hope for political engagement be realised in her own professional activities, in classroom practice? What might an effective pedagogical practice look like?

Outside the classroom, Fay was troubled by the divide that separated her from the Timorese community, but inside the classroom she recognised an opportunity to engage with students who were so keen to 'tell their own stories' of struggle and loss and hopes for a different future: '*I had the complete beginners and even within that I was really surprised about how much they wanted to say*'. And yet, with the methods and scripts that shaped the social space of the classroom, she felt there just '*wasn't sort of a mechanism there for them to do that*'. Her own ability to communicate was restrained by her professional training:

> *we just took the [TESOL] style teaching with us- that's what we know how to do. It's very difficult to think how to do things differently because that's the way we're trained to teach. It shapes my thinking so much. It's called teaching communicatively, but it's really just giving a phrase to practise on a slip of paper and getting them to use it in pairs, or getting them to learn a particular genre.*

To her dismay, Fay experienced the same confusion and frustration as Elly, caught up in a teaching system that crashed and burned in the contact zone of development. As a highly qualified and experienced English language teacher, she felt there was little she could offer her students as a way of connecting with their lived experience: '*I sort of cringe, "Hello everybody, and we're going to do this little structure today, and we'll sit in a happy little group". Because it's a bubble, mm, and because it's obviously going to go nowhere too.*' Her well-practiced scripts and performances seemed to float, detached, self-contained and directionless, while she experienced a growing sense of unreality: '*something gets lost, like communicative teaching gets very lost, even if you have a merry little group as if they are communicating, but they're not really*'. Fay's story of discrete disciplinary knowledge, and her sense of detachment from a more complex spatial engagement with heterogeneity, is a useful starting point for an exploration of the challenges associated with English language teaching in the context of international development. I turn now to a discussion of the regimes of time and space that underpin Fay's experiences and disappointments inside the development classroom.

Constructions of Time and Space in Classroom and Context

I have suggested earlier that although ELT theories emphasise the necessity of contextualising language teaching, understandings of what this means, and how it is to be achieved, vary greatly. I now want to outline the way that context might be understood in terms of the temporal and spatial construction of the classroom, and consider the effect this might have on the performance of language teaching. I begin by placing ELT within a global context of development, and outline the way ELT affirms the temporal narratives and spatial hierarchies established within that context.

Transition narratives and the discourse of progress in development education

A crucial problem for development classroom interactions arises in the inherent separation between foreign teachers and their students in host communities: between foreign teachers positioned as representatives of more advanced, developed nations and bearers of advanced knowledge or skilled techniques, and students as representatives of developing nations, and recipients of foreign guidance and expertise. This pedagogical relationship reflects the broader discourses of development where, on a global scale, geographic or spatial distance and difference has been translated into a chronological or temporal sequence: developing nations are merely at an earlier stage in a historical queue, positioned as perpetually 'catching up' to developed nations who represent 'a single standard of economic and political success to which all nations must aspire' (Spurr, 1993: 62). In Mignolo's words, this is the 'relocation of languages, peoples, and knowledges in time rather than space' (2000: 283).

Through this temporal paradigm, development discourses suggest a chronological hierarchy, a classification of nations and peoples based on one's place in an order of progress from tradition to modernity. Such discourses tend to represent the space of 'underdevelopment' in ways that suggest a deficiency to be remedied by the introduction of 'advanced' First World knowledge made available through foreign aid. As a result, developing nations are not imagined as 'having their own trajectories, their own particular histories, and the potential for their own, perhaps different, futures' (Massey, 2005: 5). And for the development expert, the temporal narrative of progress is affirmed through demonstrations of technological and economic superiority that simultaneously justify 'the authority of those in control of the discourse' (Spurr, 1993: 110).

Educational programmes fit well into this overall scheme of developmental progress, and are also internally structured according to a similarly linear narrative that shapes the classroom as a place dominated by teleological considerations. This has implications for both national development, figured within a global hierarchy of knowledge and progress, and individual development evolving along a cognitive and knowledge continuum. In the global hierarchy, despite a rhetoric that values alternative knowledges, education for development tends to be associated with the transfer to periphery institutions of knowledge generated in the First World. In this process, acquisition of English language as a technical skill supposedly confers benefits for societies and individuals in terms of socioeconomic advancement, technological progress and access to a world economic community (Pennycook, 2000; Toh, 2003). The tenets and methods of ELT associated with native speaker expertise, the communicative approach, learner-centredness and group work have, in turn, become 'synonymous with progress, modernization, and access to wealth' (Kramsch & Sullivan, 1996: 200).

On the everyday level, the modern classroom is organised, according to Foucault (1977), around the control of time and space, bodies and disciplinary knowledge, to achieve progress through the production of both learners and teachers as compliant participants. In the institutional organisation of education, the teacher is positioned as a model of disciplinary knowledge, and granted institutional authority to control the transparent space of the classroom, ushering learners through the predictable stages of achievement; learners are classified, graded, separated and examined in accordance with their attainment of certain stages in a normative continuum. Thus the conventional temporal narrative of Second Language Acquisition prescribes movement through theoretical stages (e.g. based on the acquisition of morphemes, or the demonstration of prescribed competencies) that define learner progress towards a specified, standard target, and position the language teacher in development as the 'agent of change'. In this process, the appraisal and management of both students and teachers according to the achievement of predetermined outcomes or competencies ensures the coordination of the various composite parts into a general machinery of institutional training (McHoul & Grace, 1993).

In the development classroom, bureaucratic and commercial pressures to achieve measurable progress, or 'project outputs', in a limited time tend to channel educational practice along predetermined lines, rather than allowing for the messy and unpredictable processes that accompany a more participatory construction of the classroom. And so, as recognised by Hall (1997) over a decade ago, although teachers may be aware of problems with the grading of learners and measurement of language proficiency as a technical skill, there seems to be a continuing expectation amongst donor institutions and administrative bodies that 'learning a language is a rapid and painless affair' and that 'language gain is accurately definable in terms of hours of tuition or marks on a test' (p. 266).

Connections between classroom space and context

The enclosure of the modernist classroom within firm boundaries can be seen as an attempt 'to stabilize the meaning of particular envelopes of space-time' (Massey, 1994: 5). Within this space, disciplinary knowledge is disseminated, but the content of that knowledge, with its geographic and ideological roots in the West, may not necessarily be informed by, or engage with, the cultural, social, economic or political location of the classroom. Indeed, it has been argued that it is the very abstraction, standardisation and detachment from a specific context of origin that has enabled the global spread of Western disciplinary knowledge, and its application in many different contexts (Eriksen, 2007; Giddens, 1990). One of the key debates about the nature of globalisation in education is therefore concerned with the extent to which detached, universal knowledges may be imposed, resisted or appropriated in local contexts (see, for example, Block, 2004; Block & Cameron, 2002; Canagarajah, 1999; Pennycook, 1994, 2007; Phillipson, 1992; Singh & Doherty, 2004; Toh, 2003). As I have indicated in earlier chapters, this problem of imposition and/or resistance is a central concern in the teaching of language and the transposition – or spatialisation – of ELT disciplinary knowledge into diverse locations and development contexts.

In an age of electronically mediated education we might ask to what extent classrooms can be described as enclosed, disciplinary spaces. In recent times, understandings of space in postmodernity have focused on globalisation, fragmentation, movement, and flows brought about by information technologies and space-time compression: flows, networks and speed are said to have replaced disciplinary societies organised around a sequence of enclosed spaces. In these analyses, spaces, places and localities tend to be problematically aligned with stasis, conservatism and resistance, often to the point where, once again, space is annihilated by the rush of time. For those of us working in classrooms, however, it would seem that the bounded places of the disciplinary society have not disappeared, but have instead come to be understood in different ways that account for the influences that have always crossed the boundary of the classroom wall. A crucial task of classroom boundaries is to regulate entry by determining what encounters with the outside are permissible. From this perspective, the social space of the classroom is constructed through the discipline of enclosed space *and* from the flow of interactions between the classroom and the globalised world beyond the classroom walls.

Analyses influenced by postcolonialism emphasise that *all* places are constructed over time from multiple social relations that transverse a particular location. Thus, for centuries, the flows of modernity and colonialism have ensured that locales were penetrated and shaped by distant social influences (Giddens, 1990; Massey, 1994, 2005). In addition, places are inflected not only by relations of global economic power, but also by relations of difference in terms of ethnicity, religion, gender, age and so on. These multiple global and local forces are materialised in complex spatial arrangements that help to construct the classroom as *open* to, yet at the same time relatively *autonomous* from, wider influences of social and political context (Canagarajah, 1993).

A spatial digression: What is language 'in context'?

Although it is generally accepted that English language needs to be taught 'in context', understandings of what context is, and how it is to be incorporated into English language teaching, vary widely. Context has featured prominently in theories of language as a social practice, as opposed to an autonomous technical skill, and is central to debates concerning the impacts of globalisation on local contexts. But for the English teacher, attending to language in context can mean almost anything, from applying language use to practical, everyday situations, to considering 'how the classroom, text, or conversation is related to broader social cultural and political relations' (Pennycook, 2001: 5).

In reasserting the importance of context, it is useful to highlight some difficulties in the diffusion of this term, and to highlight the ways in which a spatial analysis could extend understandings of context in English language teaching and applied linguistics. First, tracing back through what might be considered 'parent disciplines', we can see that context has been treated in both anthropology and linguistics 'as self-evident, as a given' (Dilley, 1999: 2), yet, as Goodwin and Duranti (1992: 13) observe, 'simply getting one's hands on the shape of context' remains a 'major analytic problem'. In both anthropology (Malinowski, 1923, 1935) and linguistics (Firth, 1957, 1968), context has been invoked in order to emphasise unique, local particularities and meanings that stand in opposition to universalist principles of broad application and generality. In sociolinguistics (Hymes, 1972), functional linguistics (Halliday, 1978, 1994) and critical linguistics (Fairclough, 1989, 1995), the term context carries a range of meanings: context may refer, for example, to a specific social or ethnic culture in a specific geographic location; to a particular event, social situation or set of practices within a culture; to specific genres, texts or sentences within which an item of grammar is embedded; or to specific ideological regimes. In applied linguistics, then, 'context is *potentially* everything and contextualisation is *potentially* infinite' (Blommaert, 2005: 40).

Second, in English language teaching, language as a discrete entity tends to be the primary object of study: language stands in a figure-ground relationship with context, which has remained the subordinate term, reduced to a neutral background. The resultant 'bucket' theory of context (Gardner, 2006) assumes a given background as 'reality', fails to fully realise the ways in which text and context are mutually constructed, neglects the interaction of contesting constructions of context when viewed from different positions,[1] and seldom takes context beyond singular cultures or geographic locations to engage with the place of textual activities within a wider flow of relationships and powers amongst different societies in a globalised world.

As a result, the widely espoused principle of teaching language 'in context' has been articulated in diverse and ambiguous ways. Practices of language teaching may be informed by relatively restricted, well-ordered and stable notions of context; that is, where context is limited to a stretch of language, an academic genre or a predictable social transaction (see, for example, Frodesen & Holten, 2005). Or context may be something outside of language, yet here again reduced to a neutral container, a setting or backdrop for single, local, communicative events, and providing simply a referential contribution to text-meaning (Blommaert, 2005); or it may be imagined as a set of norms and conventions against which individual agents supposedly exercise free will and choice in their language use (A. Luke, 1996). Such pedagogical approaches seem reluctant to engage with the boundlessness of social, political and historical conditions of context for fear that they 'may detract from the main task of describing [and teaching] text and talk' (van Dijk, 2006: 160). The result may be an instrumental focus for language learning that offers minimal engagement with, or challenge to, the political dimensions of teachers' and students' experiences in and perspectives on the world.

On the other hand, theories and practices of language teaching may be informed by a broader notion of context and language as mutually constituted in bodies of knowledge, or discourses. Here, discourse, and its realisation in spatial and temporal patterns of organisation (with, in turn, particular implications for the body, the institution and the nation), is used not to describe a stretch of language, but in Foucault's sense of a network of power and knowledge that regulates how we think, feel and act within a certain domain. These bodies of knowledge, rather than reifying and representing context as an objective reality 'out there', instead comprise a network of relations that constitutes the world as reality (Dilley, 1999: 33).

Given the co-existence of contested constructions of context (or 'reality') then, the question of whose construction prevails, how this is achieved and with what consequences, is significant.

Relating these concerns to a globalised world, Blommaert (2005: 67) recommends broadening our understanding of context to a 'higher-level situatedness', moving beyond the single-text level, to patterns of hegemonic, often invisible relations of power between different societies and within language itself. Such an understanding of context as a complex patterning of discourses points to an engagement with conflict, power and difference that can 'remake pedagogy as part of a broader political and social agenda for redistributing knowledge and reshaping power relations' (A. Luke, 1996: 313). It is these critical orientations towards context – bringing together the struggle over difference, and discourses of power/knowledge realised through regimes of time and space – that I use as a starting point in exploring the practices of English language teaching within international development. Taking regimes of time and space as hermeneutic tools can, I suggest, contribute to a critical, discursive understanding of the relationship between ELT and context.

Problems for teaching 'in context'

As suggested above, a primary challenge for teaching language 'in context' lies in the difficulty of defining what context is, developing an ongoing awareness of context as a contested construct, and inviting alternative interpretations into classroom practice. Within ELT there are further specific problems for teachers working to connect ELT to the notions of global and local spaces and places. First, it seems that ELT continues to mask its own situatedness, and so teachers in off-shore locations may or may not perceive their own constructions of classroom space as originating from specific geographic/cultural locations (see, for example, Duff & Uchida, 1997). Second, the notion of English language as a neutral, beneficial, technical skill also precludes scrutiny of the knowledge constructs and hierarchies, ideological and geopolitical effects within specific contexts (Auerbach, 1995; Pennycook, 1994; Toh, 2003). Third, foreign English language teachers' attempts to incorporate a spatial context from beyond the classroom may be limited not only by a lack of understanding of their students' lived context, but also by professional training that focuses on 'advanced' technical skills (Phillipson, 1992). In addition, the time pressures applied to teachers' work, and the orientation towards predetermined, standardised outcomes in language proficiency, also encourage an internal focus and reliance on Western methods and materials with a consequent neglect of the messier, contextualised processes in which that pedagogy takes place (Bax, 2003). Finally, teachers face the dilemma of whether teaching language appropriate to a given English language context would simply perpetuate structures of racism, sexism and elitism that inhabit particular English language speaking communities (Norton Peirce, 1989). The challenges outlined here are confirmed in the teachers' accounts discussed in this chapter.

Rather than negotiating complex notions of context, a default reliance on methods, materials and institutional expectations of 'standards' can be seen as a way of organising the internal space of the ELT classroom. Textbooks, routinised lessons, role plays and simulations are what Nespor (1994: 53) calls 'mobilizations of the world' that bring simplified representations of other (often Western) spaces and times into the classroom, and enable disciplinary reproduction despite geographical separation. The organisation of topics and levels in textbooks, the graded descriptors defined in international language tests, or the sequencing of competencies in a genre-based syllabus all represent an abstraction, stabilisation and ordering of time and space in textual form that, in turn, aims to regulate the time and space of the classroom. These representations of absent space-times are augmented by teaching methods as techniques for 'mobilization in the flesh' that aim to shape, stabilise and standardise the performance of teachers and students in the space of the classroom (Nespor, 1994: 14), thereby producing a 'spatialization of being' (N. Rose, 1996). Although materials, methods and curricula may be mediated and appropriated in a complex process of conscious and unconscious adjustment (Canagarajah, 1999; Kumaravadivelu, 2001; Sunderland *et al.*, 2000), they nevertheless restrict the ways in which teachers and classrooms engage with the spatial politics of other, unfamiliar spaces.

A further problem that emerges in making connections with students and the world outside the classroom relates to expectations of professional distance, and the role of the teacher as knowing subject. On the one hand, English language teachers in development are positioned as knowledgeable experts, and are expected to maintain professional standards, approaching their task and their students with an objective detachment. The native speaker status and modern methods that form the basis of the foreign teachers' expertise help to position the teacher as the rational, knowing subject in control of the space of the classroom. On the other hand, the expectation that teachers adapt their language teaching to the context of their students' lives assumes the need to develop an understanding of the students' world, and implies the building of a more democratic relation between teacher and student. The processes of

balancing detachment/authority and engagement/nurturing, and negotiating connections between the space inside and outside the classroom,
are central to teaching practice and emerged as challenges for teachers in
development contexts.

Classroom Contexts in Indonesia and East Timor

In this section I outline the educational contexts referred to by the
teachers in their discussions of classroom practice (see also Appendix A).
In Indonesia, Ann was appointed as an English language teacher at a
teacher training college, and Bree was engaged in an in-service programme to *'upgrade'* local, language teachers' skills in the use of communicative methodology. Both were working as volunteers on 2-year
appointments. In East Timor, Elly, Dana, Fay, Carol, Helen and I were
appointed on short-term contracts of 2 to 3 months, and were involved
in NGO English language teaching projects provided for students at a
disused tertiary campus in Dili prior to the reopening of the national university. Kate, Jane and Ann were also appointed on short-term contracts in
East Timor to provide language teaching and instruction in ELT methodology at a teacher training college and at various high schools in regional
and rural districts.

In both Indonesia and East Timor, English has been taught as a foreign language. Since Indonesia's independence from the Dutch in 1945,
Bahasa Indonesia has been the common national language, standing
alongside several hundred local languages, with English the first foreign language for international communication, studied by some 10% of
senior high-school students (Dardjowidjojo, 2000). Since independence,
changes in the national curricula policy for English language teaching
prescribe a shift from grammar-translation to communicative approaches,
a shift that reflects broader political changes and discourses of progress.
Under Suharto's New Order regime, which favoured rapid development
and modernisation, a compulsory communicative curriculum was prescribed for English language teaching in 1984, and modified in 1994 to
a 'communicatively oriented' curriculum, emphasising 'meaningfulness'
in language use (Dardjowidjojo, 2000: 25–6). While the communicative
approach and related learner-centred ideals are discursively aligned with
educational ideals of development and progress, contextual contingencies
and deficiencies within Indonesia are presented as retarding their adoption. Hence, Dardjowidjojo (2000: 28) claims that large class sizes, teachers'
low language proficiency, teacher-centredness and application of 'the
old [grammar translation] concepts' have contributed to the 'failure' of

English language teaching in Indonesia. Similarly, Jazadi (2000: 32) claims 'limited resources', a prescriptive national examination system and a 'top-down' curriculum with lack of local relevance, have inhibited progress towards the ideals of a 'learner-centred communicative approach' (p. 37).

In its early years of nationhood, East Timor also experienced immense political, cultural and linguistic changes and was significantly influenced by the discourses of modernisation and development. Amongst these changes, the status of English has been particularly contentious. In the specific domain of education, the sudden withdrawal of Indonesian teachers from East Timor following the 1999 referendum meant the education system had to be rebuilt from scratch, thereby opening a space for the entry of foreign English language teachers (Hajek, 2000). In the transition to independence, the development of a language policy was hotly debated, with Portuguese and Tetum eventually nominated in 2002 as the official languages, and Indonesian and English designated as working languages. However, Bahasa Indonesia had been the language of instruction for a younger generation educated under the Indonesian regime, and English had gained prominence as a result of the UN administration and the influx of foreign aid agencies. For all students in East Timor, English represented only one part of a multilingual complex since most spoke one or more Timorese languages as well as Indonesian, and some of the older adult students also spoke Portuguese. In the schools, Timorese teachers negotiated a range of local oral languages and in the early years continued to use the Indonesian curriculum until the new East Timorese course of study could be determined (Earnest, 2003; UNDP, 2002).

Following the upheaval of 1999, the influx of international agencies in East Timor meant that English appeared as the language of power and economic advancement. Despite the official move towards Portuguese as a national language, Timorese tertiary students requested the United Nations to provide English language training courses. For these students, English could be seen as a language of resistance to the power wielded by an older generation of nationalists educated under the Portuguese colonial regime.

The Spatialising Power of English Language

Instrumental expectations attached to English as a key to securing social and economic advancement rely on powerful mythologies of progress that frame English as a 'mythical hero' of development (Pennycook, 2007: 100). The presence of English language speakers, as international development consultants, experts and change-agents, positions English as the means of connection with more privileged places in a more powerful world: so closely associated with the developed world, English is the language of opportunity and privilege. Teachers' views of English often confirmed this discursive positioning. Thus, from Ann's perspective, students in Indonesia desired English because it represented *'the way out of here, a way to a better life'*, *'principally through better jobs, and jobs that might lead to contact with foreigners. If they spoke English they got better pay, maybe get a job with a foreign company, like with the gold mining company.'* Similarly, from Carol's perspective, students in East Timor *'saw for themselves that all the UN from all those countries, everybody spoke English'*, so *'to have them only speaking Portuguese, and Tetum, makes them remote in the area that they live in'*. Put simply, for Fay's students English represented a desire for *'connection with the wider world'*.

In my own classes, students wrote in their journals of their desires in a way that reflected common expectations and aspirations attached to English. The connections to a wider world that English offered were sometimes relatively specific: *'I wanted learning English language because communication language for education, industri language, for businisman, and internasional language'* (Silvina), and also specifically related to the way that an independent Timor would connect with the wider world: *'After Timor Loro Sae got freedom on August 30 1999, English language is very important because Timor can't live self'* (Antonio). Other connections, while more generalised, indicated strongly the spatially dispersed, globalised pull of English: *'all person must learn English because English is keys in the world'* (Angelo), or even more succinctly, *'language English a language the world'* (Maria). The unidirectional influence of the language situation in the immediate context was evident in at least one student's observation that *'now in Timor country many people which come from all country, where now they lived in Timor. East Timor people want to speak with people which from abroad must now speak English because majority they can't speak Tetum language'* (John).

Despite the pervasiveness of these expectations, a few teachers were more sceptical about the ability of English to fulfil its promise. Thus, while Dana recognised her students' belief that *'if they can speak English then they, then their future is just that bit better, it opens more opportunities and more doors for them'*, she also felt this was unrealistic, and perhaps *'a bit of a dream too: "if I can speak English then, yeah, I can do anything"'*. Indeed, in the early years of independence, there were few opportunities for Timorese to work with the transient English-speaking development community, and those that did exist were in jobs as drivers, domestic help and so on, paid at a fraction of the rate awarded to foreign workers. English, in this sense, created at least as many barriers as opportunities, and continued to reproduce restrictive social and economic hierarchies that allowed privilege for some, mostly those on international contracts, while excluding others.

The spatialisation of teachers and students

The powerful mythologies of progress that surround English language also establish a particular frame for the native-speaking English language teacher as expert, 'flown in on sleek jet planes' and expected to 'perform his or her role' according to 'script and plan' (Toh, 2003: 557). The script for ELT arguably remains dominated by a hegemonic commitment to a set of iconic practices (Holliday, 2005), including the communicative language teaching (CLT) method, which remains the standard for ELT in development despite its debatable applicability in EFL contexts. Although the precise nature of the communicative method is difficult to define, one of the key theoretical principles of both CLT and genre-based methods is that meaning is produced through the inseparable *combination* of language and the context of use, though context is often limited to a set of apolitical variables including setting, participants and purpose. It is the connection between language and the broader political notions of context that often seems to be severed in the routinised performances of ELT, where social context tends to appear as a 'neutral backdrop' against which 'androgynous bourgeois agents assert individual choice' (A. Luke, 1996: 311).

The notion of the communicative approach as *the* modern method, and a measure of advancement (Bax, 2003), underpinned the work of foreign teachers assigned to instruct Indonesian and Timorese teachers in the use of communicative methods. Bree's appointment in Indonesia, for example, was on the basis of her ability to introduce CLT, in accordance with the Indonesian adoption of a communicative curriculum and as an aspect of modernisation in English language education (Dardjowidjojo, 2000). CLT was also seen as central to the work undertaken by Ann, Jane and Kate in '*upgrading*' the skills of primary and high-school teachers in East Timor. Indeed, all the teachers in this study expressed an adherence to communicative approaches, and certain project documents stipulated this as a requirement; yet teachers' descriptions suggested that communicative approaches primarily meant little more than requiring students to talk in groups or pairs, with the oral activity itself seen as more important than the content or context of the talk. The drive to represent any teaching practice as communicative, and the constraints that might apply in some circumstances, were indicated in Ann's insistence that, despite the size of one particularly large class, '*I did my best to make it as communicative as I could*', with the sign of communication being that '*about a third*' of the students '*put up their hands with answers*' to her questions.

In practice, across all the projects, teachers' classroom work was organised, at least initially, according to imported texts in the form of coursebooks supplied by a donor institution or, more often, by teachers themselves: '*I brought a box of books, a grocery box, umm, just one box, of my favourite lessons or whatever I thought might be useful and I coped with that*' (Ann). Imported texts, including textbooks, curricula, genre samples, lesson plans, methods and standards, were utilised by teachers in their attempts to organise the space and time of the classroom: they constituted, for teachers and students, a 'spatialization of the self' through a set of localised routines, habits and techniques performed within the classroom (N. Rose, 1996). The impact of such routines could be seen in the teachers' conscientious habits of planning and organising sequences of work before meeting their students at the commencement of the course, and before each day's work, in a way that 'filled up' what was otherwise represented as the dauntingly 'empty' time and space of the classroom. Thus, like many others, Dana insisted '*you've got to be very organised with your own work, in terms of how you present and all that kind of thing, and what you're delivering*'.

My own observations of curriculum planning

Although a communicative approach was proposed in the NGO administrative documents describing the ELT project for Timorese tertiary students, the fuzziness of the term was evident at all stages of curriculum planning. I use the term 'planning' loosely. As events unfolded, any original pretence of programme coherence quickly unravelled under the pressures of implementation. My sense was that all those involved in the planning for our 'communicative' teaching were well intentioned, but 'things fall apart', so to speak, in the conflicting expectations that teachers face as they attempt to plan their use of space and time in advance, without adequate engagement with the community in which they will work. For our university ELT course, it was intended that content should focus on students' plans for future study, and although the 'English language training methodology' described in project documents anticipated 'students using the language in meaningful situations from the first day', the use of a standard textbook, *Headway*, was also stipulated.

Since *Headway* was found to be unavailable in the numbers required at short notice, an Australian coursebook had been substituted as a set text. In early preproject correspondence, the team leader recommended a curriculum based on 'textbook activities', some 'ESP content' and a circulated list of associated 'language functions and genres'. The list, e-mailed to teachers prior to departure from Australia, included standard items such as sequencing activities, directions, processes, classification systems, definitions, comparison and contrast, and concluded with the team leader's observation: 'There, that's the first fortnight filled in!!!' (personal communication, July 2000). This light-hearted comment, ironically signalling a desire to 'fill in' teaching time with scripted activities, recurred later in teachers' own accounts of practice, and indicates again the underlying tension between the rhetoric of contextual relevance and the stranglehold of sedimented disciplinary expertise.

Having circulated the list of functions and genres as the basis for teaching, project administrators initially planned for classes to commence just one full day after the teacher's arrival in Dili. However, this plan to 'touch down and teach' was derailed by protracted negotiations between administrators and the students' representative bodies in regard to project control, in which the struggle over whose version of the project would prevail was crystallised in a turf war: the tussle over control of the physical space of the project site. From the perspective of project staff, the militant students' ownership of the campus afforded the students an unwarranted 'added lever with which to press their demands' for greater control over project resources and processes. At one point, the students' leverage resulted in the project staff being locked out of the university. 'Turf', as Auerbach (2000: 149) observes, 'is a critical issue for students', and the location of the project in a campus that symbolised students' long history of repression and resistance, worked to shape this space as a site of struggle, not only over control of this project, but also over wider issues of engagement and consultation in the process of development.

The right to control who was allowed to participate in the programme was one such contentious issue. As enrolments were processed over the first few days, the atmosphere on campus was emotionally and physically explosive: students vented their frustrations, some threw furniture, others shouted or cried in anger. Amongst the highly politicised student body, deep divisions were apparent in heated discussions held in the campus courtyard.

Continued

Without access to an interpreter, however, the issues of debate remained obscure to teachers, who remained, at the insistence of project administrators and through their own language limitations, implacably outside student politics. Eligibility for enrolment was dependent on prospective students' completion of a 'needs analysis' that had been distributed to the student representatives by project administrators. However, the questionnaire had not been returned and, though various explanations were floated, the reasons for this also remained obscure. Perhaps the logistical challenges of distributing the needs analysis to students from all over the country had been too great: student representatives had been keen to include students from all 13 districts, yet this proved difficult with educational institutions closed, administrative documents destroyed, and in the absence of any postal service. Perhaps, as project administrators hinted, the struggles between various political factions within the student body had prevented the wider distribution and collection of the questionnaires. Or perhaps the questionnaires were seen as irrelevant because the needs identified in the forms bore little resemblance to the students' political desires and aspirations.

Without the returned needs analysis, there was no clear process for regulating registration, and far more students arrived to enrol than has been expected; disputes arose over students registering under false names, over occupation of campus rooms, over control of project equipment. However, in these and all future negotiations with student representatives, the project management decided not to involve teachers directly: it seems clear from the beginning that classroom teaching, as a technical exercise, was intended to be spatially and discursively disconnected from the students, their political activities, and the wider world beyond the classroom walls. The parameters established for the teaching programme were limited to a focus on text-level language skills for an imagined set of academic studies, with historical and political issues comprising an excluded curriculum.

In the unanticipated delay before the commencement of classes, the team leader directed teachers to prepare a curriculum based on outcomes extracted from the Australian textbook that had been purchased for the project. Our planning continued in a vacuum: at this point, East Timor had been something of a closed society for decades, and we had little knowledge of our students, or their experiences. Had the needs analysis been completed, it would have offered little assistance, having been designed primarily as a means of determining students' English language proficiency, and grading students into supposedly homogeneous classes. In this vacuum, teachers fell back on doing what they already knew. Fay proposed a curriculum based on one she had worked with in Australia, and together we fashioned an eclectic syllabus, informed by a functional approach to language and literacy. The syllabus was based on a typical teaching pattern in Australia, consisting of weekly themes (family, accommodation, work, health, leisure), together with complementary text types (such as recounts, or descriptions), language features (lexis and grammar) and competencies (such as asking for information, or making an appointment). Project reports later described this as a 'targeted, East Timor-specific curriculum to which adjustments could be made as special needs of their students became apparent'. But the parameters for classroom engagement were already in place.

Although teachers understood that their lessons should ideally be contextualised, constructed from information gathered from students and relevant to their needs, the habits of TESOL training, and the pressures of institutional time that structured their professional practice, largely worked against this happening. On Elly's project, teachers were required to provide 40 hours of classroom teaching each week and, allowing for duties before and after class, this meant 11 hours a day on campus, leaving little time to engage with the outside world. As Elly remarked, *'obviously you try to match what you're teaching to student needs'*, nevertheless *'when you've taught quite a lot of TESOL classes'*, teachers develop *'roughly an idea of the areas you might cover in an elementary class or an intermediate class or something, your basic kind of grammar areas that get covered in a certain area, and the content that you'd talk about'*. In effect, the scripts and plans of ELT, together with institutional time constraints, militated against an engagement with context:

> *When you go out teaching you're not going to spend 4 hours a night looking for that perfect piece of realia that relates to the students' experience, instead, you go to an English school and get shaped into teaching in a particular way, which is off a textbook. [. . .] The limit too is that thing of being able to have <u>time</u> to go and design the sort of materials that would be useful.*

Similarly, teachers acknowledged that imported materials, especially text-books, *'would have to be adapted to the situation, 'cause that happens anywhere you go'* (Carol), but the form of this contextualisation varied greatly. Some processes of adaptation comprised a simplification of lexis or grammatical structures to suit the students' English language proficiency; some placed the structures within what they saw as the local scene, while others found the disparity between the textbook world and the lived experience of their students made working with the textbooks impossible.

Spatial Patterns of English Language Teaching

In this section I explore diverse ways of relating teaching performances to learners and contexts, and discuss three broad categories of teaching practice, or spatial discourses of pedagogy. In each group, I use a spatial lens to discuss the ways in which teachers perceived their own and their students' educational practices; how teachers' educational texts and tech-nologies constituted classroom space; and how the relationship between space inside and outside the classroom was negotiated. From these per-spectives, I consider the implications for the status of the teacher and their disciplinary knowledge, the relationship between teacher and students, and the connections between disciplinary teaching and lived experience. In each group, I also draw on the views of particular teachers, though in doing so I do not wish to imply they are 'good' or 'bad' as individual prac-titioners; rather I use their words to illustrate the particular discourses that shape teaching practice.

In the first category, 'maintaining boundaries', teachers drew on disci-plinary practices that validate classroom control and regulate engagement with a diverse flow of ideas from the immediate context. These dis-cursive practices appeared to confirm a temporal narrative that secures global/local educational hierarchies. In the second and largest group, teachers found their professional ELT routines were inadequate to meet the specific challenges posed by a very different spatial context. The class-room space appears to be destabilised, and teachers experienced degrees of 'disorientation and disillusionment'. In a third group, 'mobilising spa-tial practices', teachers' accounts signal a more fluid connection with external influences, and a more complex opening of ELT to the tran-scultural politics of local context. These practices suggest a disruption of hierarchical boundaries, and a more productive engagement with differ-ence. None of these broad categories apply exclusively to single teachers, but rather describe different discourses and ways of doing teaching that might be taken up by teachers in specific times and places.

Maintaining boundaries

This first group of discourses represented in teachers' accounts of practice points to a modernist temporal logic that reinforced the authority of the native speaker teacher and discouraged the movement of unruly bodies and ideas from beyond the classroom wall. In accordance with this logic, outside influences were represented as a source of interference with the proper organisation of the classroom. More broadly, in these discourses, we see English language teaching as 'a pedagogical site and institution for educating the racial and linguistic "Other"' (Luke, 2004: 25).

Representing 'Our' space

A belief in the promises of English had implications for the way teachers saw themselves in the local space, where native speaker status and expertise in modern methods appeared to legitimise their presence and their intrinsic value. In volunteering to work in Indonesia, where people were *'desperate to learn'* English, Ann found herself transformed from being *'just an English teacher'* into being a *'precious commodity'* as *'the first and only ever English native speaker they'd had'*. A similar veneration of native speakers, and a conflation with good teaching, was expressed in Ann's view of herself as seen through her students in East Timor, who reportedly implored: *'we want to be taught English, and we want to have good lecturers, from America and Australia, we need good lecturers'*.

With the reverence accorded to native speaking English teachers, Kate found *'the respect that you get there that you don't get here [in Australia]'* was one of the primary attractions in teaching abroad. In her responsibility for instructing Timorese teachers in *'modern'* methods, she was aware of *'the chauvinism of the thing, of us saying "well this is obviously a much better way to teach"'*. Nevertheless, Kate believed her years of experience and familiarity with *'improved methodology'* would help to *'take them out of the Dark Ages a bit'*. Such discourses of advanced disciplinary knowledge point clearly to an inherent chronological hierarchy whereby one might progress, with expert intervention, from the Dark Ages to a more modern state.

Representing the 'Other' space

In contrast to the value attributed to supposedly advanced Western practices, the local institutional and teaching context was seen to be either messy, vague and chaotic, or immoral and corrupt. The Indonesian education system within which Ann worked was represented as one that operated on *'bribery and corruption'*, and Indonesian teaching practices were seen as static and traditional. From Ann's perspective, Indonesian teachers '*liked to teach grammar*', their methods required only '*rote learning, writing everything down*', while their materials were described as '*very out-dated, the course books, very limited*'. Similarly, Kate believed Timorese teachers' practices were '*very rigid and old fashioned, chalk and talk*'. At the same time, she found their practices lacked system and order, and so '*organisation was a big thing I thought they needed help with*'.

In these characterisations of students, teachers mirrored discourses that were also evident in NGO project documents. In administrative reports from one NGO project, there is evidence of sympathy for students' histories of resistance struggle, and experiences of torture, rape and killings amongst friends and family. At the same time, the reports describe the Indonesian educational system as having an 'authoritarian/traditional model of teaching' which had left students with 'widespread literacy problems', a 'lack of experience in management and systems', 'severely lacking' in 'conceptual maturity and study skills', and in 'skills of critical analysis and self directed learning'. The students were believed to be 'quite unaware of the extent of their lack' and of 'how far they need to progress in order to cope with tertiary level study'. 'Progress', according to the NGO, was to be facilitated initially by expert teachers who will demonstrate 'new strategies' and explain the 'advantages [these strategies] will bring'. Implicit in the documents is the notion that a key aspect of language and literacy projects in development is also to produce 'modern selves', rescued from the backwater of tradition and authority, as Fiedrich and Jellema (2003) observe in their evaluation of *Reflect* programmes. The making of modern selves, in the form of independent, self-directed, rational subjects, is a key concern of development projects driven by the temporal discourses of modernity.

Structuring space inside the classroom

Foreign teachers, being held in such high esteem, found they had great freedom to structure the classroom space and time through the introduction of 'modern' disciplinary technologies, but the resultant lessons did not necessarily emerge from or connect with spaces and times outside the classroom. For Ann in East Timor, '*favourite lessons*', developed over years of experience, framed the classroom organisation in a way that reflects conventional ELT teaching patterns. For a group of school students in a rural location she planned lessons arranged in a predetermined sequence, and based on topics and functions conceived as universal examples of '*everyday English, you know, that's what we do, don't we?*' To supplement the lessons, students were arranged into role plays of shopping, an activity of questionable relevance in rural Timor.

They were beginners so we did introductions, and shopping, telling the time, months of the year. I made it active for them and we did lots of games but they always had a language purpose. Ah, they were learning [English] at high school, but quite minimal. But I've taught lots of beginners before. It wasn't hard, that's all I can say really, because it was something I've done lots before, and I thought: okay, this is the level, and all right we start with that, we go on to that, that, that, that, that topic, that'll practically fill the whole course. So it just rattles along.

Another series of lessons connected with local geography may have had greater potential for engagement with the local context; however, the perspective embedded in the lessons suggested a spatial construction of the world outside the classroom as a landscape for consumption, a product of the tourist gaze. *'We did one on culture, leisure, directions, and we also did one on, like, geographic features of Dili and the surrounds, so Dili as a visitor would see it. So we did all this kind of "what's a good place to go swimming?" and "what can I see as a tourist?" and that sort of thing'*. Ironically, Ann's own experience of Timor, where she shunned the company of wealthy foreigners in favour of living with a Timorese family and making strong connections with Timorese friends, was quite different to the shopping and tourist discourses she drew on in her teaching, yet these apparently remained the dominant discourses for organising the space of the classroom and shaping a particular view of the world outside.

Kate's approach to structuring lessons was in many ways similar to Ann's. Kate believed the Timorese teachers in her class *'don't <u>know</u> what they don't know about ESL'*, so in the interests of time efficiency she would determine the lesson content: *'if you wait for them just to self-identify [what they need], you waste a lot of time'*. Thus, while Kate spoke of *'joint ownership'* and *'negotiation'* with the local teachers in her class, her own teaching constituted a one-way flow of expertise: *'modelling, demonstrating'* and *'setting up systems'* to expeditiously amend the deficiencies she saw in local practices. Most of her lessons were based on an Australian school textbook from the 1980s, and despite being written for upper primary aged children in a migrant/ESL rather than EFL context, she felt it was appropriate because *'the comprehension level was right at their level'*. A lesson she described as particularly successful involved the reading and rewriting of a children's picture book of *'Waltzing Matilda'*,[2] which she argued was suitable since *'everybody all over the world knows the Waltzing Matilda tune'*. However, the teachers in her class appeared to have a mixed response to this lesson, seeing it as either irrelevant to their subject matter or unworkable with a large class.

Guarding the inside, erecting barriers

Since mixed-level classes are conventionally perceived as a problem in ELT, all of the teachers expected their classes would be spatially and temporally organised to reflect a grading of students. Grading implied institutional expectations of stabilising classroom space by classifying students according to their language proficiency and determining the appropriate series of lessons to move the supposedly homogeneous body of students towards a predictable end. However, the need for teachers to police the boundaries of each level, to regulate entry and so maintain appropriate standards, proved to be a challenge, as Kate's accounts demonstrate.

As well as giving instruction in language teaching methodology, Kate was preparing her class to take the IELTS examination, so that they *'could go on and have something of substance'*. However, she had difficulty in guarding the standards of her *'high level'* class since one student with an inappropriate language proficiency had surreptitiously *'slipped into'* the class.

> *Mister Miguel was a principal of a school, and he didn't come to the first lesson, and I think this was by design. He just kind of slipped into the second one, and said oh yes, he'd been here before and he'd completed level 3. And on checking, he hadn't satisfactorily completed level 3, but there was no way he was going to go down because of losing face.*

The principal's presence was seen as an interference in the proper progress of the class: he was *'really holding things back 'cause he was so much slower'*, and so Kate believed it was fortunate that he was eventually removed: *'in the end fate decided it, he had a motor cycle accident* [laughs] *he broke an arm or broke a leg, and I went okay, you weren't meant to be here'*. The drive for a homogeneous progress in technical skills appeared to overshadow factors related to any alternative values and investments.

The interference of Timorese cultural practices and language conventions also presented challenges for Kate in her efforts to maintain what she considered to be proper standards of English language usage. Part of the problem, according to Kate, was that the teachers in her class were overly *'conscious of status'* and *'respect'*, which led to difficulties in the transfer of local forms of address into English usage. Her response, on hearing her students using *'Signor or Signora with the first name'* and addressing each other as *'Mister Miguel, and Mister Carlos'*, was to think, *'that's really weird and I'm thinking, it's wrong, from an English speaking perspective, 'cause you then get the people who put "Dear Mister Jim Jones..."'*. She explained in class that this was *'a big faux pas'* and that it *'doesn't work in English'*, but was unable to eradicate the habit:

> *They don't understand that you use the Mister with the surname, so that-you know, they're such sweet people that nobody would ever say "this is wrong". So we would call them by their first names, but they would call us and everybody else with putting a Mister or a Sister or whatever in front of it [as a sign of respect.] I don't mind doing it, as long as they're not going to have a carry over to the English.*

A further cause of frustration arose for Kate in relation to interference from her students' diverse engagements in the outside world. As one of their language learning tasks in their IELTS preparation, Kate had her students *'do a pie graph of their typical day'*, which revealed the nature of their engagements in other spaces: *'God, this guy had "visiting the sick" and "praying and leading the family in prayers" and* [laughs] *and all these different things, and I'm thinking Holy Moly!'* The local teachers, going about their daily activities, had articulated a different set of priorities that conflicted with what the foreign teacher saw to be the necessities of English language learning. Expressing annoyance that students' attendance to these religious duties and celebrations interrupted what she considered to be the more important concern for progress and achievements of the English classes, Kate exclaimed: *'it's like argh! are we ever going to get this class started?!'*

In sum, teachers' perspectives in this section suggest a confidence in professional scripts and plans as a means of efficiently delivering the promises of English. While these very familiar practices work to secure the status of the foreign teacher and ensure classroom stability and control, they also risk diminishing opportunities for critical engagement with the lived experience of students and with the social and political contexts in which the classroom is situated.

Disorientation and disillusionment

A second group of teaching discourses and practices suggest ways in which teachers resisted the status of the foreign teacher as expert, but found the habitual practices of English language teaching were inadequate in making a connection with the lives and experiences of their students.

Representing 'Our' space

While teachers in the previous group were confident that their experience, methods and native speaker status would help students achieve progress towards their goals, the teachers in this group were more suspicious of the inflated value attributed to foreign English language teachers, and felt burdened by the responsibility for delivering the promises of English expressed in their students' desires. With foreign teachers carrying the label of expert, Dana believed she and her colleagues were the ones *'that everybody had their hopes fixed on, and that they expected so much of'*, a daunting prospect given the perception that students *'expected to learn the entire English language in seven weeks!'* Similarly mindful of the excessive promises attached to the language, Elly was *'anxious to give the students what they needed'*.

> *I felt almost pressured to compensate for their reality a bit. It was kind of that thing of the urgency, the sense of urgency that they brought with them into the classroom about their situation, that anxiety about their futures, it was very hard not to feel personally like you- because they saw you essentially as a bit of a ticket out of a miserable life, like, they saw this as a huge opportunity.*

Rigid institutional expectations to deliver predetermined outcomes also placed significant pressures on teachers and increased their sense of inadequacy. Whereas a genuinely participatory development process would have necessitated a negotiation of goals and means, Fay felt the programme administrators *'basically wanted us to get off the plane and [immediately] start teaching [. . .], just to walk in and teach without any curriculum, well not actually a curriculum, but without any ideas'*. This clearly also conflicted with disciplinary expectations that teaching be relevant to the context, as Elly explained: *'you have to know what the hell's going on, so you are limited, I think your teaching's limited, the success of any project is limited when you send 15 people in blind!'*

Representing the 'Other' space

Being more inclined to question their own expert status and value as native speakers, these teachers represented local pedagogies not as stubbornly anachronistic but, rather, as emerging from local circumstances. Bree described her Indonesian colleagues as *'fantastic'* and highly competent, and was more inclined to see their 'traditional methods' as appropriate to specific conditions, such as a necessity to fulfil examination requirements, or to accommodate large class sizes. It made her *'cringe a bit that our model [of teaching] was sort of, in an unspoken way, seen as being superior'*. Although she described local practices as *'very teacher-centred'*, she argued that *'if you're in a classroom of 50 students, or 100 students, you've gotta be teacher centred!'* From this perspective, local classrooms were seen to be constructed in relation to contextual contingencies.

Figure 5.1 Old university campus, Dili

In East Timor, the immediate physical and political context of the old tertiary campus (see Figure 5.1) had a particularly disorientating effect on teachers. While these accounts may suggest certain similarities with previous descriptions of local space as chaos, they also signify an emergent engagement with phenomenal and cultural meanings attached to local places. In the student-controlled buildings, the violent memory of recent military occupation was ever present: surrounded by razor wire, the classrooms still had battle plans and weapons instructions posted on the wall (see Figure 5.2); yet with utilities and infrastructure destroyed, all that remained was a burnt-out concrete shell, pock-marked with bullet holes. These physical conditions evoked strong emotional responses from teachers. Helen wrote: '*Our campus [. . .] was razed. We went into this burnt out building still smelling of smoke, walked up the staircase which was mostly blown away and up to the first floor where the students were crowded into classrooms with no windows and doors in groups of about 70.*' In the place of windows and doors were gaping holes that let in the flow of smoke, insects and noise from the outside: '*It is incredibly noisy- tanks and trucks thunder past; helicopters rattle overhead; taxi drivers toot their horns incessantly.*'

Figure 5.2 Military instructions on campus wall

We sweat in the terrible heat with no fans and the mozzies circling. [...] My hands are grey with chalk dust and by the end of the day, my clothes are filthy and wringing wet. My shoes are wrecked and by 4:40 I am totally exhausted. [...] At first I was numbed; then shocked and then upset at the state of the campus. Then I felt anger- how could people do something so spiteful and destructive? Then I felt fear- for my health [...] Then I felt depression at all the dirt and squalor.

My observation: the physical space of the classroom

Recalling the recent military use of the University, our classroom has a title gouged into a wooden plank nailed over the doorway: TASKFORCE THUNDERBIRD BATCON. Bare wires dangle from the ceiling, there are no electric lights or power points. Large windows along the exterior walls were boarded up for security by the occupying Peacekeeping Force. There is little light, and little ventilation. Arrangements are eventually made to remove the boards, leaving a long row of large openings with no glass or shutters on both sides of the room.

Through the walls of the classroom there is a flow of noises, smells, and visual inspection by passers by. It's the dry season, and with no barrier between outside and inside, the dust from burning fields invades the room, along with smoke from students cooking food on fires directly outside my classroom. Our lessons are interrupted by a background cacophony of rooster calls, sirens, helicopters, troop carriers and the 'madwoman' of the neighbourhood clanging on the metal lamp post and railings. The students and I also pass in and out through the walls, an easier passage than through the door which is used by more official visitors, like the politicians who come waving the flag. This constant flow makes me aware of our physical connection to the environment and offers a tangible sense to our embeddedness in the practices of daily life in East Timor, and the social, cultural and political influences we carry with us in and out of this relatively autonomous space.

Structuring the inside

From Dana's point of view, the physical conditions meant *'there was nothing there, we had to go in and make it a classroom'*, by constructing the space with familiar objects and routines. However, the outspoken political demands of the student body, and their ownership of the campus, necessitated careful negotiation: teachers and team leaders had to *'go into [the students'] space and negotiate how it was all going to work'*. This was a space where Dana recalled feeling *'very much like I was on somebody else's turf'*. The university students in control of the campus were described by Elly as *'highly politicised'*, *'young Timorese guerilla fighters'* caught in a *'jostle for power'* with *'the old Portuguese [-speaking, Timorese] exiles who'd been living in other countries'*. These were students preoccupied with *'issues of sovereignty and self determination'*, and learning English was a significant element in this generational struggle in which the students were *'fighting for some- some power against the [nascent] government'* and their preference for Portuguese as the official national language. Yet Elly also saw the function of the aid programme as contributing to the students' continued marginalisation: *'they were being marginalised and we were a part of the marginalisation process. You know, "give them some teaching, let them stay on their campus and they'll be out of our hair"'*.

An awareness of these competing meanings ascribed to the project affected how teachers saw their role in the campus and in the classroom. Initially, Elly and others had seen themselves as *'kind of neutral people who just dropped in there'* with *'a kind of neutral idea [of] teaching English, and god there's no politics involved in that!'* But the salient political constitution of this space meant that teachers had to revise this apolitical view of their activities. Each was, necessarily, *'operating in a political role as a teacher'*, because *'we were seen as part of the whole machinery that had arrived, with the UN, the Australian military, the NGOs and all that kind of thing'*.

A functioning classroom space constituted through the routines of favourite lessons came to be viewed by these teachers as problematic, as we have seen in Elly's description of a tightly organised *'TESOL system'* transplanted from elsewhere onto local space. Compared to her non-TESOL colleagues, Elly observed *'we had a much more structured idea about what we were doing'*, by way of a set of standardised routines: *'We decided what we were doing before we went in, it was planned out, we went through it, and the students fitted in, really, and that was our TESOL training, [. . .] you can go anywhere, I mean, pretty much, and do the same thing'*. However, all this changed when Elly found the TESOL routines that served to structure her work in locations as diverse as Siberia, Australia and Indonesia, *'crashed and burned'* during her experience in East Timor. Her assumptions about universal teaching content and practices were *'completely transformed'* by the dynamic nature of this context: *'the thing that struck me was how my ideas of what to teach at a certain level went out the window, and how much the students kind of shaped the curriculum far more'*. In practice, project expectations implied in the adoption of a standard textbook, a routine curriculum, and notions of appropriate content for each proficiency level, were clearly inadequate in this context. Elly soon realised that there was no point in trying to *'superimpose'* teaching experience from another place *'without any attention being paid to the realities, which of course is crazy because the realities were really, really important'*. The *'realities'* situated the classroom in the specific local, national and global spatial and temporal context:

> *We're teaching in bombed out buildings, so that's one, physical location, right, [. . .] we're there as a project from another country, at a point where this country's trying to work out its self determination issues, I mean, like it's just dumb. As if we could have not come into contact with those issues, and they wouldn't come up in the classroom, it's just ridiculous really.*

As we have seen in the opening of this chapter, Fay's experience also led her to reflect on the inadequacy of an orthodox disciplinary practice, and to conclude that the routine classroom activities, focused on reproducing models and structures, constituted a *'big English bubble'*. Fay parodied her teaching routines as *'giving out little phrases for them to practice'*, and producing *'a little merry group, as if they are communicating, but they're not really'*. This not only generated a space of discomfort in the classroom, but also raised doubts about the ultimate notion of progress and development, *'because it's a bubble, and because it's obviously going to go nowhere too'*. The simulated English language use within the classroom had become, to paraphrase Baudrillard (2001), a copy without an original, a simulacrum floating directionless and free of any particular context.

The combination of a functional syllabus and a world represented on the pages of a textbook offered students little explicit opportunity to construct their own identities in English. However, the distribution of blank exercise books, purchased by two teachers at a local Chinese store and distributed amongst the university students, opened a textual space for students to engage in a different way with a new language. Initially, the encouragement for students to write in these journals was intended not only to improve their fluency, but also to provide teachers with some breathing space in a long day of lessons. Fay provided instructions that outlined a rationale and some guidelines for the written content of the journals (see Figure 5.3), but students made this textual space their own.

The idea of a journal is to make you think in English and get faster at writing in English. You should

- **Try to write quickly. Don't worry too much about spelling or grammar.**
- **Write for about 20 minutes each day.**

Write about:

- What you've done recently
- A memory/memories from your childhood
- Memories from your school or university
- An important event in your life
- An important event in East Timorese history
- Describe a place you have visited in East Timor
- A news article, book or film you've seen or read
- Your opinion on any current issue eg. The UNTAET government, the future language of East Timor
- Write a poem
- A description of your family
- The place where you grew up
- A favourite recipe – list ingredients and give instructions on how to cook it
- A hobby or activity you do in your spare time
- Write the rules for a game you know how to play
- Describe how to make or do something eg. How to make a basket or repair a bicycle tyre puncture
- What you've learnt recently in your English classes
- Any problems or difficulties you are having in your English classes
- An activity you do regularly eg. Go to church, play football etc.
- A typical day in your life
- A short story

ANYTHING ELSE YOU CAN THINK OF OR WANT TO WRITE ABOUT . . .

Figure 5.3 Journal writing guidelines

My observations: My home, your home

The lifestyle presented in our Australian textbooks, while unremarkable in an Australian classroom, when viewed in my East Timorese classroom suddenly appears middle class, materialistic, immodest, littered with irrelevant Australian slang. As I am the embodiment of this 'Western lifestyle' in the classroom, I feel acutely aware that this textbook world also constructs an identity for me: supermarket shopping, car ownership, eating in restaurants, train travel and holiday air travel comprise the normal routines; washing machines, freezers, mobile phones and computers are everyday commodities. Making appointments by phone, filling bank forms, reading street signs or EFTPOS instructions are everyday practices and form the basis of modelled texts.

In contrast, in East Timor at present there are no phones, no appointments for doctors, no trains and no bus signs, especially in English, and no libraries to join, EFTPOS machines or banks to use. As we browse the pages of the textbook, references to Australians' weekend activities, such as 'clipping the edges' on the lawn in front of the house, seem almost impossible to explain in a country where many families are still living amongst rubble or in makeshift shelters, and gardens are associated with food production rather than ornamental lawns. As one student writes,

> We live in Dili capital, but now we live in front of my house because before milisia destroyed and bombed my house. (Nelson)

Although the textbook content is not directly challenged in most of the students' journal writing, resistance to the irrelevant or alienating discourses is signalled in the students' journals. In one sense it is as if a parallel syllabus is being played out as a counter to the syllabus imposed by the abstracted spatiality of themes, functions and textbook pictures. I present one syllabus, based on my own view of the world and embodied in English language teaching practices; the students write back an alternative syllabus, constructing a different textual space, a different view of the world, different subject positions for themselves and a different configuration of classroom space.

A cogent example of students' opposition to the textbooks' alien discourses is produced after a lesson where we study pictures of supposedly typical Western houses replete with every possible item of furniture and modern appliances. While such pictures are pre-sumably intended to provide rich inspiration for vocabulary devel-opment, students respond to the message conveyed in this display of the consumer items cluttering a Western home. One student's description of his house gives some insight into the cultural distance between a house that is defined by material possessions and a house that provides shelter and peace:

> *I live in Cidade Street. West of Dili city. it is simple house and not have expencive accessoreis like expensive sofa, sterio, lamp or do not have expensive interior rooms and exterior rooms. But my family can be stay ther with shadow and piece.* (Fernando)

Another describes a house which is small and crowded but happy:

> *My house is very small but I'm very happy. in the house I have four brothers and five sisters. In the house I have four bedroom. two bed-room to my father and brothers and two another bedroom to my sisters and I. I have a garden and my garden I to plant flowers and fruit . . . In the house I'm very happy.* (Ivete)

When teachers made conscious attempts to connect the space of the classroom to the world outside, further difficulties arose. Like many teach-ers, Helen found her own limited experience of Timor prevented her from successfully adapting the spatial representations in the course books: '*there was always the problem of getting the situation right*'. When Helen '*tried to adapt my materials to the lifestyle and culture of Dili*', she realised that '*being so new to the country and living in the expatriate enclave of a hotel*' offered her '*little understanding of how most students lived*'. As a result, she '*con-tinued to make incorrect assumptions about things like where they shopped, ate and socialised*', the very topics that inhabit ELT. These assumptions were governed by her own way of seeing the world, and emerged from '*an ex-pat's experience of Dili*'. Constructing and modelling a dialogue '*about likes and dislikes, you know, and the dialogue was something like "how are you get-ting on in Dili?", "Fine, I love the restaurants"*', Helen came to realise that this was a spatial practice of the foreigner: '*that was the first mistake, you know, and because there were so many restaurants and they were so well used at the time, and I hadn't been there long enough to notice that the Timorese weren't using them*'. A similar dialogue about '*little local supermarkets, that I had seen Timorese people using*' also missed the mark, since '*most of my students in fact*' *don't use them, though I'd assumed they had'*. Lost in a different world, Helen concluded: *'I wasn't really getting close to what they really do in their lives'*.

Similarly, Elly found even the simplest questions posed for practising language use *'didn't work'*: *'like, "what do you have for breakfast?" I mean, partly they didn't work because they didn't have breakfast'*. Despairing of her ability to adapt standard lessons, Fay concluded that *'there doesn't seem to be any published material that would be appropriate'*, particularly since the textbook world presented *'a lifestyle where everyone is extremely rich and extremely articulate'*. For Helen, this was a problem not only because *'the students can't identify with it'*, but because it represented a discomforting image of herself as the teacher: *'you also feel that you're um, promoting that somehow, as the person presenting it'*.

In the face of extraordinary circumstances, these teachers' expectations of maintaining autonomous, external institutional 'standards' in their teaching practice also foundered. Helen's students, having previously experienced spatial separation and grading in an earlier aid project, vigorously resisted being classified and divided in this way: *'All pretence of grouping them has gone overboard and the groups are mixed ability. This is actually what the students lobbied for in the first place! They didn't like the idea of being placed into levels as we had been asked to do. They felt this was divisive.'* Plans for final examinations and the awarding of certificates were also subverted, this time by teachers, who resisted subjecting students to external standards of classification. As Fay recalled, the students were seen as more than the measure of their competences, so *'in the end no one really tested, there was a bit of testing and goodness knows what the results of that was'*. *'The whole going up one level was a bit of a joke anyway. I mean they all got their certificates, they had completed a course. All the ones that turned up should have got a certificate, but what does a certificate mean?'*

Relating to the 'Other' space

The Timorese students' agency in appropriating English for their own purposes, and their resistance to an institutionalised textbook world, was expressed in a strong desire to *'tell their own stories'*, but to do so by using ways and means of their own choosing. As we have seen, even with her class of *'complete beginners'*, Fay was *'really surprised about how much they wanted to say'*: *'They really wanted to talk about the Timor situation, they wanted to talk about their lives, I was actually shocked at how open they were, they didn't seem- they were quite openly saying things like- writing about their family "my sister is dead" or "my uncle is crippled", or things like that, there seemed an overall willingness to speak about what was happening'*. From inside the TESOL 'bubble' Fay felt *'there wasn't sort of a mechanism there for them to do that'*, to recreate those experiences in a new language, yet this is precisely what the students did.

Many students who were hesitant with speaking were fluent when given the opportunity to construct themselves, and their world, in written English. As an active, politicised body, the tertiary students in East Timor had a strong interest in shaping their new nation, and when Elly *'gave them a creative writing activity or, you know, a free writing exercise or a diary exercise or whatever, it was so political, which was nothing you'd ever, you just don't get here* [in Australia]'. Critical accounts of national historical events and questions about current political happenings outside the classroom filled students' writing: the role and impact of the UN, East Timor's relationship with Australia, the nation's past and future struggles were recurrent themes. Students also wrote about their personal memories, their day-to-day experiences of family survival, thoughts about people who had been tortured or had died, people who they missed. These textual representations of spaces and times outside the control of teachers allowed students, in effect, to represent themselves in the textualised spatial structures of the discipline, and at the same time challenged the stabilisation of space attempted by orthodox disciplinary texts and practices.

My own observations: Students' constructions of spatial context

Writing in their journals produced a social and historical self that locates personal experience in a larger political perspective. Providing a counter to the cultural representations of the textbook world, they write about the struggles of decolonisation, and the challenges that confront the new nation:

> *Twenty five years ago when East Timor people fight with Indonesian regime. a lot of people feels under pressure. For example: discrimination, violence, warriors, etc. and untill September one years ago we celebrated liberation of East Timor which many peoples for another country give supports to our human rights. For now East Timor peoples have be makes everything and free nation. Free for speaks, free for works and security.* (Gaspar)

They reflect on the enormity of the challenges involved in the reconstruction of physical and symbolic territory:

> *As the world know about East Timor new country because the country start to zero(0). All the goods paroporty East Timor destroid by militia pro Jakarta so we will trying make and found building, construction and than people and my lang to better.* (Ismael)

Continued

> *Understanding about nation identity and to proud as East Timor peoples like patriotism, my herroes and my country. but we have challenge on the future like the fight against illiteracy ... In our future is good can proved by what are begin now. and gived contribution for our nation and our country ... The war opposites with Indonesia regime was gone but now a new war about poverty, folly underdevelopment and globalization.* (Mouzinho)

Although the intervention by international development agencies in East Timor is mostly represented in positive terms, as the months wear on doubts about who is setting the development agenda begin to surface. In students' texts the streets of the capital are identified as a site of struggle between global and local powers:

> *Everiday if we around on the streets and see many people very busy and staff UNTAET with UN cars very busy too but what are they doing? Maibe they have a meeting and spoke about East Timor future but haw about action like development problems, educational problems and market orientation. UNTAET has progress about 10 months but can't programs for gived solution for emergency problems.* (Maria)

In these textual representations, it seems that students could 'recognise themselves in the acquisition of English' (Thesen, 1997: 509).

The spatial representations of the students' texts provided a clear contrast with those presented in conventional textbooks, and considering the students' consistent determination to write their stories, it seemed at times they were keen to integrate these experiences and views into classroom activities. However, the sensitive, emotional and political content of their writing presented the teachers with a further challenge, and raised doubts about explicitly engaging with students' concerns. Moreover, contractual obligations prohibited teachers' involvement in political issues, and by implication prevented explicit classroom engagement with students' political experiences and expressions.

Sensitivity to students' stories of personal suffering also led some teachers to draw firmer barriers to keep the outside out, so although Fay felt the students' experiences were *'something we really should have worked with'*, they also made her and others *'feel uncomfortable'*. In her professional demeanour, Fay described herself as *'fairly distanced as a teacher, I cringe away from a lot of personal contact'*, an aspect of her style that perhaps, at times, suited the protective shield provided by an ELT *'bubble'*. Engagement with these emotional experiences was seen to be *'not the role of teacher but more psychotherapist or counsellor'*: *'It's not a role I feel comfortable with, tip-toeing around these subjects. For a couple of reasons, firstly just the trauma, I don't know how to handle that, and secondly because my culture was so different from theirs, different values and beliefs.'* Despite the teachers' expressed solidarity with Timorese political activism, fear of the passions that could be invoked led some teachers to avoid contact with personal accounts of trauma and grief, and to acknowledge the significance of very different spatialised practices of response: *'They [the Timorese] would go to church and pray, so that was really different to how I might handle this trauma, so I wouldn't know how to talk about these things to them. In this way the nuns were better. For me there was a big gulf, I felt like an outsider to that culture.'*

The dilemma about whether or not to connect led to confusion for Elly, too: *'I thought I had to be so much more hands off in a lot of ways, in terms of some things, and so much more in there, in terms of others'*. Her professional scripts in ELT were inadequate in this situation:

> *I didn't have the skills, you know, someone sitting there telling you how their friend died, you know, how to give the space for them to be able to say that but also thinking I don't think I can cope with another student telling me another story like this today. I mean I've had three already, that was it, I just couldn't- that was- I found that really, really hard.*

The difficulties of addressing emotionality and memory were perceived as partly a result of the dry disciplinary construction of the classroom space: *'there was no space provided for them to talk about that kind of stuff, and again, I don't know whether that was a cultural thing or whether that was partly to do with the way the classroom was set up as well'*. Such absences and disconnections were reiterated by Dana, who sensed in the classroom there was *'a divide there that just couldn't be conquered, because of differences in background and ethnicity, and culture'*.

Teachers' accounts in this section indicate a frequent response of uncertainty and confusion, disconnection and resistance when faced with in the challenges of articulating orthodox English language teaching practices within the complex context of development. It seems that this unsettling sense of confusion, despite being painful for some individual teachers, nevertheless offered opportunities for productive change. As we shall see in the following section, by dislodging the pedagogical certainty and superiority that held prescribed teaching scripts in place, some teachers found a means for engagement with a radically different context.

Mobilising spatial practices

In this final section I explore a third group of teaching discourses, practices and experiences that suggested a movement away from stable notions of classroom time and space ordered solely by the teacher through texts, methodologies and standards. Disruptions of an ordered classroom through the intrusion of other times and spaces involved a two-way movement across the classroom walls, a taking up of spatial practices, and a shift in the roles of teacher and learner. The impact of students and contexts on these classrooms meant that a range of different times were accounted for in classroom events: historical time, personal memories, memories of particular places and an immediate, experiential now. The pace and time of the classroom also shifted to something that teachers felt was more in tune with the context of an outside world.

Representing 'Our' space and 'Other' space

As we have seen in earlier sections, foreign teachers were often placed in a position of superiority in relation to local colleagues and students, and accordingly vested with the authority to control the time and space of the classroom. But where teachers felt discomforted with 'superiority-of-being-us', they resisted the spatial hierarchy of ELT. Jane *'felt a lot of the Timorese, because I was white, it was this kind of thing* [bowing] *like especially one of the fellows who worked at the college, and [I'd say] "Domingos, please don't", and he'd be like this* [bowing], *and that was just-* [cringes] *that was just- I didn't like that'*. She was concerned that the respect her local colleagues and students gave her created a hierarchy of *'I am here and you are there* [hand gestures high and low]', and produced *'this distance'* between them that she attempted to break down. Jane's struggle was one towards dissolving the boundaries between self and other, between self and the environment, in the contact zone. Likewise rejecting the social patterns she had witnessed in the development context, Helen at the very beginning of her course wanted to show her students *'there are no Malai [foreigners] in this classroom, only friends'*. In Pratt's (1992) analysis of the contact zone, this process could be seen as one in which the separated, ordered spatiality of imperial culture, and of the autonomous, imperial Self, could be reconceived in terms of porousness and fluidity that allow for an engagement with difference. Nevertheless, any romanticised notion of an easy friendship should be approached with caution. As Bartlett (2005) argues in regard to pedagogies for development literacy, friendship between teacher and students is no substitute for critical, analytical engagement with students' 'real' social, economic and political struggles.

Attempts to shift from a position of teacher control were often accompanied by an acknowledgement that the teacher was not necessarily the one who knew what was going on either inside or outside the classroom. Resisting the position of the knower, Jane admitted that, as an outsider, she '*never* knew what was going on'; however, this '*wasn't bewildering*' or a cause of anxiety. In the end she came to realise '*it doesn't matter that you don't know, and probably you'll never know*'. In this move, rather than positing a transcendent, knowing subject, a detached 'monarch-of-all-I-survey', Jane sought to relinquish the *a priori* position of authority granted her as the expert teacher, and through contextual experiences of 'disorientation, incomprehension, self-dissolution' (Pratt, 1992: 222) became open to a different sort of engagement with place.

Unstructuring the inside

Student resistance to the imposed stabilisation of space and the orderly sequence of preplanned lessons led some teachers to revise their view of the classroom. In these revised perceptions, the classroom was experienced by Elly more as a space of struggle: '*in Timor you got much more a sense of the classroom being a place where people constructed their identity and where there were power struggles between my concept of what the classroom was going to be and what they thought it should be*'. It had become obvious that the students' engagement in classroom processes was greater when their political issues were central, and Elly realised that the ordering of classroom space and time would have to be reversed: '*you'd have to work from the students to a curriculum, [. . .] The content and the sort of skills and functions would have to be framed around experiences that make sense to the students.*' Instead of the functions and topics usually represented in international coursebooks, critical engagement with this context might be about '*getting up and having political arguments*', about the choice of national languages, or about the constitution of the national assembly. These were things she felt the students '*really related to, I think because it was part of their experience*'. When '*you actually touched on something that was quite- yeah that dominated every part of their daily life, that is, the debates of the time or whatever, they fired up, yeah, they liked it. They felt confident, they knew what they were doing.*' As students took over this space, Elly became '*a lot more responsive to the day to day, [. . .] a lot more flexible and less- actually less planned, a lot less structured*'. Her experiences changed the type of conscientious teacher she had become through TESOL training, and afforded greater openness to unexpected futures: '*I mean I'm a kind of organised planned person, and I think my personality- [. . .] I think I'd actually have to let go and loosen up quite a bit, and just take it as it comes, day by day, be a bit less frightened of the unknown, a bit less frightened of the unexpected'*.

Movement occurred, too, in and across different pedagogical routines, as teachers transgressed the edicts of TESOL methods and instead fashioned practices from a greater variety of available resources. Rather than simply dismissing local practices as 'traditional', Jane's efforts to introduce 'modern' language teaching methods recognised the value of diverse approaches and practices that could be more suitable and sustainable in the immediate conditions of Timorese schools. Shuttling between her own and her students' familiar practices provided *'a balance of what they thought was good teaching, so that they would feel they were learning, to what I felt was good teaching'*.

Challenging the TESOL orthodoxies that favour English-only communication, teachers also made a more explicit use of translingual practices in their classroom interactions. Apart from the practical value of drawing on students' linguistic repertoires, an insistence on English-only in the classroom would seem both ironic and inappropriate given the history of colonial linguistic impositions experienced within Timor. Multilingualism was clearly such a pervasive necessity in the students' lives, that my own students were amazed that the majority of Australians could be born, raised, educated, pursue a career and complete all the functions of life in one language. In Timorese classrooms, by contrast, we communicated with fragments of my Italian, tracing through Portuguese connections and finding their appropriations in Tetum. Similarly, Fay's students used processes of multilingual translation to negotiate classroom text and talk; and for Helen, translingual practices opened the way for freer connection and communication, as she moved between *'a combination of English and the odd Portuguese borrowed word in Tetum'*. Carol still felt bound by TESOL orthodoxies not to use her own second language, Bahasa Indonesia, although it was spoken fluently by her students; nevertheless, translingual processes flourished in the students' classroom negotiation of meanings in a local English language newspaper. The newspaper stories in this turbulent time generated *'a lot of debate and discussion'* that connected the classroom with reports of everyday happenings, and engaged both teacher and students in translingual processes:

> *Because a lot of the emotive words that were being used in the newspapers had Latin roots, so the Spanish and Portuguese helped them there. Those that spoke Portuguese, they were familiar with it enough to be able to pick out a lot of those words which made reading [easier], even though some of those extracts looked pretty difficult [. . .] there wasn't a lot of new vocabulary that they had to learn.*

Moving the space of the classroom

Enclosure of the modernist classroom within firm boundaries represents an attempt 'to stabilize the meaning of particular envelopes of space-time' (Massey, 1994: 5), and subjects those within to the gaze of disciplinary authority. Within these boundaries, the conventional asymmetry of power and knowledge between teacher and student is secured. However, for some teachers, a move outside the physical boundaries of the classroom fostered a reversal of teacher and students' expertise.

In an early attempt to disrupt the stable pedagogical hierarchy, and to make connections with her students, Jane drew a time-line of her own life experiences, and used this as a model in the hope of eliciting students' own life stories. But students were reluctant, resistant. When inside the space of the classroom, they were *'very non-committal about their personal stories and about the war'*, eluding the spatial schema of the panopticon and the disciplinary gaze. However, a physical move beyond the institutional envelope opened up possibilities for different, destabilising 'spatial practices' (de Certeau, 1984: 96). When outside the classroom, students' stories about the meanings of various places were more readily shared. Walking down the street, students explained the significance of particular places, as Jane listened: *'this place was bombed, the bombs came over here, this happened here, and that sort of thing'*. In this spatial practice, the students had become the experts, narrating the stories-in-walking that 'weave places together' (de Certeau, 1984: 97). In this way, although Jane had insufficient knowledge of the culture of East Timor to adapt the content of the textbook to that context, moving outside the classroom allowed a more subtle, spatially nuanced, contextualisation of language and meaning. It also enabled a different connection between the teacher, the student and the production of 'spatial history' (Carter, 1987).

Complex constructions of place also emerged when Jane visited a Timorese beach with her students after studying textbook stories and information about Australian beaches. While beaches in Australian textbooks are often represented as jolly scenes of outdoor living, these beaches had a different meaning to tell. On the beach together with her students, these other stories surfaced, through fragments and memories of other times in this place. The students told her that

> *going down to the water and swimming is not something that they did [. . .] Swimming or being in the water was avoided because, when the Indonesians were there that was part of the torture, they'd take them down to the beach and put their head down underneath and that kind of thing [. . .] it takes a bit of courage to [go there], because this is what happened.*

The beach was constructed through different experiences of different groups and individuals, as a liminal space of contested meanings, as a place 'haunted by many different spirits hidden there in silence, spirits one can invoke or not' (de Certeau, 1984: 108). Here, in verbal relics and debris, the silenced memories that emerged did so in resistance to the proper, disciplinary organisations of space and place. Through these spatial practices of narration, the talk between teacher and students turned from the routine functions set out in the textbook to talk emerging from the contingencies of place. These exchanges not only alluded to past trauma, but also concerned daily events occurring outside the classroom: the construction of a new nation built on old ties and allegiances, the writing of a new constitution, the role of the church in the new state, the impassioned speeches of Xanana on his election rounds.

Moving the time of the classroom

In the teacher's experiences discussed above, there was evidence not only of the development of a different sense of space, but also of a diverse sense of time, as personal and community histories, and potential alternative futures, were brought into the space of the language classroom. The most pressing articulation of time appeared in teachers' perception that there was never enough of it. This was particularly true for teachers on short-term contracts where the measurement of progress was tied to unrealistic time constraints. Even after her two years in Indonesia, Bree acknowledged the sense that '2 *years* sounds *like a long time, and felt like a long time, but it wasn't, to kind of make those changes'*. Her observations help to put the notion of the transient teacher as change-agent into a longer, more complex perspective of local time. Whether the transient periods of foreign teaching were long or short, almost all the teachers perceived time – and their own presence – as elusive and fleeting: as Dana lamented, '*I didn't feel like we'd done everything that we could have. I felt like there was missed opportunities and things that could have been done better.*' In this perspective, a notion of the teacher as the 'change-agent' of development is brought into doubt.

A second sense of diverse time was experienced as a more immediate, richer 'now', which emerged in classroom interactions untethered from the textbook, where something was shared apart from a planned learning experience and the mastery of a given structure. For Fay, a growing familiarity meant there was also much '*light-heartedness*' in classroom exchanges, as noises from inside and outside, past and present jostled together, '*like when the sirens went past and the students jumped and shouted "Militia! Militia!" and burst out laughing, and I thought, they seemed able to take on trauma'*. This excess of times came together when Fay, in a genuine position of not knowing, asked her students' advice about where she should visit on her weekend. The ensuing interaction brought students' personal knowledge into the classroom not in the genre of a simulated information gap, nor in a tourist's role play, but in the form of a parody: *'We asked them where to go for the weekend and it became this big joke, "Militias have destroyed it!" They'd all learned that phrase. That kind of light-heartedness, or that ability to joke about something'.*

This shifting sense of time was not without its difficulties. Outside the classroom there were communal practices of remembrance, recalling into the present personal memories of violence and trauma, 'things *extra* and *other* [that] insert themselves into the accepted framework, the imposed order' (de Certeau, 1984: 107). As we have seen in the previous section, topics that arose spontaneously in the course of everyday lessons inside the classroom recalled into the present personal memories of trauma. In these classroom events, the imposed order showed its instability. In Carol's class,

> *there'd be something about, 'There was more rain in Hong Kong than London', or something like that, and then when they made up their own sentences: 'More people were killed in Los Palos than Baucau'. And then we'd be talking about languages of East Timor, and then one student'd say: 'Oh, my brother spoke English very well', 'Oh what's he doing now?' 'Oh, he was killed at the Santa Cruz massacre'. You know, that sort of thing, it was just a shock all the time. Then one of my students had to go and dig up bodies, and then he came back, and they had to ask to go over to CIVPOL, and he said 'Very sad, bones belong my family'.*

Rather than recalling these classroom exchanges as the cause of distancing between teacher and students, for Carol they appeared to build more connections, between self and students, language and context. Histories of lived experience became part of a complex vision of classroom space, rather than something that was separate from 'the English lesson': *'there was a lot of laughter and light moments and joking, but at the same time we couldn't ignore what was happening'.*

A third sense of shifting time appeared in accounts of a different tempo or pace taking precedence over the regulated time imposed by institutional and disciplinary requirements. Classroom pace was initially set by the goal of outcomes to be achieved within a certain fixed time frame and by teachers' habitual routines. Although some teachers became frustrated when other priorities and contingencies interrupted their disciplined temporal expectations, others enjoyed the sensation of a shift to time shaped by holy days, family obligations, anniversaries and political involvements. The influence of these events in producing a different sense of time was evident in Jane's changing relationship with the teaching plan that structured her pedagogical practice. She had started her teaching in East Timor within a syllabus set by the project management and based on an Australian ESL textbook: '*I suppose initially, in a new environment and in teaching something that was new, it was like, "this is on the page, okay, I'll get through this today"'*. Through the orthodoxy of the textbook, an overall trajectory had been determined, and a set of expectations from elsewhere had governed her teaching time.

As well, her idea of professionalism had signalled a valorisation of productive time also typical of an industrial, industrious modernity. Rushing around, '*still working at Australian pace*', her embodied, pedagogical performance had reflected a regulatory politics of time that underpins development and strives for efficiency, productivity and progress. As Adam (2003: 71) points out, such notions of 'time thrift' have been ingrained in the West since the industrial revolution and have been central to the neocolonialist agenda of globalisation and development: to be modern, progressive, even civilised means to 'embrace the industrial approach to time'. But for Jane these habits were gradually challenged and then changed by a new, phenomenal sense of being in place and time:

> *Once I could slow down to East Timor, it was difficult to keep, I suppose the professionalism that- my expectations of teaching, and to be able to slow down to the pace that one has to slow down to, you know with the heat and things, and that was- I think I managed it towards the end, [. . .] I was able to sort of slow down, I didn't have to go* [gestures of speedy, robotic talking and moving].

This change of pace was realised in a release from the boundaries of the textbook: '*I mean, I didn't have to open the book and think, "Oh, my god what am I doing today?"* ' In her pedagogical practice, this meant she could be more flexible, to '*risk*', and '*begin to be creative, which I wasn't, I wasn't there in that space when I first started*'. Her own and her students' resistance to regulatory regimes allowed diverse manifestations of space and time to emerge, in the 'microbe-like, singular and plural practices' and 'surreptitious creativities' which a totalising system is designed to domesticate or suppress (de Certeau, 1984: 96). She had moved from a place of having '*conflict going on, rushing here, rushing there*', to '*slowing down*', and learning just to '*be there*'. This embodied expression of pleasure in 'being there', de Certeau describes as another spatial practice, 'under-expressed in the language it appears in like a fleeting glimmer' (1984: 108). Both inside and outside the classroom, the temporal and spatial bonds that had regulated her way of being slipped away, enabling more flexible pedagogical practices, and more creative engagements between languages and the spaces, places and times of learning in development.

*   *   *

Teaching and Spatiality in Development

In this chapter I have explored the ways in which English language teaching relates to the context of international development, and considered how this relationship is realised temporally and spatially in classroom practices. I have discussed the limiting effects of an overarching narrative of progress, and of institutional and disciplinary patterns of time and space, as they shape pedagogical discourse and teaching practices, and restrict engagement between the classroom and the surrounding context. Together, these modernist regimes of time and space sustained an orthodox performance of ELT that proved inadequate to the challenges and demands of the development context and, ironically, replicated hierarchies and exclusions that many teachers had observed and repudiated in the development context. In the previous chapter, teachers' perceptions of development communities demonstrated a rejection of the spatial boundaries and exclusions that organised social hierarchies and inequalities within development contexts. However, this chapter suggests that the temporal and spatial regulation inherent in mainstream English language teaching risked reproducing similar hierarchies and exclusions that marginalise or preclude other ways of seeing, being and doing.

A narrative of progress from tradition to modernity has linked English language to the promises of development: the promise of a better life, which students could see for themselves in the economic wealth and power of an English-language-speaking development community. This temporal trajectory also presents First World teachers' expert knowledge of ELT as more advanced than local teaching practices, thereby legitimising the process of change that would superimpose 'modern' discourse practices and mobilisations of time and space onto the educational spaces of a local context which is, in turn, rendered deficient and backward. By privileging Western language teaching expertise, the temporal narrative supports a dichotomised understanding of global and local knowledge that places the native-speaking, internationally mobile English language teacher, with embodied methods and texts, in a position of authority in the enclosed disciplinary space of the classroom.

Teachers drew on familiar institutional and disciplinary spatial and temporal regimes to organise the English language classroom as a discrete domain. These regimes were evident in the grading and segregation of students, and in the use of imported textual representations of distant, First World spaces and times, which in turn ordered and spatialised teacher performance. Teleological pressures to achieve predetermined outcomes in short project time-frames, in other words a 'quick-fix' project approach to ELT, favoured routinised pedagogical performance, rather than more exploratory, open-ended approaches. These pedagogical routines rely on the performance of specific methods, sedimented through years of professional experience, and rigidified by demands for the efficient use of time. Yet such routine teaching practices produced an inwardly focused classroom, imagined as an empty space to be filled by teachers' plans and familiar lessons.

While teachers' scripted, spatialised performances sought to stabilise the classroom, they simultaneously suppressed the flow of influences from the local context, which remained as a neutral background, or even a troublesome impediment, to the maintenance of proper standards and progress. Thus, while teachers acknowledged the necessity to adapt their disciplinary texts to context, the spatial detachment of disciplinary knowledge, and spatial separation of institutional education from the community, often precluded a fuller engagement with local spaces, places and times of students' lived experience. Brought together, these naturalised ways of reducing, partitioning and mobilising time and space helped to situate English language teaching within a larger narrative of development, and replicated exclusive, colonial spatial relations that had been rejected by teachers in their observations of the development context. Thus, while colonial discourses that insist on the superiority of Western subjectivities and knowledge were rejected in the development context, they were nevertheless reproduced in the discourses of English language teaching.

Several teachers who perceived the gulf between their familiar routines and an enormously different context experienced a sense of disorientation, confusion and ambivalence that disrupted a secure, developmental vision of linear change and temporal progress. A break in the script occurred for these teachers, and certainty about superior methods or texts dissolved, leaving space for a different type of engagement. Confronted and confused by an awareness of radical difference, and seeing themselves as intruders on someone else's turf, these teachers saw the conventional disciplinary practices of ELT crash and burn, throwing into doubt the teleological promises of the language, the value of an imported disciplinary knowledge, and the hierarchy that secured control of the classroom space. The textual rendering of local space through teachers' modelled dialogues about restaurants, supermarkets or tourist sites echoed imperial practices of exploring, reconstructing and renaming local space through Western eyes, and accentuated the disjuncture between teachers' and students' ways of seeing and experiencing place. Mirroring the ambivalence that characterised teachers' experience of the development context, the teachers' resulting sense of confusion and uncertainty highlights the way in which a spatialised awareness can undermine the story of rational progress that underpins mainstream notions of English language and development.

The modernist regimes of education and language teaching were subject to challenge, subversion and appropriation by students' spatial practices. In their resistance to separation and grading, and in their demands for time and space to articulate political and personal concerns in conjunction with the processes of language learning, students asserted a proliferation of meanings for the space of the classroom and the world outside. As they articulated their own space in the language, students also constructed a different type of spatial history, a co-existing spatial story of particular places and events that insisted on its own relative autonomy and could not be 'compressed into a supposed temporal sequence' (Massey, 1999: 281). The students' appropriations of English language, and inclusion of translocal discourses and symbols, blur the boundaries of classroom space and point to temporal and spatial practices that refuse to be wholly disciplined by modernist Western regimes. As a consequence of these practices of resistance, the colonial model of imposition was no longer clear.

An awareness of and engagement with other spatial histories and spatial practices led some teachers to a more fluid, critical performance of English language teaching in development. Within the classroom, teachers questioned, and partially relinquished, the hierarchies that aligned their teaching with the superiority-of-being-us: their own central position as the knowing, mapping subject, and their own disciplinary knowledge as the sole source of expertise was overturned. They also envisaged the classroom as a different type of space, not necessarily aligned with the temporal progress mandated by the development institution, but open to a relationship with the contingencies of another place, and the value of alternate knowledges and political imperatives offered by a different context. What this suggests is not a simplistic democratisation of the classroom in favour of learner-centredness, but rather a more critical awareness of the discourses that coexist and struggle to surface in the classroom, that organise a particular type of relationship between the classroom and its various contexts, and that signal the relative values accorded to diverse, translocal knowledges, practices and peoples. This spatialised view highlights the complex, relative autonomy that characterises the classroom, its intricate relation to the temporal pull of modernity and globalisation, and to the spatial effects of localisation; that is, of being situated in a local place which is itself always already inflected by external influences.

With regard to teaching performance, rather than being confined by sedimented routines geared to achieving predetermined outcomes, the discourses of teaching practice in this group suggested a greater awareness and affirmation of proliferous, co-existing spaces and times. An affirming engagement with diverse social and political spaces, in turn, allowed teachers and students to move out of the classroom to explore the histories, discourses and meanings articulated in local places and, as we shall see in Chapter 6, to approach questions of local ownership in alienated public spaces occupied, in the case of East Timor, by the new global invasion. These engagements with local spaces and places were accompanied by an awareness of different times related to teachers' 'being there', in the local context. Time as memory, a slowing down of the rushing, commodified time of modernity, and a greater sense of the immediate, emerged to counterpose the reduction of time to linear progress and to institutional segmentations and routines. As with the examples of students' resistance, in these spatial and temporal practices the boundaries of the classroom were subverted, allowing a critical engagement with contextual difference that resists reduction to a singular temporal narrative. Together with these shifts in space and time came a different, political understanding of what it means to be a teacher in development, a view of oneself as political agent and as an integral constituent of development's complex spatiality. Not so much an 'agent of change', facilitating development as 'the one and only narrative it is possible to tell' (Massey, 2005: 5), but rather a participant in a complex process where there are multiple trajectories, histories and different potential futures.

Notes

1. Regarding contesting views of context, see van Dijk's (2008) theory of context as formed in participants' subjective, selective mental models.
2. *Waltzing Matilda* is a traditional Australian folksong containing a range of Australian cultural concepts and colloquialisms.

Chapter 6
Doing the Washing Up: Teaching and Gender in Development

Through an exploration of teachers' narratives so far, I have discussed responses to perceived racial, economic and gendered inequalities perpetuated in the various spaces of the development context, and considered the relationship between this world outside the development classroom and the space constructed by English language teaching within the classroom walls. My consideration of classroom teaching also explored the ways in which teachers' earlier concerns regarding social inequalities were articulated with accounts of English language teaching practice. In this chapter, several threads that have arisen in these discussions come together, as I discuss aspects of gender that emerged in teachers' accounts of their English language teaching practice.

While most studies of gender in TESOL focus on learners, and studies of gender in development focus on gender 'problems' situated in host communities, I am interested here in the gender relations experienced by representatives of donor communities. This chapter looks at the ways in which several of the teachers saw themselves performing within gendered spaces that were established by the broader spatiality of development and educational institutions, and within a teaching space that was also a contact zone between different cultures. Throughout the chapter, the teachers' accounts of the way gender was played out in specific classrooms events vary significantly, and yet each account of students' experiences bears the embodied traces of history – of struggle, oppression and resistance – so close to the surface, and invites a response from the teacher as a participant in the spatiality of the classroom.

The teachers' accounts of gendered events are discussed in the light of four tensions in the teaching space. In relation to the teaching self, the first concerns the pedagogical tension between authority and nurturance, while the second concerns the tension between male–female gender relations and teacher–student pedagogical relations within the classroom. The third aspect that specifically affects the position of the Western teacher in the development context relates to the competing claims of gender equality and cultural sensitivity, while the fourth concerns the interaction of public, institutional space and personal, private space.

In the opening section of this chapter, I discuss the way these four tensions are explained in literature from feminist pedagogy and the discipline of TESOL. In the second section, I consider accounts of teachers taking authority in relation to the gendering of two differently located teaching spaces: in the classroom and in the kitchen of the teachers' residence. In the third section, I discuss the accounts of teachers' constrained authority in regard to the negotiation of difficult personal issues of gender, memory and contested spatial meanings. In one account, a young female teacher is challenged by a young male student; in another, questions of gender solidarity are examined; and in another, the extent of institutional interference in domestic space is questioned. In the final section, I consider an account of authority negotiated between teacher and students that involved dialogue across different understandings of gender and shifting boundaries of teaching space and time. In this account, teachers and students work together to approach an area of potential gender exploitation in the development context.

The Female Teacher, Gender and Culture

In Chapter 4, we have seen something of female teachers' discomforting experiences as gendered subjects within the context of international development: the experience of being read as gendered subjects and as objects of sexual discourse outside the classroom. We also saw how a sexualised identity was perceived to disappear once the women passed into the spaces established by the educational institution, and so became 'teachers'. As Gallop (1995: 81) notes, however, gender does not just disappear, since '*all* teaching takes place between gendered subjects'. Rather than disappearing, gender is merely performed differently in different spaces. In this section, I review discussions about the role of the female teacher in education and explore what the negotiation of femaleness and spatialised pedagogical authority might mean for the First World teacher in the Third World context.

Intersections of pedagogical authority and nurturance

The first theme of relevance to the teachers' accounts concerns the issue of how the female teacher performs with pedagogical authority. This theme addresses one of the hidden tensions of gendered relations in feminist pedagogy, between teacher authority and nurturance (C. Luke, 1996).

The development of a nurturing pedagogy has been historically associated with the 'march of progress' from an authoritarian, patriarchal, teacher-centred discipline towards a supposedly more 'natural', maternal, learner-centred model of teaching (Jones, 1990; McWilliam, 1999). In this modern pedagogical model of care and nurture, technologies of the self produce and govern both teacher and students as good, productive citizens and moral subjects supposedly without the intervention of external disciplinary control. However, as critical feminists have pointed out, by delineating a motherly role that 'served to keep women firmly entrenched as vital carers' and 'guardians of an impossible dream' (Walkerdine, 1992: 16, 22), such discourses reproduce essentialist notions of women as nurturers, and mask the authority inherent in the pedagogical relation.

The tension between a nurturing and authoritative role for the teacher is apparent in theories of feminist pedagogy, particularly as they relate to emancipatory ideals. More closely aligned with a discourse of nurturance, one trademark of liberal feminist pedagogies is said to be a 'blurring of boundaries between teachers and students' (Gallop, 1995: 80) and 'a decentering of the teacher's position, while students gain greater control of the classroom' (Norton & Pavlenko, 2004: 511). This democratic feminist model of pedagogy has been problematised as framing an idealised notion of the 'good teacher' and 'good teaching' as 'selfless, sexless nurturance' (Gallop, 1995: 83), while discounting the embodied, spatially specific power guaranteed the teacher by her location within hierarchical, institutional structures, and her responsibility to produce certain moral and educational outcomes. Liberal feminism has also been associated with the discourse of equal opportunity that emphasises emancipation through access and freedom of choice, but has been accused of neglecting underlying structural inequalities. In contrast, critical or radical feminist pedagogy has adopted a more transformative political agenda of actively working against structural social injustices in the form of sexism, racism, homophobia and so on. With this aim in mind, Luke (1996) urges feminist educators to 'disengage from their anxieties about authority and power' (p. 302), to 'assert her authority against the myth of the egalitarian classroom', and to lead students to 'see themselves and the world through different, and more (en)light(ening) lenses' (p. 291).

Intersections of gendered and pedagogical relations

A second, complicating paradox for the enactment of female teaching authority concerns the reversals of hierarchy implied in gender and pedagogical relations. When the normal gendered hierarchy implied between male and female is reversed in the pedagogical hierarchy between female teachers and male students, the teacher's authority can become compromised. The awkward question of sex may remain dormant as long as the student and teacher do not interact as man and woman, and the students remain in an infantilised and feminised position (McWilliam, 1999). However, in an event where a challenge is made to a female teacher's authority by a male student, the sexed bodies of both may materialise, and the assumed institutional authority of the teaching position is compromised by the reduction of the teacher to the space of her sexed body. As Gallop (1995: 80) aptly observes, '[h]owever much the teacher might dream of divesting her- or himself of authority so as to get closer to the female student, she or he clearly does not want it taken away by the insubordinate male student'.

This tension serves to remind us that, despite the obvious (female) gendering of the ELT profession, the teacher's *body* is curiously absent from TESOL studies of gender in language pedagogy, where the focus has been largely on texts (sexism in classroom materials and language use), or on gender as a variable in learners' cognition, rates of participation and achievement (Sunderland, 2000: 204). This focus on the rational and the cognitive in education has left the body as the 'excess baggage of pedagogy' (McWilliam, 1999: 133), and the complication of the sexed body of the teacher and/or the student in the classroom, where it is awkwardly out of place, is rarely discussed.

Intersections of gender and culture

The third issue of relevance concerns the teacher's classroom responsibility for relations of gender and culture, and particularly the implicit responsibility to ameliorate conditions of inequality that may exist within the students' community. This responsibility stems from the role of the school in the inculcation of moral and ethical standards, a role that historically has been at least as important as the transmission of disciplinary knowledge. More specifically, the role of the female schoolteacher as the guardian of European morality has historically involved enlightening and civilising the savages in the colonies, as the 'Other' of Western progress and culture (Jones & Ball, 1995; Loomba, 1998; Orford, 2002). Although the overt expression of such civilising discourses may be eschewed in contemporary practices of TESOL, it seems that certain traces remain. Thus, for English language teachers in development contexts, there may be an implied role, derived in part from human rights discourses, of working against the social and moral injustices of sexism, racism, poverty and so on. However, the various interests of social justice are sometimes in conflict, as can be seen in the debates between First World and Third World feminism on the issue of feminist cultural imperialism. So, for example, where distinctions of ethnicity and class place the white, middle-class teacher in a hierarchical position in relation to her students, classroom practices focusing on feminist emancipatory aims may be interpreted as part of the racist and classist 'civilizing legacies' of ESL (Schenke, 1991: 53). Critical and feminist approaches to second or foreign language education thus need to take account of postcolonial theories that deconstruct Western ethnocentrism and recognise 'important intersections between race, ethnicity, class, sexuality, geography, colonial tradition, and culture in shaping gender' (Pavlenko, 2004: 66).

The issue of potentially imposing Western feminist norms in non-Western, Third World contexts points to the risks associated with complicity in cultural and linguistic imperialism. On the one hand, the imposition of concepts seen to be derived from Western feminism may provoke a backlash from some sectors in developing countries. In East Timor, for example, Charlesworth (2008: 355) claims that the assertion of women's rights during the UN administration prompted a negative response from local groups, and 'traditional law and indigenous practices that disadvantage women were reinforced by religious conservatism and also by patriotic expressions of cultural pride by male leaders'. On the other hand, as critical scholars have pointed out, the construction of Third World women as victims of patriarchy based on 'less rational and enlightened cultural norms' reproduces the 'superiority of the West', diminishes the significance of ethnicity, class and nation (and in particular their colonial heritage), and problematically assumes that Western women are liberated and in control of their own lives (Mohanty, 2003: 41). In this regard it is useful to recall Spivak's (1994) argument that imperialism was justified as a civilising mission through the actions of 'white men, seeking to save brown women from brown men' (p. 101), misrepresenting indigenous gendered performances through Western discourses, and overlaying imperial, cultural, social, legal and religious meanings onto another cultural space, and onto the body of the Third World woman.

The potential dangers of feminist cultural imperialism may be deftly evaded by figuring TESOL as ahistorical, apolitical and therefore acontextual. Thus, the advice to foreign teachers that their role 'is not to effect change in its social and educational structure but rather to attempt to increase...students' proficiency in English as best they can within the existing structure' (McKay, 1992: ix–x) assumes that ELT *can* be detached from social context. However, this rule of non-interference is also problematic given the intertwining of social relations and language work, the complex positioning of foreign female teachers within translocal social and institutional networks, and donor requirements for the incorporation of approaches to address gender inequality in development programmes. For these reasons, for Western teachers in development contexts the question of *whose* gender norms are to apply is crucial.

Intersections of public and private space

A fourth related paradox for the female teacher involves the intersection between public space (the masculine sphere of civic, political life) and private space (the feminine sphere of domestic, family life). Two particular projections of this division are relevant here. First, on a global scale, the public domain has been mapped onto a vision of colonised space as the realm of heroic, masculine endeavour, where white women have traditionally been relegated to the private sphere in nurturing and civilizing roles as teachers and nurses (Mills, 1994). Second, in the educational domain, the civilising, nurturing role of the teacher has been incorporated into the public, institutional space of the school, and into the school's agenda of social regulation as it extends into the private spaces of the home and the family. According to Foucauldian analyses, the development of the modern school entailed 'a network of advice that linked the child to the school and the school to the family' in a complex 'technology for locating the urban family more precisely in a regime of power/knowledge' (Jones & Ball, 1995: 46). The nurturing teacher, in a caring and advisory relationship with the home, thus took up a tutelary interest in social relationships outside the classroom, specifically those concerned with the reproduction of society in the domestic space.

There are advantages (and risks) in an educational approach to social and political transformation that articulates the private and public domains through an engagement with students' lived experience and the historical and discursive construction of gender. Working with gendered discourses and lived experience in TESOL necessarily shifts the spatial focus of language learning outwards, beyond the classroom, to consider how gender and language are constructed in workplaces, homes, communities and so on. The increasing importance attributed to lived experience and social context beyond educational spheres has thus seen gender, language and education 'pushing the boundaries', 'moving out of classrooms' and out of English language environments (Davis & Skilton-Sylvester, 2004: 392).

At the same time, engaging with students' lived experience requires sensitivity to the balance between teacher authority and student privacy, between the institutional, panoptic spaces of the classroom and the spaces that students may not want to have colonised by the institutional gaze. Feminist pedagogy, combined with the imperatives of a communicative approach, encourages an engagement with difference by allowing speakers to communicate their personal experiences in a new language (Kramsch & van Hoene, 2001). However, while the teacher's desire for engagement can open up possibilities, these practices may also be read as coercive or as an act of appropriation that draws private lives into the domain of power, and risks colonising the learner 'as fodder for pedagogic talk and put[ting] on public display what should be after all a moment of private insight' (p. 299). Sensitivity to these potential intrusions requires that teachers do more than just 'replicate the power practices of benevolent, helping relations' (Schenke, 1996: 158) by interrogating their own complicity in the discourses that feminist pedagogy seeks to contest.

Working across the paradoxes

The paradoxes outlined above produce contradictory discourses within which the language teacher in development must perform, working within a masculinised public realm, with a framework that confers institutional authority, yet responding to a call to democratise the classroom; working against perceived gender inequalities, while remaining sensitive to cultural difference, and to the heterogeneity within that cultural difference. None of the teachers in this study professed to focus on gender as an issue in their classrooms, confirming Sunderland's (2000) observation that gender as a category remains of little importance in teacher perceptions of classroom practice. Gender nevertheless emerged in narratives of certain events where it is tied in with other axes of difference such as age, culture, political allegiance and institutional status. These accounts are arranged loosely in order, and move from images of authoritative spatial control, to images of a fragile and constrained spatial authority, and then to images of a more openly interactive exploration of gender and representation in the contact zone of language learning.

Teacher Authority and Gender Equality

In this section, I explore examples of how teachers utilised their institutional authority to implement practices of gender equality. As we have seen, the female teachers in development contexts experienced spatially confining gendered regimes, and had attempted to modify their own gendered performance in terms of dress, comportment and mobility, to comply with perceived culturally specific gender norms. However, as teachers entered the educational space of the campus, these gendered constraints were seen to diminish. As a product of the mutual constitution of social and spatial relations within the institution and the classroom, the teachers were conferred with institutional status and authority and, in this domain, no longer saw themselves as sexed or gendered subjects. Being invested with institutional authority, most teachers expressed a relative sense of control and comfort in the space of the classroom: in this space, gender wasn't perceived as 'a problem'.

Helen: Who speaks?

Teachers often suggested that gender was also not a problem of relevance for students inside the classroom, despite the low number of female students compared to male students enrolled in the English language programmes. In their recollections, teachers drew on discourses of equal opportunity, and an attribution of meaning to speaking and silence, to explain gender in terms of differences in classroom participation. Helen's view of the gender mix in her classroom recalled:

> *it wasn't- it was equal, it wasn't an issue, girls weren't- some girls were quiet, but so were some boys. I didn't find the girls were holding back at all. They were quite ready to criticise, they might wait for you, you know, to call them or something, nothing unusual about that. And the boys would be the sort of spokesmen, spokes-people, but not, certainly not in every case.*

Helen's hesitations here suggest some of the uneven ground teachers walk on when addressing or interpreting issues of gender in the classroom, where the focus is often on participation rates and talk time. In the context of Helen's experiences in the contact zone, gender disparities amongst her students were of less concern than problems of racial oppression and economic disparity between First World aid workers and the East Timorese community, and the realisation of her own uncomfortable location within First World privilege.

Elly: Equal access

However, in cases where equal access to educational resources *was* seen as a problem, teachers felt confident in using their authority to oppose what they perceived as relatively straightforward examples of sexism, and to reorganise the classroom space and time to enable gender equality. In Elly's classroom, *a minority of students in the class were women, and they tended to defer to the blokes, in the sense that the guys'd get on the computer [for writing practice] and just tap away and the women'd just sit back a little bit. But also, the women were often also running households at home and trying to feed kids and doing all that sort of stuff as well.*

Computer resources were limited, and to ensure equal access

we instituted a half-half rule so when half time was up they would change seats, so most of them would go with that, a couple of guys would hang on and hang on and hope that I wouldn't notice and the girls wouldn't say anything. And I'd just go over and chuck 'em off their chairs and put the women in the seat. And they didn't really mind, they were going to try it on, but they didn't chuck a fit when they got thrown off or anything. So I'd say they had a 'fair's fair' kind of concept, I think they just tried it on. [...] there were a few little things like that that I just kind of made practices 'cause otherwise they [the women] were missing out on little things.

Elly's authority in reorganising the classroom can be seen as a product of the mutual constitution of social and spatial relations within the institution, where the power to exercise spatial control is vested in the teacher. However, when reflecting on these interventions, Elly pointed to some of the contradictory discourses and doubts that troubled her in this simple exercise of authority. Like Helen, Elly had distanced herself from the patriarchal relations she perceived amongst the international community in the development context, and in her teaching role had expressed a desire to break down the hierarchies that positioned her above her students. At the same time, she expressed conflicting desires to be, on the one hand, a nurturing teacher, involved with students' lives, *'in there, proving my commitment to them'*, but, on the other hand, to be *'hands-off'* so as not to trample on privacy and cultural sensitivities. The possibility that her insistence on gender-equality practices may potentially represent an imposition that contradicted perceived Timorese cultural norms led to *'all sorts of contradictions in my head [...] I don't know the answer to this one. This is like a cultural relativism versus human rights argument and I never know what to think.'*

In line with her Marxist ideology, she concluded that eventually gender equality would come about in East Timor as a result of *'social and economic transformations'* in the *'phases of development'*, thus positioning women's development within the framework of temporal and materialist progress. In the meantime, she speculated that foreign teachers' introduction of gender-affirmative, equal opportunity practices may have achieved little in terms of addressing any underlying economic, cultural and political structures that hold women in a particular position within a particular society:

> I think that introducing some of those ideas, whether they get adopted now by say Timorese communities or not, is as much of an intervention as can be made. [. . .] But it doesn't surprise me at all that- you know, [hearing] that the NGOs withdraw and the village groups go back to their traditional ways, because none of the social structures have changed.

In these views, Elly confirms the observations of Charlesworth (2008) and Corcoran-Nantes (2009): the teacher was caught between the public institutional space of authority, which might insist on a formalised meaning of equality and access, and cultural structures that were assumed to be organised along different lines. Of course, at any stage of economic development, in both developing and developed societies, it is characteristically women who are working, studying, 'running households at home and trying to feed kids and doing all that sort of stuff as well', maintaining responsibility for the domestic/reproductive role of society despite gaining access to the public domain of productive labour.

Kate: Into the kitchen

Elly's authority to organise the space of the classroom according to liberal ideals of gender equality was apparently received with little resistance. However, greater difficulties arose where educational authority met with the gendered meanings of spaces outside the classroom, and where issues of gender equality confronted issues of cultural difference. In her teaching practices, Kate drew on TESOL discourses that presented Western language teaching qualifications and methods as more advanced than those practised in East Timor, thereby validating her authoritative role as a Western expert assisting the progress of development. The demonstration of these 'modern' methods was also seen as the primary organising principle of her lessons, with elements arising from the context, including issues relating to gender or cultural difference, remaining as a background for the lesson sequence.

Kate's lessons were mostly designed to demonstrate a mixture of text types and teaching methods, drawing on genre approaches that have been influential in a strand of critical literacy teaching in Australia. Such approaches claim to empower marginalised students through explicit instruction in 'powerful' forms of writing and speaking; however, they can tend to neglect local contingencies and be conservative of prevailing (or in the case of EFL, externally imposed) norms and hierarchies (A. Luke, 1996). For one particular lesson, Kate *'invited [the students] to all come to the house where we [foreign teachers] were living, and I got all the resources and we made pancakes'. 'We did it as a recount of our own experience, a language experience approach, and then converted it to a procedure thing, a recipe, for Shrove Tuesday [a Christian celebration], which turns out is a big deal up there [in East Timor].'*

Since the teaching method was to be *'hands-on'* and *'experiential'*, the class had shifted from the conventional classroom to the domestic space of the home, a move that raised particular aspects of the gendered meanings of space. In this account the teacher's authority to organise the teaching and learning space of the classroom was carried over into the domestic space of the home: *'I made a little bit of a cross-cultural faux pas, with insisting that everybody had to participate at all levels and that included the men washing up. [. . .] Carlos's eyes got as big as saucers, "You want me to do the washing up?!"'*

At this point, with Carlos indicating his resistance to Kate's directions, a number of different cultural discourses could have been invited into the discussion, and formed the basis of open enquiry. Considering that the cultural politics of Timor were at this point a relative unknown for the teacher, these might have included enquiries about patterns of interaction in Timorese domestic space or, since this event was situated in relation to a religious festival, the patterns of gender played out in Timor as a deeply Catholic country. Yet, in Kate's recollection, only one cultural perspective was made available:

> *I said* [flippantly] *'yeah, everybody can have a go'* [laughs]. *So I just made the point that if you're doing this sort of thing you just have it as an across the board rule that everybody has to wash their hands, everybody has to have some hands-on experience and participate, and that includes the cleaning up, and you don't get to- I said this is an English lesson, so although maybe it's culturally inappropriate in Timorese society, if we're exploring English and Australian styles of education it's something to explore. So I didn't impose it that it was better, I usually- and I probably told them that line too that, [when I was teaching] in Taiwan I very strongly said that it wasn't Western education practice or business practice was better than their style, but I wanted them to know how to eat with a knife and fork as well as with chop sticks, and to choose when it was appropriate to do it either way. So that got over a few humps in Taiwan, and I think I used the same story up there [in East Timor]. But I- at the time I didn't realise how strongly ingrained it was that a man would <u>never</u> do the washing [up].*

Despite the seeming simplicity and apparent triviality of the point at issue, the story invites some complex questions about the teacher's use of authority and expertise in different locations, the conflation of English language and Western moral and cultural norms, the balance between gender equality and cultural sensitivity. On the one hand, we see in this story the use of pedagogical authority to promote gender equality; we might also see, on the other hand, an imposition of stereotypes about gender and culture made through the moral gaze of the teacher and the eyes of Western discourse. Within a liberal framework of equality ('*everybody has to . . .*') and tolerance towards difference ('*it wasn't Western education . . . was better*'), Kate's account implies a set of confident generalisations: about gender equality being synonymous with English language communities; about the nature of gender *in*equity in other cultures; and about individual freedom to choose particular ways of performing gender. Presented through a singular authoritative position, and relying on constructions of Third World women and men as subjects of unenlightened patriarchy, these gender stereotypes maintain the superiority of the West, diminish the significance of ethnicity, class and nation (particularly in their relation to colonial heritage), and can misleadingly imply that Western men and women enjoy equality in relation to such domestic drudgery.

In this incident, negotiating the balance between norms of gender equality and cultural sensitivity became more difficult as teacher and students moved outside of the classroom to a non-institutional domestic space, and the requirement for the students' bodily, hands-on performance of gender seemed to provoke a degree of resistance. The invocation of cultural appropriacy also opened questions of *which* cultural context is assumed to be relevant, and *whose* cultural norms should apply, leaving a rather shaky connection between the language lesson and the supposed context of use. With these sticky problems, the teacher is working in a difficult terrain, at the boundary between (contested) Western notions of gender and the domain of cultural sovereignty that remains unknowable when opportunities for interrogation and enquiry are bypassed.

Curiously, in some locations beyond the educational domain, Kate held Timorese cultural/gender norms to be paramount, and expected that foreign women should conform to those geographically specific standards. We might recall from Chapter 4, for example, that the beach was a site of intense transcultural struggles over gender performance and appropriateness, conformity, visibility and agency. It was in this contested public domain that Kate ardently upheld what she saw as a Timorese gender code, to the extent of condemning Western women who flouted what were deemed to be spatially appropriate norms:

I think some of the young Americans and Australians are begging for trouble with what they wear to swimming and stuff like that and, you know, they just think what's appropriate for us here [in Australia] is appropriate for us there [in East Timor], whereas we [Kate and her colleagues] all went [to the beach] in these long legged things.

The tricky crossroads of gender and culture emerge yet again at this site. In a place well outside the English language classroom, where her professional authority was significantly lessened, Kate identified with a different set of authoritative regulations. Identifying with those who have the moral superiority and power to effect spatial control in the public domain, Kate upheld the gender rules that veil the female form, implicitly approving the 'punitive consequences' for young Western women who 'fail to do their gender right' in this particular place (Butler, 1990: 193).

If we return now to look again at the domestic domain in the immediate, intercultural context, a further aporia is evident: my own observations of the domestic space of aid workers' houses indicated that Timorese staff mostly performed the domestic labour for foreign professionals who worked in the public domain. In these houses, it seemed neither the white women nor the white men ever did the washing up. In that particular context, domestic work was marked not only by gender and culture, but also by ethnicity and class. Thus, it seems despite the liberal, nurturing discourse of equality, the neglect of specificities of context and the traces of cultural superiority that linger in the tenets of ELT risked producing an authoritative speaking position for the teacher 'that sees the "other" as the problem for which they are the solution' (Lather, 1992: 132).

The movement of teacher and students outside the classroom has the potential to disrupt settled patterns of knowledge and power that inhere in the space of the classroom; however, this move is not without risk, given the power of the institution and the language to reach into other spaces and impose different (and purportedly superior) cultural meanings. A way forward for teachers struggling with such difficulties could be to start with an exploration of 'spatial practices' (de Certeau, 1984) that resist universalist narratives of progress and univocal, authorised versions of how gendered spaces should be constituted. Spatial practices are those that engage with the multiplicity of stories and memories in any context or place, and may emerge when students (and teachers) are invited 'to present their own stories, on their own terms, and through their own eyes' (Asher & Smith Crocco, 2001: 135). Opening up enquiry into situated, gendered experiences could highlight, on the one hand, a less than ideal domestic situation in the teacher's Australian home location, where women continue to spend much more time in unpaid domestic work than do men (Australian Bureau of Statistics, 2006). Alternatively, a closer look at the immediate intercultural, development context of Timor would have demonstrated how gender is entangled with other dimensions of difference in the domestic and public domains, in the kitchen and on the beach. These diverse experiences of domestic and public space would seem to offer fruitful places for enquiry, for disrupting colonial legacies, and developing critical insights and agency amongst both teachers and students.

Constrained Authority and Student Consent

Although teachers are vested with the institutional authority to control the space of the classroom, the performance of authority is also relational, and dependent on student consent. In the following accounts, the teachers' authority was constrained by student resistance, and an awareness of being outsiders on someone else's turf. In the first account, the teacher perceived that a male student's overt challenge to her authority was enabled by gendered relations within the contested space of the classroom. In the remaining accounts the restraint on teachers' authority to act or speak about gender relations was self-imposed and founded on the teachers' sensitivity to being the outsider in another cultural space.

Dana: The male student's challenge

In the student-controlled university campus of East Timor, the normal presumptions of teaching and administrative authority were clearly contested by student agency. The students' rights to control the educational space rested not only on their ownership of the campus, but also on their ownership of the programme they had lobbied the United Nations to initiate. Moreover, the majority of the students were young males, a number of whom had been actively involved in the fight for liberation, and were currently involved in the struggle for representation in national governance. In this context, the teaching space was a highly contested site and several teachers commented that they moderated their usual performance of authority in consideration of their own status as interlopers in this political domain. For Dana, the youngest of the female teachers, the experience of teaching in the student-controlled campus was particularly unsettling.

Her story demonstrates how the normal rules that prescribe authority in the space of the classroom were destabilised by the unexpected eruption of performances that, from her point of view, belonged outside the classroom, but were enabled by the gendered relation between a young female teacher and a young male student.

As a relatively recent university graduate, Dana expressed a sense of being 'out of place' in the position of authority on the campus:

> *I remember walking in on that first day and it feeling a little bit, um, intimidating, and um, I don't know- on the one hand it was great to be working in the university, but it was weird to be um, like, the university administration, where, you know, we'd been used to- I'd been used to being the student when I was on campus, so it was kind of weird to be in a different role.*

Her sense of place was further troubled as she became aware of the political implications of the teaching role. Like other teachers and project managers, she had believed that teaching itself was not a political activity, and that politics did not belong in the classroom; but because of the contested nature of the physical site she became aware of the political position she occupied:

> *I remember those first couple of meetings we had [between teachers and student leaders] and there were problems with organisation and all that kind of stuff, that was quite sort of disorienting, 'cause we were there to just teach and there were all these political problems and that was sort of quite- was a little bit difficult at the start.*

Dana's uncertainty about her institutional authority also accentuated the gap between herself and the students in the classroom: '*I found the whole situation of being there pretty tricky*'. Her unease focused on an incident in the classroom where one student, angry with the misadministration of the whole project, stood up in class to make a public declaration.

> *I had one student who was so angry about everything that had happened that he decided to stand up in my class and make a declaration against the whole project and, um, you know, give a big speech about how the project was not working and, um, you know, a list of complaints about the classes and that sort of thing.*

Dana felt that most of the complaints were unreasonable demands for greater access to the limited resources; however, one complaint which she felt was '*totally justified*' was that the students '*should have been taught in Indonesian*' by Indonesian-English bilingual teachers, since that was the language of instruction most familiar to the students. As a monolingual language teacher, Dana saw herself as the victim of institutional and disciplinary policies that favoured native speakers of English: *'I felt horrendous, I felt attacked, and pretty kind of freaked out. I found it was very hard not to take it on personally as a criticism of my teaching, 'cause there I was teaching in English, you know, because I'd been put in that position'*. On the whole, however, the young man's challenge to the teacher's authority to control the space of the classroom was interpreted as a misplaced performance by the student: it was *'inappropriate'* in that space. Dana surmised that the student's behaviour was probably related to his history of involvement in student politics, the liberation struggle and *'fighting the Indonesians'*. This *'culture of political activism'* had been transferred into the classroom, but *'it was not the appropriate forum to raise the issues that he was raising'*. An example, perhaps, of learner-centred democracy gone too far?

As Dana's sense of authority slipped, the male student's challenge recalled the gendered vulnerability she experienced in the public spaces outside the classroom: *'I always find that as a young female teacher that you always get challenged a bit more, because of your gender and because of your age'. 'I don't think he would have done that in [a male teacher's] class for example. And you know, I think I was less confident at that point too, so as soon as you've got a young female teacher who isn't maybe quite as confident as, say an older male teacher, sometimes that can be tricky.'*

Dana's confidence and sense of control had relied on the predictable performance of well-planned lessons unfolding in an orderly sequence of activities but, following this incident, her scripted control appeared to be compromised by the fear of unpredictable challenges from her male students. The classroom now became an unknown terrain, a space of uncertainty: *'I found it difficult to relax with the students, I found it difficult to relax with them. And you know, there were times when I was a little bit, um, a little bit wary of what was gong to happen next, um, that was mainly with the male students, some of the younger male students.'* In this space, simultaneously constituted by the weight of educational authority, by gendered hierarchies, and by a student politics of liberation struggles, who gets to be *'standing up in class and doing the speech'*?

In this event the disordering of classroom space may appear to signal what Gallop (1995) identifies as the intrusion of conventional gender relations ('male–female games') into the expected pedagogical hierarchy between teacher and student ('student–teacher games'). However, the added complication of the teacher being a cultural and political outsider, rather than in a position of institutional ownership and control, further confused what could be considered appropriate in this contested space, and points to a reading that focuses on the student's challenge to traces of cultural imperialism in the structuring of the educational programme, as evidenced, for example, in the appointment of monolingual English speakers. In this sense, our focus shifts away from the bodies of the individual female teacher and the individual male student to the location of gender within conventional ELT and development policies and practices that potentially disadvantaged both the teachers and students.

Despite Dana's objection to the challenge posed by her student, and her awareness of the tenuous nature of her (gendered) authority in the classroom, the lesson she described here cannot be understood in isolation. It could be juxtaposed with her pleasure in a contrasting lesson where students initiated a more collaborative resistance to outsider control, by generating a spontaneous *'discussion on Timor and what was the future, problems that Timor is facing and solutions'*. Like the declaration made by her young male student, this discussion also arose from students' dissatisfaction with a development agenda controlled by international organisations, and yet it offered for Dana a more productive engagement across difference. Abandoning her well-practised lesson plan and relinquishing her own desire for a class controlled by teacher-designed activities, Dana stepped back as students took the floor, arranging themselves into groups to name pressing problems facing the new nation, and to work on their own proposals for future action. She saw herself neither as the teacher-in-authority providing technical instruction and expertise in *'the mechanics of learning a language'* nor as a victim of masculine anger. Rather, she was a *'special guest'*, a witness who could listen to students' concerns and proposals to shape different futures. This instance of language use went beyond being relevant, and instead opened up the space of the classroom to chance (from the teacher's point of view), to student agency in creating something new, and to 'the openness of the future, its relative connection to but also freedom from the past, the possibilities of paths of development, temporal trajectories uncontained by the present' (Grosz, 1999: 4). In a landscape that was overrun with masculinised, international plans for development, this forum facilitated students' agency to construct and embody their own plans for a new nation, moving towards a critical engagement between language and translocal space. For Dana, these experiences provoked a disturbance to previous ways of seeing the world and the place of teaching in that world, and *'raised a great deal of political awareness'* about the nature of English language teaching and of her own location within structures of racial authority, economic privilege and cultural imperialism that disadvantage others. Despite Dana's awareness of the tenuous nature of her authority in the classroom, on reflection she described her teaching in East Timor as '*the most rewarding thing I have done in my life thus far*'.

Ann: Not my place

Cultural sensitivity, an awareness of not necessarily being in a position of knowing, and uncertainty surrounding their outsider status prevented most teachers from initiating the explicit incorporation of questions relating to gender as a topic for discussion into their classroom teaching. This was particularly the case in regard to the impact of gender-specific torture and trauma in students' lives which several teachers believed was manifest in an immobilising fear amongst their female students who were, in Fay's words, '*just totally freaked out [...] all those poor students, like those girls, who sat there and couldn't do anything [they] were just totally freaked out. One or two of them persevered, but they just sat there rigidly, and I don't think actually finished [the course]. They were just terrified by the whole thing.*' Sensitivity on the part of teachers, and resistance from students, appeared to foreclose the possibility of historical engagement with gendered memories in the public arena of the classroom (Schenke, 1996); instead, the following accounts suggest how teachers allowed students to regulate the extent and the ways in which gender was explicated.

The notion of a boundary between what could or could not be used for pedagogic talk emerged in Ann's reflections on her experience with a group of Timorese women activists. During her time in East Timor, Ann had become aware of the activities of GFFTL (Grupo Feto Foinsa'e Timor Lorosa'e: East Timor Young Women's Group), a '*group of young female university students [who] took it upon themselves to organise a literacy campaign and to help women in particular*'. These women students had recounted to Ann their experiences of private trauma, and in their current role as educators had taken on a more active, public approach to gender-related problems. Ann's encounter with the young women affected her own personal experience and sense of place in East Timor, but was separated from her more public role in teaching:

> *I went with them and I went to their locations, I travelled with them and then I also interviewed those young women, about the official language and the national language and about their memories of the Indonesian times, was there anything positive in the Indonesian period, lots of things that therefore were political. This was not to do with my teaching, but it was very much to do with my experience. And that's when I heard the stories and where I lay awake at night. [...] Yes, they had people chopped to death in front of them. Some of them had to hide in the mountains for two years with nothing, no*

shoes on their feet and no food, begging for food from farmers. And it shook me to the core, it really did.

Although the stories the women told her were deeply affecting, they were not hers to colonise for pedagogic talk in the classroom: '*I had immense admiration for them, and it affected me very much. But in my teaching it really didn't come up at all, it wasn't alluded to and I could see it was not my place to allude to it.*' Ann's deep concern for students' personal lives outside the classroom, where she became, at times, intimately involved in their family lives, health problems and economic difficulties, stood in marked contrast to her technical approach to ELT, where she constructed her professional performance through conventional discourses of method, native speaker standards and a predictable sequencing of language lessons that just '*rattled along*'. As well as respecting the students' private space, her dislocation of the private and public/pedagogic domains in this way was also in accordance with her resolve not to become enslaved by a nurturing pattern of teaching that had seen her personal life consumed by her professional life and left her '*physically, mentally and emotionally worn down in Sulawesi*'. In East Timor, her determination to maintain the boundary of her own private space meant '*I wasn't on overload like I was in Sulawesi, and I felt like I was in control*'.

Yet Ann had her own experiences of diminished control within gender relations in East Timor, and these she might have shared, had the boundaries of public and private, teaching and non-teaching remained porous. Her experiences of walking in the streets of Dili had initially been carefree, she '*never felt any threat to my security*', and the regard she felt from the Timorese community was similar to the value she was accorded in Sulawesi:

> *I didn't mind walking anywhere, and I didn't mind walking in the pitch dark where there were no lights, and [I thought] all the people round here know me, and I felt there was safety in that. Walking through the markets every day, even though people would say, 'oh the marketplace is dangerous', but all the shop keepers knew me and called out to me and I always thought, if there's ever any trouble, I think they'd help me, I really do.*

However, this sense of regard and protection collapsed when, walking home alone one night, she was followed and grabbed by a man: '*I guess I was shocked, and my reaction was to yell at him, and I yelled at him in Indonesian, and I said: "I live here, I have lots of friends here, if I yell right now you are in big danger. Get out of here! Go!"*'

The man fled, but the incident changed her sense of self in public space:

> *What I found after that, I was so furious because I thought: you've just spoilt it for me, up till now I didn't mind walking anywhere, [...] but after that, I thought: I can't go out on my own any more. Suddenly I was really conscious of that, especially at night time, but I was more wary all the time. I was so angry that I should have to be. And I did think later: come on, you know, that can happen anywhere in the world, not just in Timor.*

In contrast to the adoration that she had felt in Sulawesi, where gender *'wasn't really a problem'*, this incident prompted Ann to reconsider her position in the social order; however, the incident was not framed as a story about white women needing protection from the malevolent desires of brown men. Anger over the individual attack, and its implications for her sense of worth and freedom, her sense of belonging, was rationalised, naturalised and transformed into a recognition of what she saw as women's universal experience: a restriction on mobility enforced by the threat of violence. This was an experience that could have been shared, but then again, with its dynamic interplay of gender and ethnicity, it is a story that could be read in many different ways, with the attendant risks of reinforcing racial stereotypes. Perhaps not every personal struggle can be displayed in the classroom for political or gender solidarity.

Jane: Don't talk about it

Like Ann, Jane felt her students actively separated from the classroom space those issues she assumed arose from on-going gender relations in their personal lives. Her experiences indicated the complex movement of gender between a public, institutional space of the school, and a private space of home and family. In a class of students she described as *'quiet'* and less *'politically active'*, her account of one event suggested how the students used the organisation of space within the classroom to keep private issues secluded from the panoptic gaze of the classroom.

> *In the [class] I had a woman who- she came in one day with a black eye and word had it that her husband had bashed her, but it was very much, 'Don't talk about it, don't mention it' [...] She came in and she was very- there were two women and one sort of protected the other, like, she kind of slid into the seat. [She normally] never sat to the back of the room, she was always at the front, and she and this friend sat up the back, close to the window. I guess from body language, I knew she had been abused. [...] The one that had been abused was sitting against the wall, so the other one- so there was no way that I could get around her.*

This created a deal of uncertainty for the teacher in knowing whether and how to acknowledge the situation. Her deliberations initially indicated a pull towards a nurturing discourse in which the teacher assumes responsibility to intervene, to extend her pedagogical interest into the private domain of family life:

Fay: *I certainly needed to go back to the college, back to the [person in charge] and say, 'What do I do, how do I deal with this? Or don't I? Or, what is it?' [. . .]*

Ros: So how did you decide to deal with it?

Fay: *Um, I didn't. I didn't like myself for not doing anything, um, and, but I did speak about it, not about it [in class], I sought guidance in it.*

Jane's institutional enquiries confirmed suspicions that her student had been identified as a victim of domestic violence, but any move towards pedagogical intervention risked aligning her with an intrusive institutional agenda of social monitoring and regulation. Her discussion of various options with another development worker touched on the spatial complexity of this dilemma, and ultimately pointed to her own impotence as an outsider: *'Well okay, what <u>can</u> you do? You can say, "You need to go somewhere", [but] where does this woman go when this happens? Um, there is nowhere for her to go. You can say, "Come here" [to my house], and then you have, then you are, you don't <u>know</u> culturally what you're doing.'*

Jane's account does not confine the problem in question to a specific culture or national location, thereby avoiding the implication that gendered violence had been solved in the West, and could be solved in the Third World by Western intervention. The teacher's deliberations suggested how the sensitive issue of gender relations linked the spaces of the home, the community and the classroom, demonstrating how the social, cultural and spatial aspects of the dilemma were mutually constituted. Yet, despite this tacit intersection with the classroom, the boundaries marked by the students and by the community limited the teacher's authority and involvement in these experiences, and in turn constrained her authority within the classroom to approach the problem of violence as a significant dimension of gender relations. To engage with the complexity of factors at play without breaching students' privacy, Jane might have taken up the work of autobiography (Schenke, 1991), and generated enquiry into her own experiences in the contact zone of development. As we have seen in Chapter 4, on the streets and on the beaches, female teachers had been exhorted to modify their dress, only venture into public space in pairs, and stay home at night, inducing a sense of gendered spatial restriction and fearfulness. Bearing in mind the potential risks, identified in Ann's experience, of reinforcing racial stereotypes, sharing these personal, situated experiences could potentially have supplied a rich source of gender-focused discussion that drew on the cultural and political perspectives and expertise of both students and teacher.

In sum, far from describing a transparent institutional space controlled by the teacher as a knowing subject, and a linear progress towards emancipatory goals, the teachers' accounts in this section have demonstrated how spaces and places were co-constructed through the various gendered and racialised relations and meanings brought to the classroom by teachers and students. As outsiders to East Timorese politics, history and culture, the institutional authority exercised by the teachers was rendered tenuous and contingent, open to contestation around issues of territoriality, students' agency and rights to ownership and privacy. Gendered meanings were entangled with culturally and contextually embedded patterns of public and private space that also limited the power of the First World teacher to institute normative visions of social justice. The authority of the female teacher was therefore spatially structured not only in a complex set of power, gender and knowledge relations within the classroom, but also between the classroom and communities beyond the classroom walls.

Negotiating Authority and Difference

While Jane's story demonstrates some of the constraints on the outsiders' potential to effect change across cultural boundaries, Carol's experience illustrates an approach that addresses gender explicitly at the site of cultural difference in the contact zone *between* communities. Rather than seeing the students' community as the location of gender trouble, this last story explores gender as a complex interplay of discursive representation and lived experience between two cultures that have come into contact both inside and outside the language classroom.

Carol: Out to see for ourselves

Carol's class comprised a group of students at the university with a higher level of English language proficiency, and her account illustrates the way her own authority meshed with a flow of bodies, texts and ideas across the classroom wall, prompting a revision of her institutional authority and enabling student control in constituting the classroom space. Of her classroom authority, she recalled:

> *it took me a little while, I was trying to be an English teacher, and wanting them to follow my course, and suddenly I realised, they didn't only want*

English, they needed to communicate with each other about what was happening [outside the classroom]. English became the medium for it, and of course the discussions went on in breaks and lunchtime, when they were out of the classroom, it would continue in Tetum then. But in class they endeavoured to express what they felt in English.

The students insisted on selecting '*the issues they talked about*', signalling the flow of political and personal ideas that entered the classroom. The organisation of space within the classroom then became a negotiation between this flow of ideas and the structure that Carol felt her students still expected her to provide, yielding a crucial connection between the political meanings of the local place, disciplinary knowledge and language learning: '*if they were going to give a narrative of something that had happened, we did narrative, past tense, you know, we did the grammar associated with it*'. This combination of grammatical structure and emotional memories might seem odd, but Carol believed the routines of the English class allowed for an escape, and for moving on. She felt her students wanted neither '*for us to just be sympathising with them*' nor to '*dwell on*' all that had happened in the past. Rather, English classes perhaps represented a way '*to get back, get back on track, get back to routine*', a way to '*get back to a structure and get things moving again*' into the future.

Carol had initially assumed the relatively small number of women in the class '*was because they were a macho society*', but then '*one of the women told me that during the- a lot of the women weren't educated to that level because, when they set off to school during the Indonesian occupation they didn't come home. Parents would keep them at home, hide them, because the soldiers would wait for them.*' Yet despite, or perhaps because of this history, in Carol's class the young women students were particularly outspoken on matters of gender politics: '*I had a fair few really strong women in the afternoon group and they used to often clap, spontaneously, when it came to an issue talking about women playing a strong role, there were very strong feelings about things*'. In an indication of their strength and solidarity, the young women introduced private experiences into the public domain, raising issues to do with the specific effects of Indonesian occupation on Timorese women, and women's present subordinate position in Timorese society. The critical point here is that the women students themselves opened these discussions and, in doing so, voiced the concerns of female Timorese scholars that a 'strong culture of patriarchy has developed over a long time in Timor-Leste, however, it can change' (de Araujo, 2007: 16).

In deference to the students' expertise and ownership, Carol initially took the role of a bystander and listener in students' discussions on women's roles and experiences. Rather than seeing herself as the author and centre of classroom action: *'I tried not to give an opinion actually. [. . .] I didn't want them to think the Western way, 'cause I was still trying to understand what- how the men and women's roles were in East Timor, I didn't feel I could impose our ideas until I knew what was happening there really'.* Although Carol was aware of serious debates within the Timorese community about the perception and treatment of women who had suffered under the occupation, as an outsider she was reluctant to use her pedagogical authority to initiate a classroom discussion focusing directly on these topics. Listening, rather than proffering solutions, suggested a contingent reversal of the hierarchies she perceived as inherent in the development context.

When she did speak, instead of directly expressing her opinion on the issues of gender subordination and reconciliation, she chose to share her own memories and embodied experiences as a Western woman, and the way she felt she was perceived as a white female teacher in Indonesia:

> *[The Indonesians] looked on Western women as prostitutes really, and so I talked about that, and I talked about some of my experiences in Bali, how it was supposed that I was a prostitute by some of the Muslim teachers, and I told them about- I told them of a couple of experiences I had [. . .] to add fuel for their own debates, to get them going, to motivate discussion, to get them all going on it really.*

Drawing connections between her own experiences in Indonesia and the Timorese context, Carol felt that open displays of sexual behaviour by some Western women aid workers, including teachers, had led Timorese men to draw similar conclusions about all Western women: *'they thought all Western women were going to do it'.* The students' concerns about the negative influence of Western sexual mores centred on rumours about the *Hotel Olympia*, a floating hotel docked in Dili harbour to provide accommodation for UN personnel. The *Olympia* became the site for the students' and teacher's engagement and exploration of difficult gender issues: *'Amongst the students, yes they did talk about that, they talked about not wanting their women to be like Western women, and that the boat, Olympia, was being used for prostitution. So that's when I thought, well we'd better go down and see for ourselves.'* A trip to the *Olympia* was planned.

Approaching the *Olympia* was also set in the context of Carol's beliefs about Timorese ownership in the reconstruction process. For Carol, an important aspect of the students' learning English was to equip them with *'confidence to participate in the UNTAET governing and reconstruction of their country'*; she wanted them to use English to *'know what was happening and to seek correct information'*. With this purpose in mind, classroom practice in asking and answering questions prepared students for excursions into institutions in which English functioned as a lingua franca, such as the UN offices. Together, Carol and her students had ventured into several UN and NGO locations, at the heart of the development bureaucracy, to enquire about plans for reconstruction, and about potential employment opportunities. These institutional domains were places that might not otherwise have been easily accessible to Timorese students, since they were heavily guarded against unofficial entrants. In this regard, the teacher's and students' collaborative movement beyond the classroom was aimed at *'giving them confidence to enter institutions and make them realise that the country was now theirs'*.

In the company of a foreign teacher, and equipped with questions practiced in the English classroom, the students visited the *Olympia*, where *'they were seeing for themselves, because they were hearing rumours, and they hadn't been- they didn't know they were allowed to go to these places, 'cause under Indonesian rule and under Portuguese rule, I guess they were not easily able to go into public places, they were intimidated by these places'*. Working with her students' sense of sovereignty and territoriality, Carol used her teaching authority not to impose Western ideals and solutions, but as a means of gaining access to a place normally off-limits to Timorese students, and so to leverage a practical interrogation of gendered effects in a specific transcultural context of development. Gender trouble was not perceived or presented as a problem solely confined to the Timorese community, to be judged through a normative liberal vision of equality. Rather, gender was discussed in Carol's language lessons as a series of discursive constructions, and approached through an engagement with the lived experiences of both teacher and students in the cultural contact zones *between* communities. In this sense, a focus on the multiple contact zones where diverse cultures interact opened up enquiry about the way in which the very presence of a hypermasculine foreign community could impact on the construction of gender relations between communities in a specific context. In the case of the *Olympia*, any gender problems that existed were sustained not by presumed patriarchal relations in the host community, but by the presence of a wealthy, masculine, international community.

Threaded through this teacher's account was a pedagogical practice that focused on how women's bodies were read in a range of conflicting discourses, from different points of view, and in different cultural locations. As well as making space for the students' interests in and experiences of gender, the teacher incorporated her own lived experience into the classroom discussion, forming a counterpoint to the usual image of the teacher as a disembodied, sexless professional (Gallop, 1995). However, this not only raised challenging topics in the classroom (prostitution and overtly sexual behaviour) but also, for a time, placed the teacher's body at the centre of attention, a move that could prove uncomfortable and confronting for some classroom teachers. For this particular teacher with a particular group of forthright students, an approach of reading gender in different contact zones enabled a negotiation of conflicting gender norms, and addressed slippery questions around cultural assumptions and representations as they intersected with highly contextualised questions of territorial and colonial occupation, cultural juxtapositions and societal change.

In one sense, the outcome of the class's investigation was inconclusive, in that we have no firm knowledge that practices of prostitution on the *Olympia*, if they did exist, were abolished. Indeed, reports of sexual exploitation by militarised donor organisations continue to surface not only in relation to Timor (Joshi, 2007; Murdoch, 2006), but also on a global scale (Mazurana *et al.*, 2005). Nevertheless, Carol's story points to an alternative, more exploratory way of addressing certain experiences or effects of gender in the context of language teaching and learning, one that avoids an easy rhetoric of solutions imposed from a position of supposed Western superiority, and begins to work collaboratively with the various interests, values and agency of both students and teacher.

Gender as Spatial Pedagogy

In these narratives, we have seen some of the challenges that English language teachers face when attending to gender as a dynamic dimension of their intercultural ELT practice. Although international development policies that frame the teachers' work propose an ideal notion of progress towards gender equality, the teachers' dilemmas and difficulties highlight a challenge to the imposition of Western norms in other cultural contexts, and are evidence of a practice that comprises significant complexities and contradictions. The relative detachment of the classroom from the world beyond allowed the teacher, in some instances, to establish certain gender rules applicable to the contained space of the classroom, but this authority did not necessarily extend to an engagement with cultural practices of gender as they were experienced in the world outside the classroom. For most of the teachers in these development contexts, it was not simply a matter of acting with a spatially conferred, institutional authority to help their students towards enlightenment (C. Luke, 1996) or to develop intercultural competence in gender issues (Norton & Pavlenko, 2004). Rather, their pedagogical practice was a matter of working in a borderland that was inscribed with strong but contradictory demands.

The challenges that teachers faced as they moved outside the institutional space were particularly pronounced in the physical and symbolic shift from the classroom to the domestic domain: this shift potentially opened up more difficult questions of cultural difference and the presumed knowability of gendered meanings in diverse spaces. The transfer of the teacher's institutionally conferred authority raised questions about the privilege of an outsider to ascribe the appropriate norms and gendered meanings within another cultural context. For teachers to diagnose and propose solutions for gender problems identified within a host community seems particularly ironic when, in the contact zone of development, gender equality rhetoric sits uneasily with the patriarchal regimes of development and hegemonic masculinities of military intervention. The spatial shift from public to private, and across cultural boundaries, thus opens a difficult area for teachers as local gender relations are too easily subject to ethnocentric stereotyping and generalisations, and become an object of improvement. Through these discourses and practices, classroom agendas are drawn into a narrative of progress that privileges an imagined Western ideal, and the relics of colonial hierarchy are potentially reinscribed in the active interventions and civilising legacies of English language work.

Rather than focusing on gender as a problem located within the host community, a more productive approach could involve teachers and students engaging with gender as a meaning making activity in the transcultural encounters and relationships of the postcolonial contact zone. In these difficult circumstances, rather than rushing to a quick success by advancing principles of gender equality derived from a position of supposed cultural superiority, there is value in staying within the grey area of uncertainty, 'remaining open and vulnerable' to 'what is not, or cannot, be fully known and controlled' (Ellwood, 2006: 68). Although there are no prescriptions possible with a practice that emerges from contingency, we might begin by framing gender within transcultural encounters, and question the effects on gendered embodiment and spatiality of being in the contact zone of development. This then entails opening a space for exploring the ways in which gender and other dimensions of difference are played out in students' experiences and perceptions; and for examining the teachers' own gendered, yet ambiguously complicit, experiences in the contact zones between communities engaged in development. In either case, teachers and students together need to step outside the classroom, physically or symbolically, to engage with the way gender is taken up in the social, economic and political visions and performances of development as a postcolonial, transcultural process.

Chapter 7
Conclusion: Spatial Practices in the Contact Zone

What the map cuts up, the story cuts across.
de Certeau, 1984: 129

The narrative accounts of teachers, in their stories of alienation and disorientation, anxiety and engagement have, I hope, given some new insights into a politics of English language teaching and gender relations in the context of international development. By exploring teachers' narrative accounts of living and teaching in development, through an interpretive framework of time and space, I have drawn attention to the complex relationship between the everyday micro-processes of living and teaching, and the broader social, political and historical discourses of education and development that privilege time and progress over space in the construction of a complex, intercultural sense of place. In proposing the notion of spatiality as a useful tool for exploring English language teaching, my aim has been not only to illuminate struggles and challenges, but also to identify opportunities for a critical, political, engagement with context. In this final chapter, I draw together the arguments that have arisen in the discussion of teachers' accounts, and consider implications for the practice of English language teaching as a critical contextualised performance.

In my engagements with the teachers' narratives, I have attempted to explore the problems of approaching English language teaching as a certain script, or map, of 'what we already know'. Through the teachers' eyes, we have seen how conventional discourses and practices of English language teaching, gender and development mobilise understandings of time and space that limit interaction between communities, teachers and students, language and contexts, and channel the present towards a narrow vision of the future. On the other hand, we have looked at practices that take the disorientation of uncertainty, ambivalence and 'not knowing' as a point of departure for moving towards a more flexible, social and pedagogical engagement with temporality and spatiality,

209

in ways that open up different possible futures for a globalised world. A spatial hermeneutic has, hopefully, extended understandings of English language teaching in the context of development, and offered some insight into how and why familiar pedagogical routines crash and burn in the heat of racial and gendered encounters in the contact zone, and how productive possibilities can emerge from uncertainty, by opening our practice to a critical spatiality. This has been a process of rethinking the relation between everyday social and pedagogical experiences and the constraints of historical development, gender regimes and disciplinary knowledge; and a process of reconnecting English language teaching with the translocal and transcultural movements and flows of a globalised world.

In all, analysis of the teachers' narratives suggests that orthodox ELT principles and practices provide an inadequate basis for a critical engagement between language, gender and the development context. All teachers espoused the conventional wisdom of relating language learning to the context of use, and many recognised the development context as one divided by the deeply worn, discursive and material hierarchies that sustained unequal privilege and devalued local communities in their interaction with development communities. Yet the scripting of teachers' discourse and performance by, on the one hand, an overarching temporal narrative of developmentalism and, on the other hand, modernist institutional, industrial and disciplinary regimes of time and space, tended to exclude possibilities for teachers' and students' productive, transformative engagement with knowledges and experiences available in the world outside the classroom. Just as temporal relations in the development context support social, cultural, economic, gender and political hierarchies between donor and recipient communities, so related hierarchies of knowledge and practice may be structured into the performance of language teachers through the temporal narratives and orthodoxies of ELT in a way that replicates development patterns of domination and subordination. In effect, the dominant emphasis on time in English language teaching, geared towards a liberal vision of progress, has neatly aligned orthodox ELT with mainstream notions of international development, and has tended to overshadow an engagement with a spatial politics that values and affirms a complex, coexisting, transcultural multiplicity. By contrast, spatial practices and critical engagements with the specificities of place offered teachers a means of challenging developmental hierarchies that both devalue local discourse and knowledges, and sustain social, political and economic patterns of inequality.

Teachers' Journeys in Development

The contact zone of development

Through the teachers' engagements with development as a context for English language teaching we have seen the contrast between teachers' desires for connection with something meaningful and their disillusionment with the perceived patterns of inequality in the spatial organisation of adjacent communities. On the one hand, teachers disidentified with the spatiality of development hierarchies. From the teachers' perspective, the exclusive, masculinised spaces produced by a large foreign aid community, and vigorously policed to determine insiders and outsiders, were seen to form a barrier between foreign workers and local communities, and to establish exclusions based on racial and economic stereotypes that replicated colonial discourses. Aid workers' communities were also seen as inwardly focused and internally fragmented by contradictory assertions of economic advantage or moral superiority. These internal hierarchies tended to marginalise teachers who, branded as lightweight, uncommitted and middle class, felt excluded by the muscular pursuits of a militarised development mission, or reviled for missing out on the gravy train of development privilege.

While teachers felt dislocated from the wealthy development community, and disidentified with the superiority-of-being-us that the community exemplified, they also recalled feelings of alienation from local communities, thus experiencing a double sense of otherness. Together, these experiences of marginalisation, fragmentation and conflict signalled a deep ambivalence with regard to the project of development, and with regard to the teachers' presence in the development context. However, the teachers' narratives also expressed possibilities for different ways-of-being and connecting to local spaces and places, experienced through spatial practices such as walking, listening, engaging and reflecting, outside the bounds of exclusive enclaves and institutional classrooms. These spatial practices helped to move teachers beyond relations of dislocation, dominance and detachment, towards relocation and engagement with places and people across the cultures of the contact zone: a shifting sense of self, a shifting sense of being there in the world, a shifting translocal, transcultural identity.

Temporal designs of teaching

Despite the teachers' disidentification with the hierarchies and exclusions of the development contact zone, their narratives demonstrated how naturalised temporal and spatial patterns are constitutive of similar hierarchies in the practices of English language teaching. To begin with, a belief in the power of English as the key to a better future, or at least an escape from the past, held sway over teachers and students, reproducing a modernist temporal trajectory that links language and development in 'potent mythologies of progress' (Bhabha, 1990b: 209). The consequent value ascribed to the native speaker teacher as the expert in modern methods, and to externally determined credentials as a measure of success, signalled an effort to displace local knowledges, and echoed the traces of colonial discourses evident amongst the wider development community. Institutional processes of spatial and temporal organisation involving the testing and grading of students were initially taken for granted, despite the social and linguistic difficulties this produced, but became a site for student and teacher resistance. Once in the classroom, teachers mostly relied on textbooks, favourite routines or scripts imported from elsewhere to fill the imagined 'empty' space and time of lessons, quashing the flow of ideas, histories, struggles and lived experiences from the immediate context beyond the classroom walls. Looking out from the classroom, familiar teaching processes of reconstructing and renaming local spaces and spatial practices suggested the extent to which ELT is complicit in development's 'colonial dominion over space' (Crush, 1994: 336). Through these conventional discourses and practices of English language teaching, context is reduced to a passive background or stage for the proper work of the classroom; context becomes a receptive space to be developed by the introduction of advanced Western knowledge.

Given this restrictive temporal and spatial framework, teaching practices and discourses tended to fall into three groups: those that just 'rattled along', confirming a linear teleology of progress that overlooked (in both senses, as either ignoring/dismissing or surveying/incorporating) local dimensions and lived experiences of space and time; those that became lost in uncertainty and ambivalence as the conventions of ELT crashed and burned, proving insufficient in the face of a radically different and challenging context; and those that demonstrated a spatial flexibility – or translocal spatiality – in moving across and between the conventional practices of ELT and the transcultural relationships and discourses arising in the contact zone. The physical and metaphorical movement of teachers and students beyond the spatial and temporal constraints of the classroom offered a different way of engaging with political and social meanings in the contact zone, as students' expertise emerged from their knowledge of place. Teachers' and students' manipulations and appropriations of English language teaching practices thus signalled a blurring and transgression of spatial boundaries, and undermined colonial relations of power and knowledge implicit in conventional discourses of ELT in development.

Gender regimes and English language teaching

Despite the incorporation of gender equity principles into development with policies aimed at social progress for recipient communities, persistent patriarchal and sexist regimes had a significant impact on teachers' engagement with the world of international development and with host communities. In many ways, the contemporary development context appeared to support hegemonic discourses and spatial practices of gender inherited from readings of imperial space as a context for heroic, white, masculine endeavour. Where the foreign population was largely male, female teachers became an object of the male gaze, and a target of concern in regard to the supposed threat of local (male) violence. While teachers' narratives indicated a rejection of the restrictive gendered spatiality they observed within foreigners' social and professional domains, their reactions to the gaze of non-Western males were tempered by a sense of their own embodied inappropriacy as Western women in the local space. Their more complex and ambivalent responses to these transcultural gendered relations point once again to the ambiguous inside–outside position of white women in these contexts: on the one hand, complicit in the dominant economic, political and racial privileges of an international (white, English speaking) elite, and on the other hand subordinated by the (Western and non-Western) male gaze that produces the female form, and strictly curtails its spatial mobility.

The institutional spaces of education enabled a somewhat different gendered performance for Western teachers, since in those spaces they saw themselves primarily as professional beings (with the productive potential of authority that implies) rather than as sexual beings (rendered as objects of a controlling male gaze). Teachers' institutionally conferred authority was, nevertheless, relational and dependent on a complex set of factors including the ambiguous status of teachers as supposed experts but outsiders to the culture of the communities in which they worked, and the limits of institutional interference in private or cultural spaces. To an extent, the ambiguities and dilemmas affecting teachers' experience of gender relations with other cultures outside the classroom produced similar feelings of uncertainty and ambivalence with regard to gender issues in their professional performance.

While the space inside the classroom could be organised by teachers to reflect their own culturally mediated views of gendered social justice, for example, insisting on equal access to educational resources, the extension of that authority to spaces outside the educational domain raised certain difficulties. It seemed that students resisted institutional and pedagogical colonisation of these personal and cultural domains, illustrating the inextricable links between gender and other dimensions of difference, and the extent to which pedagogical authority was co-constructed in interaction. When gender-related problems emerged in the course of English lessons, teachers were at times torn between a desire to act with authority for (their own ideas of) social justice and conflicting responsibilities to respect cultural autonomy and difference. The limited knowability of gender relations in another culture thus significantly diminished the scope of teachers' performance in this regard. Temporal and spatial constraints (short time frames of projects, and emphasis on efficiency in teaching practices), and the specific dilemmas faced by teachers in approaching Otherness, worked against opening up lines for exploring gender relations more fully. Yet here again, moving outside the conventional space of the classroom allowed the teacher opportunities to engage with gender not as an object of improvement in the local society, but as a dynamic dimension of the relationships *between* cultures.

Implications for English Language Teaching and Gender: Beyond Development

A number of issues that have consequences for the practice of English language teaching emerge from a temporal and spatial interrogation of teachers' journeys in development contexts. One central issue, arising from beliefs in the power of English as a means of accessing a better life, is that ELT falls into the slipstream of a pernicious developmentalism: aligned with a discourse that categorises communities and knowledges along a chronological scale, ELT carries an implicit promise of progress 'out of the Dark Ages' towards an imagined goal of civilised modernity. Thus, in East Timor, English was seen as providing a way forward by guaranteeing access to economic, social or political possibilities, the benefits of which were evident in the powerful and wealthy English-speaking international population. In Indonesia, while the material evidence of success associated with English may have been less apparent in the lives of volunteer teachers, their professional status and the presence of professional white men in dominant positions served to sustain those delusional promises. In combination, English language, development and policies of gender equality form powerful mythologies of progress that shape expectations of ELT for both teachers and students, and perpetuate colonial discourses of Western superiority. Such potent temporal forces not only divert attention from the prevailing social, political and spatial dimensions of uneven development, but also limit the potential for a more productive and affirming pedagogical dialogue across difference.

The association of ELT with developmentalism foregrounds the uncomfortable conjunction between ELT as a gendered profession and the active, masculinised nature of the development enterprise. Echoing the paternalism and patriarchy of colonialism, development work as experienced by the teachers in this study favours a mode of heroic, masculine endeavour and simultaneously produces female subjects as both subordinate and as passive objects of masculine control. The greater number of men in development ELT (than in the feminised profession of the teachers' home country) would appear to do little to remedy the gender problems of ELT if, as in this study, men predominate in positions of authority and economic privilege, leaving the supposedly lightweight, and effectively marginalised work of classroom teaching to women. Although education still tends to be regarded as women's work, in the development contexts of this study the division of labour within education replicated traditional patriarchal hierarchies, while beyond the educational domain, a complex network of patriarchal and sexist discourses also served to keep women in their place. Focusing on gender as a problem located within recipients' communities, and an object for the West's civilising mission, draws attention away from these continuing structural imbalances and practices of gender divisions that privilege white, masculine authority in development work and in language teaching more broadly.

Dominant temporal narratives in education and development also have significant implications for the positioning of English language teachers within global hierarchies, and for the regimentation of pedagogical performance. The nature of development as change in a specified direction, and the importation of expertise from elsewhere to effect this change, is supported by a normative classification of nations, cultures and knowledges that sees 'advanced' Western expertise as the end point of progress. The presence of the First World teacher as the agent of change implies the key to individual, community and national progress lies in the application of the latest disciplinary knowledge. Regardless of how individual teachers might accept or resist the label of expert, the discourses of development teaching place the teacher, and her expert knowledge, in a position of responsibility to deliver the goods in the form of the (often illusory) promises of English. To fulfil these expectations, teachers can therefore tend to assume disproportionate authority and responsibility, exerting spatial control on the basis of the advanced status of their knowledge in a way that militates against their performing as 'coexplorers' in a participatory process of learning (Kumaravadivelu, 2001).

The *way* teaching performance is regimented, what spatial and temporal organisations of being are envisaged and enacted in the classroom, is of crucial importance in maintaining or challenging existing temporal and spatial regimes. Meaning and power are constituted through spatial and temporal organisations. In taking up the temporal logic of replacing 'traditional' teaching methods with supposedly more advanced pedagogical theories and practices, teachers may rely on spatial representations of disciplinary knowledge (in the form of lessons plans, maps and diagrams, curricula, prestige credentials), and formulated spatialisations of being (inherent in scripts of method and practice), to stabilise the meanings of the classroom space. However, the use of imported models and practices risks directing our activities into the same 'deeply worn channels' (Nespor, 1994: 15) that have produced uneven development. A focus on scripted performance and dissemination of 'modern' methods leaves little room for a critical orientation towards ELT, an orientation that might return the disciplinary gaze in order to examine the inflated claims of English language itself, and the complicity of English in the patterns of social, economic and political hierarchies of development.

Under the sway of linear temporal imperatives that privilege First World techniques, routine representations and performances can constitute a professional bubble, a free-floating simulacrum of an English-speaking world, detached from the heterogeneous context of local spaces, places and times. Although professional rhetoric encourages the adaptation of language texts to context, and disciplinary theories stress the interdependence of context and meaning, the way that context is conceptualised in mainstream ELT practice may support this bubble-like detachment. Institutional constraints and ingrained beliefs about the progress afforded by Western methods of ELT continue to shape taken-for-granted practices of how we perform English language teaching, and to structure understandings of context as subordinated not-yet-modern other. So influential are these temporal and spatial patterns that, even when teachers in this study recognised that something was drastically wrong, thinking and doing differently was rarely possible. The consequences would seem to be that in spite of good intentions, the abstractions and simulations of the classroom were too often disconnected from the everyday lived experiences of teachers and students, and from the situation of these experiences within wider historic, cultural, economic and political conditions that affect everyday lives.

The discussion thus points to the importance of finding ways to interrogate, and perhaps escape from, the temporal and spatial logic of ELT and/as developmentalism, and to allow different ways of relating teaching and language to a critical, political notion of context. Along these lines, we might ask, with May and Thrift (2001: 37), how we can 'inhabit the present as if it were a place, a home rather than something we pass in a mad scramble to realise the future?' and to seek a politics 'which can help us stop and ponder what we are doing'. Given the temporal and spatial patternings of social and economic exclusion associated with English in the particular discomfort zones of this study and in the broader geopolitics of uneven development, we might ask *what* sort of language use would provide more open possibilities for teaching and learning? To rephrase Crush (1994), what would a decolonised, dewhitened, postcolonial English language teaching actually look like? Rather than a language use and pedagogy synchronised with the temporal rhythms and spatial patterns of the global elite, and complicit in the colonial dominion over space, it seems that one way forward is to locate our language works not in singularly imagined cultures or nations, whether they be Western or non-Western, but rather in the nexus *between* global exigencies and the challenge presented by local claims to spaces, places and times: in the translocal, transcultural relationships of the contact zone. As the teachers' narratives have demonstrated, where the bubble of ELT becomes porous or disintegrates, there is potential for teachers to exploit their own in-between position and bring diverse spaces/places/times into dialogue, through spatial practices of being there, and engaging with difference and multiplicity in the contact zone of development.

Questions for a critical practice of English language teaching

An escape from the bubble would imply, as an initial step, an interrogation of the ways and the extent to which performing ELT is colonised by given, naturalised notions of time and space that tie the discipline of ELT into hegemonic systems and stratified cultural politics of specific locations. An interrogation of temporality and spatiality is not an end in itself, but offers an avenue of enquiry into social relations and political engagement. Rather than starting with a set of quick-fix solutions for the 'problems' of development, then, teachers might pause to consider some timely questions as a means of taking a different slant on their teaching project. Following Massey (2005), these questions focus on political notions of space as the product of interrelations, as the sphere of multiplicity and plurality, and as always open to the possible futures.

Thinking about the broader meaning and context of our teaching activity, we might ask questions such as: what temporal relationships are assumed between teachers' and students' languages, communities, cultures, nations? What identities are produced through these temporal schemes? In the context of the teaching project we might ask: What layers of external interactions (histories of international, economic, linguistic and cultural exchange) have formed this place? What spatial relationship arrangements are evident and how do they reflect assumed chronologies? What temporal and spatial geometries of power are enabled in this site? How do such geometries shape this site as a contact zone between cultures or communities? What social hierarchies are constituted in particular physical or imagined spaces and places? What spatial and temporal geometries underlie the organisation of gender in our different communities?

Thinking more specifically about classrooms as particular sites, we might ask: what geometries of power, or forms of authority, are enabled in and by this enclosure? What are the pressures and consequences of temporal regimes that apply in this site? What forms of knowledge are legitimised or refused? What knowledge, identities and representations of other places do I embody and bring with me into this place? What possible futures do I embody or assume? Who is included or excluded from this site, and to what effect? What gender relations are constituted or legitimised in this space? What are the articulations, and accountabilities, between this classroom and power relations in the world outside? What opportunities might be opened if we left this classroom/site? What other sites of contact between relevant communities or cultures could be investigated? What potentialities (of gender, ethnicity, nation, knowledge) could teacher and students leverage to facilitate a co-exploration of other sites? What type of places, and futures, do we want to create between us? Such interrogations would contribute towards a critical approach to English language teaching, in the sense of framing a 'problematizing practice' (Pennycook, 2001). Rather than providing a set of proven solutions, they offer a means of thinking differently about the taken-for-granted contexts, relationships and practices of English language teaching.

A critical contextual practice would engage with heterogeneous aspects of time, turning away from an obsession with a singular view of the past in order to imagine different futures, refusing the drive towards efficiency and its reliance on easy answers, and decoupling ELT from the classifications, separations and limitations of an industrial approach to time. This would mean opening ELT practice to various personal and collective histories, to a sense of spontaneity in the present, and to a notion of change unrestricted by limited, predefined visions of progress. At the same time, it would imply a questioning of the way spaces, places and people are connected, disconnected or categorised through language and

language teaching, and an opening out of the classroom space to the phenomenal, cultural and political influences and knowledges of (trans)local
places. In this study, the expertise of students, and their contestations and
appropriations of spatial and temporal practices, pointed to possibilities
for this type of questioning and reconnection. This is a process similar to
Gruenewald's (2003) decolonisation and reinhabitation of place, a process
that implies learning new ways of being in a postcolonial world, and for
the teacher it signals time and space as dimensions with which to critically
rethink the textual and political relation across translocal, transcultural
spaces. A critical notion of context moves beyond efforts to make language
relevant by aligning language learning with a liberal, developmentalist
vision of progress, or adapting texts and resources to suit passive spatial
representations of a particular location. It is based in a notion of context
as a political spatiality, and in a notion of space as the medium and the
expression of relations of power.

Approaching gender issues in the contact zone of development teaching has proven particularly challenging, and perhaps goes some way
towards explaining the absence of situated studies of gender and ELT
in Third World contexts (Sunderland, 2000). Gender was a significant
problem for the women teachers in this study, where the perpetuation
of patriarchal and sexist regimes affected the negotiation of gender both
inside and outside the classroom. The teachers' accounts signal not only
the naturalisation and invisibility of gender imbalances within the classroom and the institution, but also the considerable limitations on the
ability of First World teachers, with their First World baggage, to work
with students interrogating gender and/as culture in diverse geopolitical
locations. Negotiating gendered spatiality in relation to another culture,
and in relation to other axes of difference such as ethnicity and economic
status, is a process that requires sensitivity and reflexivity, humour and
generosity, listening rather than speaking, and a willingness to reflect on
one's own position in relation to diverse communities and spaces. Given
the unknowability of gender in relation to other cultures, active political interrogation of gender and ELT in Third World contexts needs to
proceed in conjunction with a continuing interrogation of what might be
more accessible or knowable. In this case, the aspects of gender I regard as
knowable are the entrenched patriarchal spatiality of international development, and the gender-related marginalisation experienced by women
in ELT. Alongside these concerns, a productive place for the interrogation
of gender, ethnicity and economic difference is in the very relations that
arise *between* the different communities and individual circumstances of
participation in the contact zone.

In terms of drawing conclusions which may be of relevance to other English language teaching situations, the particularities of Indonesia and East Timor, and my own partial, positioned perspectives need to be borne in mind. Although many of the issues outlined above concerning time and space as parameters of constraint and possibility could be relevant in other development contexts, the particular dynamics of political and linguistic conditions in Indonesia and East Timor presented specific conditions for language teaching. In both these locations we might see history at a turning point, as the nations (re)invent themselves, and reach out into economic, political and cultural global flows. For both Indonesia and East Timor, these were years of rapid change and a rush of possible futures seemed to lie ahead. Were we present at something like a pivot point in history? I think, on reflection, this was so: it was a time of tumultuous change, and whole communities were turning on a point where possibilities for fashioning the future seemed to proliferate. Yet, perhaps we need to think about our place in the present as always resting, fleetingly, on a pivot point, and that those prolific possibilities are only hidden from view by that image of a future contained by the past. Following Grosz's (1998: 37) project, we might dare to 'think temporality and futurity, in all their richness, as modalities of difference', to move beyond normative visions of progress, and into 'the more disconcerting notion of unpredictable, disordered or uncontainable change, which lurks within the very concept of change or newness [and] seems to disconcert scientific, philosophical and cultural ideals', yet opens the present to the richness of 'futures yet unthought'.

So, given the historical and geographic contingency of the teachers' narratives, and my own contingent readings of those texts, what can be offered here for other pedagogical possibilities? There can be no pre-given means for escaping the limitations of regulated time and space. But perhaps, using a framework of time and space, we can open up our practices to a different way of thinking about and performing English language teaching that brings together translocal links between language and gender, text and context. What can be generalised to other contexts of language teaching is a questioning stance, and an invitation to explore alternative conceptions of taken-for-granted temporal and spatial meanings that underpin social and political relations of power and knowledge.

Appendix A Teachers and Projects

Teacher	Location	Institution (students) [EFL proficiency]	Role as language teacher
Bree*	Indonesia	Vocational high schools (teachers) [advanced]	Teacher training in CLT
Bree	Vietnam	Teacher training and language college (teachers) [advanced]	Teacher training in CLT + EAP
Ann*	Indonesia	Teacher training college (Pre-service teachers) [advanced]	EFL + English literature
Ann	East Timor	University (undergraduates) [mixed]	EAP
		High schools (teachers) [intermediate]	ELT methodology
		High schools (students) [beginners]	EFL
Carol*	Indonesia	Technical and vocational college (teachers) [advanced]	ESP (Hospitality)
Carol	East Timor	University (undergraduates) [intermediate]	EFL/EAP
Roslyn	East Timor	University (undergraduates) [elementary]	EFL/EAP
Fay*	East Timor	University (undergraduates) [beginner]	EFL/EAP
Dana*(+ email)	East Timor	University (undergraduates) [elementary]	EFL/EAP + computer skills
Elly*	East Timor	University (undergraduates) [beginner]	EFL/EAP + computer skills
Helen (+letters and email)	East Timor	University (undergraduates) [intermediate]	EFL/EAP
Kate	East Timor	Teachers training college (teachers) [mixed]	EFL + Teacher training in CLT + IELTS preparation
Jane*	East Timor	Teacher training college (teachers) [beginners]	EFL + Teacher training in CLT

* indicates that this was the teacher's first development project experience

Appendix B *Transcription Codes*

[...]	Ellipsis in square brackets indicates some original text has been omitted
[text]	Italics in square brackets indicates text inserted by researcher to ensure clarity of grammatical or referential meaning
text-	Hyphen indicates a speaker's false start or self-interruption
<u>never</u>	Underlined text indicates emphasis by speaker
[laughter]	Text in square brackets describes non-verbal communication (sounds and gestures)
gotta	Unconventional spelling in participants' interview data generally follows pronunciation
Everiday	Unconventional spelling and syntax in participants' writing is retained from the original script

References

Abbott, G. (1992) Development, education and English language teaching. *English Language Teaching Journal* 46 (2), 172–179.

Abbott, G. (2000) Language in lifelong education for Third World development. *Development in Practice* 10 (2), 216–222.

Abeles, M. (2008) Rethinking NGOs: The economy of survival and global governance. *Indiana Journal of Global Legal Studies* 15 (1), 241–258.

Adam, B. (2002) The gendered time politics of globalization: Of shadowlands and elusive justice. *Feminist Review* 70 (2), 3–29.

Adam, B. (2003) Reflexive modernisation temporalised. *Theory, Culture and Society* 20 (2), 59–78.

Adam, B. (2004) *Time*. Cambridge: Polity.

Addison, T. (2000) Aid and conflict. In F. Tarp (ed.) *Foreign Aid and Development: Lessons Learned and Directions for the Future* (pp. 392–408). London: Routledge.

Aidwatch (2005) *Australian Aid: The Boomerang Effect*. Retrieved 1 June 2005, from http://aidwatch.org.au.

Altbach, P.G. (1998) *Comparative Education: Knowledge, the University, and Development*. Greenwich, CN: Ablex.

Anderson, B. (1991) *Imagined Communities: Reflections on the Origin and Spread of Nationalism*. London: Verso.

Anderson, B. (1993) Imagining 'East Timor'. *Arena Magazine* 4 (April–May), 23–27.

Appadurai, A. (1996) *Modernity at Large*. Minneapolis, MN: University of Minnesota Press.

Appleby, R. (2004) The political context of English language teaching in East Timor. In A. Hickling-Hudson, J. Matthews and A. Woods (eds) *Disrupting Preconceptions: Postcolonialism and Education* (pp. 235–249). Flaxton, Australia: Post Pressed.

Appleby, R., Copley, K., Sithirajvongsa, S. and Pennycook, A. (2002) Language in development constrained: Three contexts. *TESOL Quarterly* 36 (3), 323–346.

Archer, D. (2003) Appendix 1: Reactions to this report from Reflect practitioners. In M. Fiedrich and A. Jellema (eds) *Literacy, Gender and Social Agency: Adventures in Empowerment* (pp. 195–203). London: ActionAid.

Archer, D. and Cottingham, S. (1997) REFLECT: A new approach to literacy and social change. *Development in Practice* 7 (2), 199–202.

Archer, D. and Newman, K. (2003) *Communication and Power: Reflect Practical Resource Materials*. CIRAC The International Reflect Circle. On WWW at http://www.reflect-action.org.

Arenas, A. (1998) Education and nationalism in East Timor. *Social Justice* 25 (2), 131–148.

Arnove, R.F. (1980) Comparative education and world systems analysis. *Comparative Education Review* 21 (1), 48–62.

Ashcroft, B., Griffiths, G. and Tiffin, H. (1998) *Post-Colonial Studies*. London: Routledge.

Asher, N. and Smith Crocco, M. (2001) (En)gendering multicultural identities and representations in education. *Theory and Research in Social Education* 29 (1), 129–151.

Auerbach, E.R. (1995) The power of the ESL classroom: Issues of power in pedagogical choices. In J.W. Tollefson (ed.) *Power and Inequality in Language Education* (pp. 9–33). Cambridge: Cambridge University Press.

Auerbach, E.R. (2000) Creating participatory learning communities: Paradoxes and possibilities. In J.K. Hall and W.G. Eggington (eds) *The Sociopolitics of English Language Teaching* (pp. 143–164). Clevedon: Multilingual Matters.

Australian Agency for International Development (AusAID) (2000) *Progress for East Timor: A Stronger Future for East Timor*. On WWW at http://www.ausaid.gov.au/hottopics. Retrieved 22.11.2005.

Australian Agency for International Development (AusAID) (2001) *Australian Development Cooperation with East Timor: Interim Strategy Outline Paper*. Canberra: AusAID.

Australian Agency for International Development (AusAID) (2007) *Better Education: A Policy for Australian Development Assistance in Education*. Canberra: AusAID.

Australian Bureau of Statistics (2006) How Australians use their time. On WWW at http://www.abs.gov.au. Retrieved 9.4.2008.

Bartlett, L. (2005) Dialogue, knowledge, and teacher-student relations: Freirean pedagogy in theory and practice. *Comparative Education Review* 49 (3), 344–364.

Bartlett, L. (2008) Literacy's verb: Exploring what literacy is and what literacy does. *International Journal of Educational Development* 28 (6), 737–753.

Baudrillard, J. (2001) Simulacra and simulations. In M. Poster (ed.) *Jean Baudrillard: Selected Writings* (2nd edn) (pp. 169–187). Cambridge, UK: Polity Press.

Bax, S. (2003) The end of CLT: A context approach to language teaching. *ELT Journal* 57 (3), 278–286.

Benwell, B. and Stokoe, E. (2006) *Discourse and Identity*. Edinburgh: Edinburgh University Press.

Bertrand, N. (2003) Language policy and the promotion of national identity in Indonesia. In M.E. Brown and S. Ganguly (eds) *Fighting Words: Language Policy and Ethnic Relations in Asia*. Cambridge, MA: MIT Press.

Bhabha, H.K. (1990a) DissemiNation: Time, narrative, and the margins of the modern nation. In H.K. Bhabha (ed.) *Nation and Narration* (pp. 291–322). Routledge: London and New York.

Bhabha, H.K. (1990b) The third space: Interview with Homi Bhabha. In J. Rutherford (ed.) *Identity: Community, Culture and Difference* (pp. 207–221). London: Lawrence & Wishart.

Bhabha, H.K. (1994) Remembering Fanon: Self, psyche and the colonial condition. In P. Williams and L. Chrisman (eds) *Colonial Discourse and Post-Colonial Theory: A Reader* (pp. 112–123). London: Pluto Press (original publication 1986).

Bhattacharya, R., Gupta, S., Jewitt, C., Newfield, D., Reed, Y. and Stein, P. (2007) The policy-practice nexus in English classrooms in Delhi, Johannesburg, and London: Teachers and the textual cycle. *TESOL Quarterly* 41 (3), 465–488.

Bingham, N. and Thrift, N. (2000) Some new instructions for travellers: The geography of Bruno Latour and Michel Serres. In M. Crang and N. Thrift (eds) *Thinking Space* (pp. 281–301). London: Routledge.

Block, D. (2004) Globalization and language teaching. *ELT Journal* 58 (1), 75–77.

Block, D. and Cameron, D. (eds) (2002) *Globalization and Language Teaching*. London: Routledge.

Blommaert, J. (2005) *Discourse*. Cambridge: Cambridge University Press.

Blunt, A. and Rose, G. (1994) Women's colonial and postcolonial geographies. In A. Blunt and G. Rose (eds) *Writing Women and Space: Colonial and Postcolonial Geographies* (pp. 1–25). New York: The Guilford Press.

Boughton, B. (2008) East Timor's national literacy campaign and the struggle for a post-conflict democracy. Paper presented at the 17th Biennial Conference of the Asian Studies Association of Australia 1–3 July, Melbourne, Australia.

Bourdieu, P. and Passeron, J. (1970) *Reproduction in Education, Society, and Culture*. London: Sage.

Bowcott, O. (2005) Report reveals shame of UN peacekeepers. *The Guardian*. On WWW at http://www.guardian.co.uk/international/story/0,3604,1445537,00.htm. Retrieved 20.4.2005.

Bowers, C.A. (1983) Linguistic roots of cultural invasion in Paulo Freire's pedagogy. *Teachers College Record* 85 (3), 365–390.

Brunnstrom, C. (2003) Another invasion: Lessons from international support to East Timorese NGOs. *Development in Practice* 13 (4), 310–321.

Bruthiaux, P. (2002) Hold your courses: Language education, language choice, and economic development, *TESOL Quarterly* 36 (3), 275–296.

Brutt-Griffler, J. (2002) *World English: A Study of its Development*. Clevedon: Multilingual Matters.

Burke, A. (2001) *In Fear of Security: Australia's Invasion Anxiety*. Annandale, Australia: Pluto Press.

Butler, J. (1990) *Gender Trouble: Feminism and the Subversion of Identity*. New York: Routledge.

Butler, J. (1993) *Bodies That Matter: On the Discursive Limits of 'Sex'*. New York: Routledge.

Cabral, E. and Martin-Jones, M. (2008) Writing the resistance: Literacy in East Timor 1975–1999. *International Journal of Bilingual Education and Bilingualism* 11 (2), 149–169.

Canagarajah, A.S. (1993) Critical ethnography of a Sri Lankan classroom: Ambiguities in student opposition to reproduction through ESOL. *TESOL Quarterly* 27 (4), 601–626.

Canagarajah, A.S. (1999) *Resisting Linguistic Imperialism in English Teaching*. Oxford: Oxford University Press.

Canagarajah, A.S. (2002) Globalization, methods, and practice in periphery classrooms. In D. Block and D. Cameron (eds) *Globalization and Language Teaching* (pp. 134–150). London: Routledge.

Canagarajah, A.S. (2005) Accommodating tensions in language-in-education policies: An afterword. In A.M.Y. Lin and P.W. Martin (eds) *Decolonisation,*

Globalisation: Language in Education Policy and Practice (pp. 194–201). Clevedon: Multilingual Matters.

Canagarajah, A.S. (2006) TESOL at forty: What are the issues? *TESOL Quarterly* 40 (1), 9–34.

Carnoy, M. (1980) International institutions and educational policy: A review of education-sector policy. *Prospect* 10 (3), 265–286.

Carter, P. (1987) *The Road to Botany Bay*. London: Faber & Faber.

Carter, P. (1992) *Living in a New Country: History, Travelling and Language*. London and Boston: Faber & Faber.

Castells, M. (1999) An Introduction to the Information Age. In H. MacKay and T. O'Sullivan (eds) *The Media Reader: Continuity and Transformation* (pp. 398–410). London: Sage.

Charlesworth, H. (2005) Not waving but drowning: Gender mainstreaming and human rights in the United Nations. *Harvard Human Rights Journal* 18, 325–334.

Charlesworth, H. (2008) Are women peaceful? Reflections on the role of women in peace-building. *Feminist Legal Studies* 16, 347–361.

Charlton, S.E. (1997) Development as history and process. In N. Visvanathan, L. Duggan, L. Nisonoff and N. Wiegersma (eds) *The Women, Gender and Development Reader* (pp. 7–13). London: Zed Books.

Chesterman, S. (2001) East Timor in Transition: From Conflict Prevention to State-Building, *ciao working papers*. On WWW at http://www.ciaonet.org/wps/chs03/.

Chopra, J. (2000) The UN's kingdom of East Timor. *Survival* 42 (3), 27–39.

Chopra, J. (2002) Building state failure in East Timor. *Development and Change* 33 (5), 979–1000.

Clarke, M. (2006) Aid and development in conflict environments: An introduction and summary. In M. Clarke (ed.) *Aid in Conflict* (pp. 1–8). New York: Nova Science.

Clarke, M. (2008) *Language Teacher Identities: Co-constructing Discourse and Community*. Clevedon: Multilingual Matters.

Clifford, J. (1997) *Routes: Travel and Translation in the Late Twentieth Century*. Cambridge, MA: Harvard University Press.

Coleman, H., Gulyamova, J. and Thomas, A. (eds) (2005) *National Development, Education and Language in Central Asia and Beyond*. Uzbekistan: British Council.

Coleman, H. and Sigutova, M. (2005) Sustainability in education development projects: What are the limits? In H. Coleman, J. Gulyamovea and A. Thomas (eds) *National Development, Education and Language in Central Asia and Beyond* (pp. 108–117). Uzbekistan: British Council.

Cope, B., and Kalantzis, M. (1993) The power of literacy and the literacy of power. In B. Cope and M. Kalantzis (eds) *The Powers of Literacy: A Genre Approach to Teaching Writing* (pp. 63–89). London: The Falmer Press.

Copley, K., Haylor, G. and Savage, W. (2005) Facilitating languages, participation and change: National and regional cases. In H. Coleman, J. Gulyamova and A. Thomas (eds) *National Development, Education and Language in Central Asia and Beyond* (pp. 124–132). Uzbekistan: British Council.

Corbidge, S. (1995) Thinking about development. In S. Corbidge (ed.) *Development Studies* (pp. 1–16). London: Edward Arnold.

Corcoran-Nantes, Y. (2009) The politics of culture and the culture of politics – a case study of gender and politics in Lospalos, Timor-Leste. *Conflict, Security and Development* 9 (2), 165–187.

Cottingham, S., Metcalf, K. and Phnuyal, B. (1998) The REFLECT approach to literacy and social change: A gender perspective. *Gender and Development* 6 (2), 27–34.

Crang, M. (2001) Rhythms of the City: Temporalised space and motion. In J. May and N. Thrift (eds) *Timespace: Geographies of Temporality* (pp. 187–207). London: Routledge.

Crang, M. and Thrift, N. (2000) Introduction. In M. Crang and N. Thrift (eds) *Thinking Space* (pp. 1–30). London and New York: Routledge.

Craven, E. (2002) *Development Discourses and Australia's Assistance for Human Resource Development in Vietnam*. Unpublished EdD thesis, The University of Sydney, Sydney.

Crush, J. (1994) Post-colonialism, de-colonization, and geography. In A. Godlewska and N. Smith (eds) *Geography and Empire* (pp. 333–350). Oxford: Blackwell.

Crush, J. (1995) Imagining development. In J. Crush (ed.) *Power of Development* (pp. 27–43). London: Routledge.

D'Cruz, J.V.D. and Steele, W. (2003) *Australia's Ambivalence Towards Asia: Politics, Neo/Post-colonialism, and Fact/Fiction* (2nd edn). Monash University, Australia: Monash University Press.

Dardjowidjojo, A. (2000) English teaching in Indonesia. *EA Journal* 18 (1), 22–30.

Davis, K.A. and Skilton-Sylvester, E. (2004) Looking back, taking stock, moving forward: Investigating gender in TESOL. *TESOL Quarterly* 38 (3), 381–404.

de Araujo, M. (2007) Oxfam and partners in East Timor: Creating a voice for women and carving a space for that voice. In D. Grenfell and A. Trembath (eds) *Challenges and Possibilities: International Organizations and Women in Timor-Leste* (pp. 13–16). Melbourne: Globalism Institute, RMIT University.

de Certeau, M. (1984) *The Practice of Everyday Life* (S. Rendall, trans.). Berkley: California University Press.

Deleuze, G. (1992) Postscript on the societies of control. *October* 59 (Winter), 3–7.

Denham, P. (1997) Eight autumns in Hanoi. In B. Kenny and W. Savage (eds) *Language and Development: Teachers in a Changing World* (pp. 193–207).

Dilley, R. (1999) Introduction: The problem of context. In R. Dilley (ed.) *The Problem of Context* (pp. 1–46). New York and Oxford: Berghahn Books.

Djite, P. (2008) *The Sociolinguistics of Development in Africa*. Clevedon: Multilingual Matters.

Do, H.T. (2000) Foreign language education policy in Vietnam: The emergence of English and its impact on higher education. In J. Shaw, D. Lubelska and M. Noullet (eds) *Partnership and Interaction: Proceedings of the Fourth International Conference on Language and Development* (pp. 29–42). Bangkok: Asian Institute of Technology.

Downer, A. (1996) *Education and Training in Australia's Aid Program (Policy Statement by the Minister for Foreign Affairs)*. Canberra: Australian Agency for International Development.

Downer, A. (7 April 2000) *Education for All*. Speech delivered to a public meeting in Adelaide coordinated by Community Aid Abroad. On WWW at http://www.ausaid.gov.au/media/release.cfm?BC=Speech&ID=2228_5089_736_5142_608. Retrieved 16.9.2009.

Duff, P. A. and Uchida, Y. (1997) The negotiation of teachers' sociocultural identities and practices in postsecondary EFL classrooms. *TESOL Quarterly* 31 (3), 451–486.

Duffield, M. (2002) Social reconstruction and the radicalization of development: Aid as a relation of global liberal governance. *Development and Change* 33 (5), 1049–1071.

Earnest, J. (2003) Education reconstruction in East Timor: The case of a transitional society. Paper presented at the Educational Research, Risks, Dilemmas: NZARE/AARE Conference, 29 November–3 December 2003, Auckland, New Zealand.

Edwards, M. (1999) *Future Positive: International Cooperation in the 21st Century*. London: Earthscan Publications.

Edwards, R. and Usher, R. (2000) *Globalisation and Pedagogy: Space, Place and Identity*. London: Routledge.

Eisenstein, A. (2007) *Sexual Decoys: Gender, Race and War in Imperial Democracy*. London: Zed Books.

Ellwood, C. (2006) On coming out and coming undone: Sexualities and reflexivities in language education research. *Journal of Language, Identity, and Education* 5 (1), 67–84.

Eriksen, T.H. (2007) *Globalization: The Key Concepts*. Oxford; New York: Berg

Errington, J. (1998) *Shifting Languages: Interaction and Identity in Javanese Indonesia*. Cambridge: Cambridge University Press.

Escobar, A. (1995) *Encountering Development: The Making and Unmaking of the Third World*. Princeton: Princeton University Press.

Escobar, A. (2004) Development, violence and the New Imperial Order. *Development* 47 (1), 15–21.

Eversole, R. (2003) Managing the pitfalls of participatory development: Some insights from Australia. *World Development* 31 (5), 781–795.

Fabian, J. (1983) *Time and the Other: How Anthropology Makes its Object*. New York: Colombia University Press.

Fairclough, N. (1989) *Language and Power*. London: Longman.

Fairclough, N. (1995) *Critical Discourse Analysis: The Critical Study of Language*. London: Longman.

Fiedrich, M. and Jellema, A. (2003) Literacy, gender and social agency: Adventures in empowerment. London, UK: ActionAid.

Firth, J.R. (1957) *Papers in Linguistics, 1934–1951*. London: Oxford University Press.

Firth, J.R. (1968) A synopsis of linguistic theory, 1930–1955. In F.R. Palmer (ed.) *Selected Papers of J. R. Firth, 1952–1959* (pp. 168–205). London: Longman.

Foucault, M. (1977) *Discipline and Punish*. New York: Pantheon.

Foucault, M. (1980) The eye of power (C. Gordon, L. Marshall, J. Mepham and K. Soper, trans.). In C. Gordon (ed.) *Power/Knowledge: Selected Interviews and Other Writings 1972–1977* (pp. 146–165). New York: Pantheon.

Foucault, M. (1984a) Nietzsche, genealogy, history. In P. Rabinow (ed.) *The Foucault Reader* (pp. 76–100). London: Penguin.

Foucault, M. (1984b) Space, knowledge, and power. In P. Rabinow (ed.) *The Foucault Reader* (pp. 239–256). New York: Pantheon.

Foucault, M. (1986) Of other spaces. *Diacritics* 16 (1), 22–27.

Fox, C. (1999) Girls and women in education and training in Papua New Guinea. In C. Heward and S. Bunwaree (eds) *Gender, Education and Development: Beyond Access to Empowerment* (pp. 33–48). London: Zed Books.

Frank, A.G. (1969) *Latin America: Underdevelopment or Revolution*. New York: Monthly Review Press.

Freire, P. (1972) *Pedagogy of the Oppressed*. Harmondsworth: Penguin.

Freire, P. and Macedo, D. (1987) *Literacy: Reading the Word and the World*. Massachusetts: Bergin & Garvey.

Frodesen, J. and Holten, C. (eds) (2005) *The Power of Context in Language Teaching and Learning*. Boston, MA: Thomson/Heinle.

Gallop, J. (1995) The teacher's breasts. In J. Gallop (ed.) *Pedagogy: The Question of Impersonation* (pp. 79–89). Bloomington and Indianapolis: Indiana University Press.

Gardner, R. (2006) Conversation analysis. In A. Davies and C. Elder (eds) *The Handbook of Applied Linguistics* (pp. 262–284). Malden, MA: Blackwell Publishing.

Geertz, C. (1996) Afterword: Senses of place. In S. Feld and K. H. Basso (eds) *Senses of Place* (pp. 259–262). Santa Fe, New Mexico: School of American Research Press.

German, T. and Randel, J. (2002) Never richer, never poorer. In J. Randel, T. German and D. Ewing (eds) *The Reality of Aid: An Independent Review of Poverty Reduction and Development Assistance* (pp. 145–157). Manila: IBON Books.

Giddens, A. (1990) *The Consequences of Modernity*. United Kingdom: Polity.

Gillen, P. and Ghosh, D. (2007) *Colonialism and Modernity*. Sydney: University of New South Wales Press.

Giroux, H. (1988) *Schooling and the Struggle for Public Life: Critical Pedagogy in the Modern Age*. Minneapolis: University of Minnesota Press.

Glassman, J.F. (2003) Structural power, agency and national liberation: The case of East Timor. *Transactions of the Institute of British Geographers* 28 (3), 264–280.

Goldsworthy, D. (2003) Introduction. In P. Edwards and D. Goldsworthy (eds) *Facing North: A Century of Australian Engagement with Asia. Volume 2: 1970s to 2000* (pp. 1–12). Melbourne: Melbourne University Press.

Goodwin, C. and Duranti, A. (1992) Rethinking context. In A. Duranti and C. Goodwin (eds) *Rethinking Context: Language as an Interactive Phenomenon* (pp. 1–42). Cambridge: Cambridge University Press.

Goody, J. (1986) *The Logic of Writing and the Organisation of Society*. New York: Cambridge University Press.

Gordon, R.G. Jr. (ed.) (2005) *Ethnologue: Languages of the World* (15th edn). Dallas, TX: SIL International. On WWW at http://www.ethnologue.com/.

Gray, J. (2002) The global coursebook in English language teaching. In D. Block and D. Cameron (eds) *Globalization and Language Teaching* (pp. 152–167). London: Routledge.

Griffin, K. (2003) Economic globalization and institutions of global governance. *Development and Change* 34 (5), 789–807.

Grin, F. (2001) English as economic value: Facts and fallacies. *World Englishes* 20 (1), 65–78.

Grinberg, J. and Saavedra, E.R. (2000) The constitution of bilingual/ESL education as a disciplinary practice: Genealogical explorations. *Review of Educational Research* 70 (4), 419–441.

Grosz, E. (1995) *Space, Time and Perversion: The Politics of Bodies*. St Leonards, Australia: Allen & Unwin.

Grosz, E.A. (1998) Thinking the new: Of futures yet unthought. *Symploke* 6 (1–2), 38–55

Grosz, E. (ed.) (1999) *Becomings: Explorations in Time, Memory, and Futures*. Ithaca, NY: Cornell University Press.

Gruenewald, D.A. (2003) The best of both worlds: A critical pedagogy of place. *Educational Researcher* 32 (4), 3–12.

Gulson, K.N. and Syme, C. (2007) Knowing one's place: Space, theory, education. *Critical Studies in Education* 48 (1), 97–110.

Hadi-Tabassum, S. (2006) *Language, Space and Power: A Critical Look at Bilingual Education*. Clevedon: Multilingual Matters.

Hajek, J. (2000) Language planning and the sociolinguistic environment in East Timor: Colonial practice and changing language ecologies. *Current Issues in Language Planning* 1 (3), 400–414.

Hajek, J. (2006) On the edge of the Pacific: Indonesia and East Timor. In D. Cunningham (ed.) *Language Diversity in the Pacific: Endangerment and Survival* (pp. 121–130). Clevedon: Multilingual Matters.

Hall, S. (1989) The meaning of new times. In S. Hall and M. Jacques (eds) *New Times: The Changing Face of Politics in the 1990s* (pp. 116–133). London: Lawrence & Wishart.

Hall, D. (1997) Why projects fail. In B. Kenny and W. Savage (eds) *Language and Development: Teachers in a Changing World* (pp. 258–267). London: Longman.

Halliday, M.A.K. (1978) *Language as a Social Semiotic: The Social Interpretation of Language and Meaning*. London: Edward Arnold.

Halliday, M.A.K. (1994) *An Introduction to Functional Grammar* (2nd edn). London: Edward Arnold.

Harrison, G. (2004) Why economic globalization is not enough. *Development and Change* 35 (5), 1037–1047.

Harvey, D. (1989) *The Condition of Postmodernity: An Enquiry into the Origins of Social Change*. Oxford: Basil Blackwell.

Heryanto, A. (2007) Then there were languages: Bahasa Indonesia was one among many. In S. Makoni and A. Pennycook (eds) *Disinventing and Reconstituting Languages* (pp. 42–61). Clevedon: Mulitlingual Matters.

Heyer, P. (1993) Empire, history and communications viewed from the margins: The legacies of Gordon Childe and Harold Innes. *Continuum: The Australian Journal of Media and Culture* 7 (1), 91–104.

Hickey, S. and Mohan, G. (2005) Relocating participation within a radical politics of development. *Development and Change* 36 (2), 237–262.

Hill, H. (2001) Tiny, poor and war-torn: Development policy challenges for East Timor. *World Development* 29 (7), 1137–1156.

Holliday, A. (1994) *Appropriate Methodology and Social Context*. Cambridge: Cambridge University Press.

Holliday, A. (2005) *The Struggle to Teach English as an International Language*. Oxford: Oxford University Press.

Howard, J. (1999) *Prime Minister's speech in the House of Representatives in the East Timor debate*. On WWW at http://parlinfoweb.aph.gov.au/PIWeb/view_document.aspx?id=2365277&table. Retrieved 6.6.2005.

Hull, G. (2000) *Current language issues in East Timor. (Text of a public lecture given at the University of Adelaide, 29 March, 2000)*. On WWW at http://www.ocs.mq.edu.au/~leccles/easttimor.html. Retrieved 6.6.2005.

Hunt, J. (2004) Gender and development. In D. Kingsbury, J. Remenyi and J. Hunt (eds) *Key Issues in Development* (pp. 243–265). Basingstoke and New York: Palgrave Macmillan.

Hymes, D. (1972) Models of interaction and social life. In J. Gumperz and D. Hymes (eds) *Directions in Sociolinguistics: The Ethnography of Communication*. New York: Holt-Rinehart.

Jazadi, I. (2000) Constraints and resources for applying communicative approaches in Indonesia. *EA Journal* 2000 (1), 31–40.

Jeffrey, L.A. (2002) *Sex and Borders: Gender, National Identity and Prostitution Policy in Thailand*. Vancouver: University of British Colombia Press.

Jeffreys, A. (2002) Giving voice to silent emergencies. *Humanitarian Exchange* 20, 2–4.

Jolliffe, J. (1 December 2001) AIDS spectre looms over Dili. *The Age*. On WWW at http://www.theage.com.au/issues.easttimor.index.html. Retrieved 5.2.2002.

Jones, D.M. (1990) Genealogy of the urban schoolteacher. In S.J. Ball (ed.) *Foucault and Education* (pp. 57–77). London: Routledge.

Jones, D.M. and Ball, S.J. (1995) Michael Foucault and the discourse of education. In P. McLaren and J. Giarelli (eds) *Critical Theory and Education* (pp. 37–51). New York: State University of New York Press.

Joshi, V. (2007) Creating and limiting opportunities: Women's organizing the UN in East Timor. In D. Grenfell and A. Trembath (eds) *Challenges and Possibilities: International Organizations and Women in Timor-Leste* (pp. 13–16). Melbourne: Globalism Institute, RMIT University.

Kachru, B. (1996) English as an Asian language. In M.L. Bautista (ed.) *English is an Asian Language* (pp. 1–24). Sydney: MacQuaine.

Kagawa, F. (2005) Emergency education: A critical review of the field. *Comparative Education* 41 (4), 487–503.

Keith, M. and Pile, S. (1993) The politics of place. In M. Keith and S. Pile (eds) *Place and the Politics of Identity* (pp. 1–22). London: Routledge.

Kennett, P. (2002) Language, development and political correctness. In J. Lo Bianco (ed.) *Voices from Phnom Penh: Development and Language: Global Influences and Local Effects* (pp. 235–242). Melbourne: Language Australia.

Kennett, P. (2005) The new prescriptivism. In H. Coleman, J. Gulyamovea and A. Thomas (eds) *National Development, Education and Language in Central Asia and Beyond* (pp. 100–107). Uzbekistan: British Council.

Kenny, B. and Laszewski, M. (1997) Talkbase in Vientiane. In B. Kenny and W. Savage (eds) *Language and Development: Teachers in a Changing World* (pp. 129–140). London: Longman.

Kenny, B. and Savage, W. (eds) (1997) *Language and Development: Teachers in a Changing World*. London: Longman.

Kingdon, S. (1999) Contesting development. In R. Le Heron, L. Murphy, P. Forer and M. Goldstone (eds) *Explorations in Human Geography: Encountering Place* (pp. 173–202). Auckland: Oxford University Press.

Kingsbury, D. (2002) *The Politics of Indonesia* (2nd edn). South Melbourne: Oxford University Press.

Kingsbury, D. (2004a) Introduction. In D. Kingsbury, J. Remenyi and J. Hunt (eds) *Key Issues in Development* (pp. 1–21). Basingstoke and New York: Palgrave Macmillan.

Kingsbury, D. (2004b) Community development. In D. Kingsbury, J. Remenyi and J. Hunt (eds) *Key Issues in Development* (pp. 221–242). Basingstoke and New York: Palgrave Macmillan.

Kirby, K.M. (1996a) *Indifferent Boundaries*. New York: The Guilford Press.

Kirby, K.M. (1996b) Re: Mapping subjectivity: Cartographic vision and the limits of politics. In N. Duncan (ed.) *BodySpace: Destabilizing Geographies of Gender and Sexuality* (pp. 45–55). London: Routledge.

Kramsch, C. and Sullivan, P. (1996) Appropriate pedagogy. *ELT Journal* 50 (3), 199–212.

Kramsch, C. and van Hoene, L. (2001) Cross-cultural excursions: foreign language study and feminist discourses of travel. In A. Pavlenko, A. Blackledge, I. Piller and M. Teutsch-Dwyer (eds) *Multilingualism, Second Language Learning, and Gender* (pp. 283–306). Berlin: Mouton de Gruyter.

Kubota, R. and Lin, A. (eds) (2009) *Race, Culture, and Identity in Second Language Education: Exploring Critically Engaged Practice*. New York: Routledge.

Kumaravadivelu, B. (2001) Toward a postmethod pedagogy. *TESOL Quarterly* 35 (4), 537–560.

Larsen-Freeman, D. (2000) On the appropriateness of language teaching methods in language and development. In J. Shaw, D. Lubelska and M. Noullet (eds) *Partnership and Interaction: Proceedings of the Fourth International Conference on Language and Development* (pp. 65–71). Bangkok: Asian Institute of Technology.

Lather, P. (1992) Post-critical pedagogies: A feminist reading. In C. Luke and J. Gore (eds) *Feminisms and Critical Pedagogy* (pp. 120–137). New York: Routledge.

Leach, P. (2002) Valorising the resistance: National identity and collective memory in East Timor's constitution. *Social Alternatives* 21 (3), 43–47.

Lee, A. (1996) *Gender, Literacy, Curriculum: Re-writing School Geography*. London: Taylor & Francis.

Lefebvre, H. (1991) *The Production of Space* (D. Nicholson-Smith, trans.). Oxford: Blackwell (original publication 1974).

Lo Bianco, J. (2002) Destitution, wealth, and cultural contest: Language and development connections. In J. Lo Bianco (ed.) *Voices from Phnom Penh: Development and Language: Global Influences and Local Effects* (pp. 3–22). Melbourne: Language Australia.

Loomba, A. (1998) *Colonialism/Post-Colonialism*. London: Routledge.

Luke, A. (1996) Genres of power? Literacy education and the production of capital. In R. Hasan and G. Williams (eds) *Literacy in Society* (pp. 308–338). London: Longman.

Luke, A. (2004) Two takes on the critical. In B. Norton and K. Toohey (eds) *Critical Pedagogies and Language Learning* (pp. 21–29). Cambridge: Cambridge University Press.

Luke, C. (1996) Feminist pedagogy theory: Reflections on power and authority. *Educational Theory* 46 (3), 283–302.

Lyotard, J.F. (1984) *The Postmodern Condition: A Report on Knowledge.* Manchester: Manchester University Press.

Lysandrou, P. and Lysandrou, Y. (2003) Global English and proregression: Understanding English language spread in the contemporary era. *Economy and Society* 32 (2), 207–233.

Makoni, S. and Pennycook, A. (2007) *Disinventing and Reconstituting Languages.* Clevedon: Multilingual Matters.

Malinowski, B. (1923) The problem of meaning in primitive languages. In C.K. Ogden and I.A. Richards (eds) *The Meaning of Meaning* (pp. 296–336). New York: Harcourt Brace & World.

Malinowski, B. (1935) *Coral Gardens and their Magic* (Vol. 2). London: Allen & Unwin.

Manderson, L. and Jolly, M. (eds) (1997) *Sites of Desire/Economies of Pleasure: Sexualities in Asia and the Pacific.* Chicago: University of Chicago Press.

Martin, J.R. (1993) Genre and literacy: Modelling context in educational linguistics. *Annual Review of Applied Linguistics* 13, 141–172.

Massey, D. (1994) *Space, Place and Gender.* Cambridge: Polity Press.

Massey, D. (1999) Spaces of politics. In D. Massey, J. Allen and P. Sarre (eds) *Human Geography Today* (pp. 279–294). Cambridge: Polity Press.

Massey, D. (2005) *For Space.* London: Sage.

May, J. and Thrift, N. (2001) Introduction. In T. Skelton and G. Vallentine (eds) *TimeSpace: Geographies of Temporality* (pp. 1–46). London: Routledge.

Mayo, M. (1997) *Imagining Tomorrow: Adult Education for Transformation.* Leicester: NIACE.

Mayo, P. (1995) Critical literacy and emancipatory politics: The work of Paulo Freire. *International Journal of Educational Development* 15 (4), 363–379.

Mazurana, D. (2005) Gender and the causes and consequences of armed conflict. In D. Mazurana, A. Raven-Roberts and J. Parpart (eds) *Gender, Conflict, and Peacekeeping* (pp. 29–42). Lanham: Rowman & Littlefield.

Mazurana, D., Raven-Roberts, A., Parpart, J. and Lautze, J. (2005) *Gender, Conflict, and Peacekeeping.* Lanham: Rowman & Littlefield.

McHoul, A. and Grace, W. (1993) *A Foucault Primer: Discourse, Power and the Subject.* Melbourne: Melbourne University Press.

McKay, S. (1992) *Teaching English Overseas: An Introduction.* Oxford: Oxford University Press.

McKay, J. (2004) Reassessing development theory: Modernization and beyond. In D. Kingsbury, J. Remenyi and J. Hunt (eds) *Key Issues in Development* (pp. 45–66). Basingstoke and New York: Palgrave Macmillan.

McWilliam, E. (1999) *Pedagogical Pleasures.* New York: Peter Lang.

Merrell, M. (2001) Reading their reality: The REFLECT methodology – a sketch of literacy education in East Timor. *Fine Print* 24 (4), 26–27.

Mignolo W.D. (2000) *Local Histories/Global Designs: Coloniality, Subaltern Knowledges, and Border Thinking.* Princeton, New Jersey: Princeton University Press.

Mills, S. (1994) Knowledge, gender, and empire. In A. Blunt and G. Rose (eds) *Writing Women and Space: Colonial and Postcolonial Geographies* (pp. 29–50). New York: The Guilford Press.

Mohan, G. and Stokke, K. (2000) Participatory development and empowerment: The dangers of localism. *Third World Quarterly* 20 (2), 247–268.

Mohanram, R. (1999) *Black Body: Women Colonialism and Space*. Sydney: Allen & Unwin.

Mohanty, C.T. (1988) Under Western eyes: Feminist discourse, scholarship and colonial discourses. *Feminist Review* 30, 60–88.

Mohanty, C.T. (2003) *Feminism Without Borders: Decolonizing Theory, Practicing Solidarity*. Durham and London: Duke University Press.

Morgan, B. (2004) Teacher identity as pedagogy: Towards a field-internal conceptualization in bilingual and second language education. *Bilingual Education and Bilingualism* 7 (2&3), 172–188.

Moss, D. (2006) *Gender, Space and Time: Women in Higher Education*. Lanham: Lexington Books.

Mosse, D. (2004) Is good policy unimplementable? Reflections on the ethnography of aid policy and practice. *Development and Change* 35 (5), 639–671.

Murdoch, L. (30 August 2006) UN acts at last on sex crimes in Timor. *The Sydney Morning Herald*. On WWW at http://www.smh.com.au/news/world/un-acts-at-last-on-sex-crimes-in-timor/2006/08/29/1156816901149.html. Retrieved 3.9.2008.

Muthwii, M. and Kioko, N. (2004) *New Language Bearings in Africa*. Clevedon: Multilingual Matters.

Nandy, A. (1983) *The Intimate Enemy: Loss and Recovery of the Self Under Colonialism*. Delhi: Oxford University Press.

Nespor, J. (1994) *Knowledge in Motion: Space, Time and Curriculum in Undergraduate Physics and Management*. London: The Falmer Press.

Neverdeen Pieterse, J. (1995) The development of development theory towards critical globalism. *Institute for Social Studies, Working Paper Series, No. 187*.

Neverdeen Pieterse, J. (2001) *Development Theory: Deconstructions/Reconstructions*. London; Thousand Oaks; New Delhi: Sage.

Newfield, D. and Stein, P. (Guest eds) (2006) English education in Africa [Special Issue]. *English Studies in Africa*, 49 (1).

Nicolai, S. (2004) *Learning Independence: Education in Emergency and Transition in Timor Leste Since 1999*. Paris: International Institute of Educational Planning: UNESCO.

Norton, B. (2000) *Identity and Language Learning: Gender, Ethnicity and Educational Change*. London: Longman.

Norton, B. and Pavlenko, A. (2004) Addressing gender in the ESL/EFL classroom. *TESOL Quarterly* 38 (3), 504–514.

Norton Peirce, B. (1989) Toward a pedagogy of possibility in the teaching of English internationally: People's English in South Africa. *TESOL Quarterly* 23 (3), 401–420.

O'Kane, M. (1–7 February 2001) Revolution turns against its own. *The Guardian Weekly*, p. 21.

Ong, W. (1982) *Orality and Literacy: The Technologizing of the World*. London: Methuen.

Orford, A. (2002) Feminism, imperialism and the mission of international law. *Nordic Journal of International Law* 71, 275–296.

Papen, U. (2004) Literacy and development: What works for whom? Or, how relevant is the social practices view of literacy for literacy education in developing countries? *International Journal of Educational Development* 25, 5–17.

Pateman, C. (1989) *The Disorder of Women*. Stanford, CA: Stanford University Press.

Paulson, J. and Rappleye, J. (2007) Education and conflict: Essay review. *International Journal of Educational Development* 27, 340–347.

Pavlenko, A. (2004) Gender and sexuality in foreign and second language education: Critical and feminist approaches. In B. Norton and K. Toohey (eds) *Critical Pedagogies and Language Learning* (pp. 53–71). Cambridge: Cambridge University Press.

Pearson, R., and Jackson, C. (1998) Interrogating development: Feminism, gender and policy. In C. Jackson and R. Pearson (eds) *Feminist Visions of Development* (pp. 1–16). London and New York: Routledge.

Pennycook, A. (1989) The concept of method, interested knowledge, and the politics of language teaching. *TESOL Quarterly* 23 (4), 589–619.

Pennycook, A. (1994) *The Cultural Politics of English as an International Language*. London: Longman.

Pennycook, A. (1995) English in the world/the world in English. In J. Tollefson (ed.) *Power and Inequality in Language Education* (pp. 34–58). Cambridge: Cambridge University Press.

Pennycook, A. (1998) *English and the Discourses of Colonialism*. London: Routledge.

Pennycook, A. (2000) Development, culture and language: Ethical concerns in a postcolonial world. In J. Shaw, D. Lubelska and M. Noullet (eds) *Partnership and Interaction. Proceedings of the Fourth International Conference on Language and Development* (pp. 3–24). Bangkok: Asian Institute of Technology.

Pennycook, A. (2001) *Critical Applied Linguistics: A Critical Introduction*. Mahwah, NJ: Lawrence Erlbaum.

Pennycook, A. (2007) *Global Englishes and Transcultural Flows*. Oxon and New York: Routledge.

Pennycook, A. (2010) *Language as a Local Practice*. London: Routledge.

Peters, M. (1996) *Poststructuralism, Politics and Education*. Westport: Bergin & Garvey.

Petras, J. and Veltmeyer, H. (2002) Age of reverse aid: neo-liberalism as catalyst of regression. *Development and Change* 33 (2), 281–293.

Pham, H.H. (2000) The key socio-cultural factors that work against success in tertiary English language training programs in Vietnam. In J. Shaw, D. Lubelska and M. Noullet (eds) *Partnership and Interaction: Proceedings of the Fourth International Conference on Language and Development* (pp. 187–197). Bangkok: Asian Institute of Technology.

Phan, L.H. (2008) *Teaching English as an International Language: Identity, Resistance and Negotiation*. Clevedon: Multilingual Matters.

Phillipson, R. (1992) *Linguistic Imperialism*. Oxford: Oxford University Press.

Philpott, S. (2000) *Rethinking Indonesia: Postcolonial Theory, Authoritarianism and Identity*. London: Macmillan.

Philpott, S. (2001) Fear of the dark: Indonesia and the Australian national imagination. *Australian Journal of International Affairs* 55 (3), 371–388.

Pratt, M.L. (1992) *Imperial Eyes: Travel Writing and Transculturation*. London: Routledge.

Prinsloo, M. (2005) New literacies as placed resources. *Perspectives in Education* 23 (4), 87–98.

Rahnema, M. (1992) Paricipation. In W. Sachs (ed.) *The Development Dictionary*. London: Zed.

Ramanathan, V. (2005) *The English-Vernacular Divide: Postcolonial Language Policies and Practice*. Clevedon: Multilingual Matters.

Ramazanoglu, C. (ed.) (1993) *Up Against Foucault*. London: Routledge.

Rassool, N. (1999) *Literacy for Sustainable Development in the Age of Information*. Clevedon: Multilingual Matters.

Rassool, N. (2007) *Global Issues in Language, Education and Development: Perspectives from Postcolonial Countries*. Clevedon: Multilingual Matters.

Remenyi, J. (1994) The meaning of development reconsidered. *Development Bulletin. The Australian Development Studies Network, ANU* 32 (Briefing paper no. 35), 1–5.

Richardson, L. (1997) *Fields of Play: Constructing an Academic Life*. New Brunswick, NJ: Rutgers University Press.

Rist, G. (2002) *The History of Development: From Western Origins to Global Faith* (P. Camiller, trans., 2nd edn). London: Zed Books.

Rist, G. (2008) *The History of Development: From Western Origins to Global Faith* (P. Camiller, trans., 3rd ed.). London: Zed Books.

Robinson-Pant, A. (2000) Women and literacy: A Nepal perspective. *International Journal of Educational Development* 20, 349–364.

Robinson-Pant, A. (2008) 'Why literacy matters': Exploring a policy perspective on literacies, identities and social change. *Journal of Development Studies* 44 (6), 779–796.

Robinson-Pant, A. (2010) Changing discourses: Literacy and development in Nepal. *International Journal of Educational Development*.

Rogers, A. (1999) Improving the quality of adult literacy programmes in developing countries: The 'real literacies' approach. *International Journal of Educational Development* 19 (3), 219–234.

Rogers, A. (2000) Literacy comes second: Working with groups in developing societies. *Development in Practice* 10 (2), 236–240.

Rose, G. (1993) *Feminism and Geography: The Limits of Geographical Knowledge*. Cambridge: Polity Press.

Rose, N. (1996) Identity, genealogy, history. In S. Hall and P. du Gay (eds) *Questions of Cultural Identity* (pp. 128–150). London: Sage.

Rostow, W.W. (1960) *The Stage of Economic Growth: A Non-Communist Manifesto*. Cambridge: Cambridge University Press.

Said, E. (1978) *Orientalism*. London: Routledge & Kegan Paul.

Said, E. (1993) *Colonial Discourse*. New York: Alfred Knopf.

Said, E. (1994) *Culture and Imperialism*. New York: Vintage Books.

Savage, W. (1997) Language and development. In B. Kenny and W. Savage (eds) *Language and Development: Teachers in a Changing World* (pp. 283–337). London: Longman.

Schenke, A. (1991) The 'will to reciprocity' and the work of memory: Fictioning speaking out of silence in E.S.L. and feminist pedagogy. *Resources for Feminist Research* 20, 47–55.

Schenke, A. (1996) Not just a 'social issue': Teaching feminist in ESL. *TESOL Quarterly* 30 (1), 155–159.

Sen, A. (1999) *Development as Freedom*. New York: Knopf.

Serres, M. (1982) *Hermes: Literature, Science, Philosophy*. Baltimore: Johns Hopkins University Press.

Serres, M. and Latour, B. (1995) *Conversations on Science, Culture and Time*. Ann Arbor: University of Michigan Press.

Sharp, A. (1998) ELT project planning and sustainability. *ELT Journal* 52 (2), 140–145.

Shaw, J., Lubelska, D. and Noullet, M. (eds) (2000) *Partnership and Interaction: Proceedings of the Fourth International Conference on Language and Development*. Bangkok: Asian Institute of Technology.

Simon, R.I. (1987) Empowerment as a pedagogy of possibility. *Language Arts* 64, 370–382.

Singh, P. and Doherty, C. (2004) Global cultural flows and pedagogic dilemmas: Teaching in the global contact zone. *TESOL Quarterly* 38 (1), 9–42.

Slater, D. and Bell, M. (2002) Aid and the geopolitics of the post-colonial: Critical reflections on New Labour's overseas development strategy. *Development and Change* 33 (2), 335–360.

Soja, E.W. (1989) *Postmodern Geographies: The Reassertion of Space in Critical Social Theory*. London and New York: Verso.

Soja, E.W. (1996) *Thirdspace: Journeys to Los Angeles and Other Real-and-Imagined Places*. Cambridge, MA: Blackwell.

Soja, E.W. and Hooper, B. (1993) The spaces that difference makes: Some notes on the geographical margins of the new cultural politics. In M. Keith and S. Pile (eds) *Place and the Politics of Identity* (pp. 183–205). London and New York: Routledge.

Somerville, M. and Perkins, T. (2003) Border work in the contact zone: Thinking indigenous/non-indigenous collaboration spatially. *International Journal of Intercultural Studies* 24 (3), 253–266.

Spivak, G. (1994) Can the subaltern speak? Speculations on widow sacrifice. In P. Williams and L. Chrisman (eds) *Colonial Discourse and Post-Colonial Theory: A Reader* (pp. 66–111). New York and London: Harvester Wheatsheaf (original publication 1988).

Spivak, G. (1999) *A Critique of Postcolonial Reason: Toward a History of the Vanishing Present*. Cambridge: Harvard University Press.

Spurr, D. (1993) *The Rhetoric of Culture: Colonial Discourse in Journalism, Travel Writing and Imperial Administration*. Durham: Duke University Press.

Stoler, A.L. (1995) *Race and the Education of Desire: Foucault's History of Sexuality and the Colonial Order of Things*. Durham: Duke University Press.

Street, B.V. (1984) *Literacy in Theory and Practice*. Cambridge: Cambridge University Press.

Street, B. (ed.) (2001) *Literacy and Development: Ethnographic Perspectives*. New York: Routledge.

Summers, A. (1975) *Damned Whores and God's Police: The Colonization of Women in Australia*. Middlesex: Penguin.

Sunderland, J. (2000) Issues of language and gender in second and foreign language education. *Language Teaching* 33, 203–223.

Sunderland, J., Cowley, M., Rahmin, F.A., Leontzakou, C. and Shattuck, J. (2000) From bias 'in the text' to 'teacher talk around the text' an exploration of teacher discourse and gendered foreign language textbook texts. *Linguistics and Education* 11 (3), 251–286.

Sword Gusmao, K. (2003) *A Woman of Independence*. Sydney: Pan Macmillan.

Tabulawa, R. (2003) International aid agencies, learner-centred pedagogy and political democratization: A critique. *Comparative Education* 39 (1), 7–26.

Taylor, C. (27 August 2000) East Timor's Two Worlds. *Sunday Territorian*, pp. 19–20.

Taylor, J.G. (1991) *Indonesia's Forgotten War: The Hidden History of East Timor*. Leichhardt, NSW, Australia: Pluto Press.

Taylor, J.G. (1999) *East Timor: The Price of Freedom*. London: Zed Books.

Taylor-Leech, K. (2009) Quick-fix English: Discontinuities in a language development aid project. *English Teaching: Practice and Critique* 8 (1), 97–111.

Tembe, J. and Norton, B. (2008) Promoting local languages in Ugandan primary schools: The community as stakeholder. *Canadian Modern Language Review* 65 (1), 33–60.

Thesen, L. (1997) Voices, discourse, and transition: In search of new categories of EAP. *TESOL Quarterly* 31 (3), 487–511.

Thomas, N. (1994) *Colonialism's Culture: Anthropology, Travel and Government*. Princeton, NJ: Princeton University Press.

Thomas, P. (2004) Gender and development: Bridging policy and practice. *Development Bulletin, The Australian Development Studies Network, ANU* 64, 4–7.

Thompson, E.P. (1967) Time, work discipline and industrial capitalism. *Past and Present* 38, 56–97.

Thorne, S.L. and Lantolf, J.P. (2007) A linguistics of communicative activity. In S. Makoni and A. Pennycook (eds) *Disinventing and Reconstituting Languages* (pp. 170–195). Clevedon: Multilingual Matters.

Todaro, M.P. and Smith, S.C. (2009) *Economic Development*. Harlow: Addison-Wesley.

Toh, G. (2003) Toward a more critical orientation to ELT in South East Asia. *World Englishes* 22 (4), 551–558.

Tollefson, J.W. (2000) Policy and ideology in the spread of English. In J.K. Hall and W.G. Eggington (eds) *The Sociopolitics of English Language Teaching* (pp. 7–21). Clevedon: Multilingual Matters.

Tooth, G. (2000) Doing the business in East Timor [Radio Broadcast], *Background Briefing*. Sydney: ABC Radio National.

Townsend, J.G., Porter, G. and Mawsley, E. (2002) The role of the transnational community of non-government organizations: Governance or poverty reduction. *Journal of International Development* 14, 829–839.

Traub, J. (2000) Inventing East Timor. *Foreign Affairs* 79 (4), 74–89.

Tupas, R. (2006) Anatomies of linguistic commodification: The case of English in the Philippines vis-à-vis other languages in the linguistic marketplace. In P. Tan and R. Rubdy (eds) *Language as Commodity: Global Structures, Local Marketplaces* (pp. 90–105). London: Continuum.

UNDP (United Nations Development Programme) (2008) Human Development Reports – Indonesia. On WWW at http://hdrstats.undp.org/countries/data_sheets/cty_ds_IDN.html. Retrieved 1.6.2008.

UNDP (United Nations Development Programme) (2002) *The Way Ahead: East Timor Human Development Report*. Dili: UNDP.

van Dijk, T.A. (2006) Discourse, context and cognition. *Discourse Studies* 8 (1), 159–177.

van Dijk, T.A. (2008) *Discourse and Context: A Sociocognitive Approach*. Cambridge: Cambridge University Press.

Varghese, M., Morgan, B., Johnston, B. and Johnson, K.A. (2005) Theorizing language teacher identity: Three perspectives and beyond. *Journal of Language, Identity, and Education* 4 (1), 21–44.

Virilio, P. (1991) *The Lost Dimension* (D. Moshenberg, trans.). New York, NY: Semiotext(e).

Visvanathan, N. (1997) General introduction. In N. Visvanathan, L. Duggan, L. Nisonoff and N. Wiegersma (eds) *The Women, Gender and Development Reader* (pp. 1–6). London: Zed Books.

Walkerdine, V. (1984) Developmental psychology and the child-centred pedagogy: The insertion of Piaget into early education. In J. Henriques, W. Hollway, C. Urwin, C. Venn and V. Walkerdine (eds) *Changing the Subject: Psychology, Social Regulation and Subjectivity* (pp. 153–202). London: Methuen.

Walkerdine, V. (1992) Progressive pedagogy and political struggle. In C. Luke and J. Gore (eds) *Feminism and Critical Pedagogy* (pp. 15–24). New York: Routledge.

Watkins, K. and Fowler, P. (2002) *Rigged Rules and Double Standards: Trade, Globalisation, and the Fight against Poverty*: Oxfam International. On WWW at http://www.oxfam.org.uk/resources/papers/tradereport.html. Retrieved 6.2.2009.

Watson, K. (2007) Language, education and ethnicity: Whose rights will prevail in an age of globalisation? *International Journal of Educational Development* 27 (3), 252–265.

Wax, E. (21 March 2005) Congo's desperate 'one-dollar U.N. girls'. *The Washington Post*. On WWW at http://www.washingtonpost.com/ac2/wp-dyn/A52333-2005Mar20.htm. Retrieved 20.4.2005.

Wheeler, N.J. and Ddunne, T. (2001) East Timor and the new humanitarian interventionism. *International Affairs* 77 (4), 805–827.

Woods, D. (2001) Good guys, bad guys: Images of the Australian soldier in East Timor. *Media International Australia* (98), 143–159.

World Bank (2005) *Reshaping the Future: Education and Postconflict Reconstruction*. Washington, DC: The World Bank.

Yeoh, B.S.A., Teo, P. and Huang, S. (2002) Women's agencies and activisms in the Asia-Pacific region. In B.S.A. Yeoh, P. Teo and S. Huang (eds) *Gender Politics in the Asia-Pacific Region* (pp. 1–16). London and New York: Routledge.

Young, R. (1990) *White Mythologies*. London and New York: Routledge.

Zachariah, M. (1997) Education's role in empowering the poor to alleviate their poverty. In W. Cummings and N. McGinn (eds) *International Handbook of Education and Development* (pp. 421–487). Oxford: Pergamon.

Zuengler, J. and Miller, E. R. (2006) Cognitive and sociocultural perspectives: Two parallel SLA worlds? *TESOL Quarterly* 40 (1), 35–58.

Index